The NEW
Wilderness
& Camping

The NEW Wilderness Canoeing & Camping

Cliff Jacobson

Illustrations by Cliff Moen

ICS BOOKS, INC.

MERRILLVILLE, INDIANA

THE NEW WILDERNESS CANOEING & CAMPING

Copyright © 1986 by Cliff Jacobson

10 9 8 7 6 5 4 3 2 1

Printed in U.S.A.

Published by:
ICS Books, Inc.
1000 E. 80th Place
Merrillville, IN 46410

Distributed by:
Stackpole Books
Cameron and Kelker Street
Harrisburg, PA 17105

Library of Congress Cataloging-in-Publication Data

Jacobson, Cliff.
    The new wilderness canoeing & camping.

    Rev. ed. of: Wilderness canoeing & camping. 1st ed. 1977.
    Includes index.
    1. Canoes and canoeing.   2. Camping.   3. Wilderness areas -- United States.
4. Wilderness areas -- Canada.
I. Jacobson, Cliff. Wilderness canoeing & camping.   II. Title. III. Title: New
wilderness canoeing and camping.
GV789.J32   1986   797.1'22   85-31711
ISBN 0-934802-29-7

To Peggy Roman

Contents

A Note from the Publisher

The NEW WILDERNESS CANOEING & CAMPING was first published by E.P. Dutton Co. in 1977 as "WILDERNESS CANOEING & CAMPING" and received rave reviews for its clarity, thoroughness, and honest-to-goodness "usefulness." Though a decade has passed since the introduction of this book, demand for it has remained strong. So when Cliff Jacobson suggested to us (ICS BOOKS) that we publish an updated, expanded edition, we were naturally enthusiastic. After all, where else can you learn how to "tune a canoe for improved performance"..."discover the art of paddling a solo canoe"..."build a one-match fire in a driving rain"..."effectively waterproof your gear without spending a lot of money"..."make an enjoyable trip with toddlers"... "lead a group of teenagers"..."confidently navigate big lakes *without* devoting a lifetime of study to the intricacies of map and compass"...and more!

The NEW WILDERNESS CANOEING & CAMPING retains all the solid information and money-saving tips which made its predecessor so popular a decade ago. But now, Cliff Jacobson has updated the material and included new procedures, new chapters, new photos and exquisite pen/ink illustrations by Cliff Moen, noted Minnesota artist.

Even old dogs can learn valuable new tricks from THE NEW WILDERNESS CANOEING & CAMPING.

Acknowledgements

Special thanks should be extended to: Cliff Moen, for his spectacular artwork. Bob Brown, for his advice and patient reading of the Manuscript. Harry Roberts and Phil Sigglekow, for photos of the solo canoe; Dr. Bill Forgey and Tom Todd, for their support and enthusiasm. John Viehman, editor of CANOE magazine, and Art Michaels, editor of BOAT PENNSYLVANIA magazine for their encouragement and support. Ken Saelens, for his ingenius tumpline invention. Farid Saed, for custom photography.

The following publications for permission to use portions of my articles:

BACKPACKER
January 1985, "Weathering The Storm."
CANOE
November, 1980, "How To Get What You Want In A Canoe."
March, 1985, "Nose Jobs."
June, 1985, "Canoe Tent Evaluations."
March, 1979, "Leading The Pack."
October, 1983, "Backwoods Pyrotechnics."
BOAT PENNSYLVANIA
May/June, 1984..."The Joy Of Soloing."
July/August, 1984..."Canoeing With Children."
Nov./Dec. 1984..."Making Your Canoe Equipment Last."
March/April, 1985..."How To Pick A Paddle.
May/June, 1985..."Canoeing With Teenagers."
Sept., 1985, "Neglect And The Proper Way."
OLD TOWN CANOEING GUIDE
1982, "The Solo Experience."
Vol. 1, No. 2, "Best Ways To Cartop Your Canoe."

A Note to the Reader

A decade ago, wilderness canoeing was in transition; paddlers were just beginning to discover the joy of lean quick canoes and lightweight equipment. Now, "going light" -- or reasonably so -- is accepted practice. However, some well-meaning trippers have abused the go-light ethic by selecting outfits which are much too spartan to provide for the uncertainties of wilderness travel. Tents which are flimsy and confining can't possibly provide safety and comfort in severe weather. And canoes which are too small to negotiate the waves of a wind-tossed lake are no bargain, no matter how light and fun-to-paddle they may be.

On the other hand, there are a number of canoe campers who scorn all ultra-light ways and stubbornly cling to the bone-crushing weight of proven traditional outfits. To each his own. As for myself, I prefer a more logical "middle ground" approach.

As you can see, expounding a personal canoe philosophy is a lot like trying to tell someone what constitutes good art. Naturally I believe that my way is the best way, but there are a lot of equally knowledgeable canoeists who would disagree. I've found that if you want to get along with other paddlers, you'd better keep an open mind. You can easily get into a hassle over what constitutes the best canoe tent, the most comfortable footwear, the most waterproof way to pack for a wilderness trip, and so on. Often what works for one canoeist won't work for another. For example, I prefer lightweight, rubber-bottom, leather-top boots for canoeing. But I weigh only 135 pounds, so this type of footgear works fine for me. A friend of mine weighs 240 pounds; he went through a pair of similar boots in just four weeks, on one canoe trip.

The type of wilderness experiences a canoeist has also influences his or her methods and choice of equipment. If you've ever tipped over and had your canoe swept under a submerged tree, there to remain until low water sets it free, you might be very much opposed to tying your gear in the canoe. But if your canoe and outfit have been saved because of the extra buoyancy of tightly lashed packs, then you may be a real believer in tying *everything* in.

In the NEW WILDERNESS CANOEING & CAMPING, I've detailed all the basic skills (even the most obscure ones!) you need to know to make an enjoyable trip in the backcountry -- be it a gentle Missouri stream or a remote route in Canada. I could have cluttered the book with "obvious" information; instead, I elected to pursue a "practical" course.

The equipment and methods which I recommend here are the result of much personal experience and collaboration with others whom I know and trust. Nonetheless, I am continually revising my ideas of what is best. Possibly by the time you read this I will already consider some of my recommendations outdated. If you take canoeing seriously (or plan to), you should read every canoe book in print -- not once, but many times. Only after you have studied the ways of others and paddled many miles -- will you know what's best for you.

I won't pretend this book is a complete treatise on wilderness canoeing and camping. It's not; no single book of reasonable length could be. I offer this work as a thorough introduction, with high hopes you'll find some worthwhile hints contained within these pages, and in the process develop profound respect for all of our wild places.

Cliff Jacobson, 1986

The NEW
Wilderness Canoeing
& Camping

1.
The Wilderness Challenge

It is difficult to pinpoint what makes canoeing so attractive a pastime. The inexpensiveness of the sport attracts some, and the thrills of competition lure others. For me it is the wilderness challenge. Many of the really wild places in North America are easily accessible only by canoe, and even in the most crowded cities there is always a little-used river which can be floated to get away from it all. But a canoe is more than wilderness transportation and white-water excitement. It is a tonic for tedium and a unique form of family therapy -- togetherness. The green revolution, the ecology movement, a suffering economy, and too much war have all contributed to the popularity of canoeing. Americans are at last becoming reattuned to nature. We are trading in our Vanbagos for nylon tents and hiking boots; we are rediscovering the wilderness.

But the wilderness has changed. It is becoming increasingly difficult to find places to be alone -- places which do not show the scars of man. Virtually all of the great northern rivers are now paddled regularly. Even in the arctic it is unusual to travel for weeks at a time in complete isolation from other human beings or evidence of them. If our wild places are to survive the brunt of the thousands who are returning to nature, we must do more than provide lip service to the modern wilderness ethic; leave only footprints, take only pictures. And that is the beauty of the canoe; not even footprints are left. For this reason canoeists are more fortunate than back-packers. We don't have to look at mile after mile of littered, eroded trails and crowded or nonexistent campsites. We can simply pitch a tent on a passing sandbar and time will eliminate any trace of our presence.

Nevertheless, the environmental crisis is here -- for the canoeist as well as the packpacker. During the past decade canoeing has grown so popular that today well over a hundred manufacturers find a profitable livelihood in the production of more than seven hundred canoe and kayak models. New designs, materials, and construction methods have resulted in canoes which are lighter, faster, and tougher than anything the Indians ever built. Canoe tripping equipment has changed, too. Tents, sleeping bags, cooking gear -- everything has become lighter, stronger, and more compact. As a result, thousands of new paddlers are taking to our waterways each year. Already the impact of these canoeists is being felt upon the wildness of the wilderness.

Although lightweight equipment and new techniques have sig-nificantly reduced the risks of canoe trips in isolated areas, your most important skill on a difficult venture is still your own good judgment. Many significant canoe voyages have been successfully completed by relatively incompetent canoeists. That these individu-als survived can best be attributed to their good sense in portaging a set of complex rapids rather than dashing heedlessly downstream for a quick and final ego trip.

In 1930, Eric Sevareid, the noted news commentator, and Walter Port paddled from Minneapolis, Minnesota, to Hudson Bay via the Gods River. No white person had ever completed this trip and neither Eric nor Walter had much canoeing or camping experi-ence. They survived the hazardous journey because of their cool and accurate appraisal of dangerous situations and a portage-rather-than-perish attitude.

Only the foolhardy will take unnecessary risks which endanger their lives. Every modern canoe club has a few of these carefree individuals, and some of them are excellent paddlers. Such persons should, for your own safety, be left out of your wilderness trip plans. Don't think you have to be an Olympic canoeist to undertake a voyage of significance. Of course you need skill and the right gear, but mostly you need to keep your wits about you.

Most canoes have excellent resale value, even when they are many years old. If you are on a limited budget and can afford to buy an inexpensive canoe now, you can work your way up to a better model within a few years with little financial loss. As you paddle you will gain experience and learn more efficient ways to camp and canoe. When you are ready for a really fine canoe, you will have developed the knowledge and skill to appreciate it and you will damage it less in difficult waters because your apprenticeship will have been served.

Because the canoe is such a versatile and wonderful craft, it deserves your study if you are to derive the greatest benefits from its use. Loaded and handled properly, a well-designed canoe will ride out running waves that would frighten most powerboaters. And the same canoe that can carry you hundreds of miles across wilderness waters will drift quietly along peaceful local rivers, filled with kids and dogs and coolers, providing you and your family with an inexpensive and enjoyable way to discover nature.

2.
The Wilderness Canoe – An Investment in Freedom

My love affair with canoeing began in 1966 when a friend invited me to join him on a float trip down a small Indiana stream. It sounded like fun and rekindled memories of the good times I'd had on trips taken as a boy scout. It was a glorious day for a river float -- warm, bright, and with a persistent breeze. The river was pleasant but not spectacular; the canoe was a badly made fiberglass model that weighed at least ninety pounds. But no matter; the gentle beauty of the experience captured my heart. From then on, I vowed to never be without a canoe of some sort.

Within the year, I'd purchased my first canoe -- a fifteen foot fiberglass cheapie about like my friend's. I'd pinched pennies for months to buy that boat and was very paranoid about the possibility it might be stolen. So when I camped out, I confidently chained it to a tree or the doors of my car!

I paddled that canoe in blissful ignorance for more than a year before I purchased my first high performance boat -- a 17-foot, 9-inch Sawyer Cruiser. After that, came three aluminum Grummans of various lengths and weights, another Sawyer, two Old Town's, four Mad River's, and three cedar strip canoes I built myself. Ultimately, I ran out of storage room in my garage and was forced to sell some off -- a terribly painful experience for someone who loves canoes as much as I. Fortunately, I recently acquired a canoe trailer so the possibility of adding to my five canoes excites me.

As you can see, canoe fever is incurable. One remedy is to simply paddle at every opportunity -- mill ponds, lazy rivers, wilderness lakes; makes no difference. It's "time on the water" that counts. Admittedly, this is not a realistic solution for there are always new streams, new rivers, and new lakes to explore. And of course everything changes as water levels rise and fall, which means you can re-do a route each week and never repeat yourself. Even if you confine your paddling to your home state, you'll be hard pressed to discover all the wonders of its waterways. And that is the versatility of the canoe. It is the only craft I know that is as much at home on tiny creeks as on giant lakes and reservoirs. I've even paddled mine on the ocean with complete confidence!

Unfortunately, not all canoes are suitable for touring the back-country. Some are too small, some are too fragile, and some are just inappropriately designed. To most people a canoe is a canoe, and this compounded by the fact that most canoe builders are not canoeists, keeps the sales of badly designed poorly constructed models booming. Many are merely producing a popular product at an attractive price. Even the powerboater fares better in this respect, for when he goes to a marina to buy a new or used craft, the salesman has at least some idea of what makes a good speedboat. Few canoe salespeople have ever paddled the canoes they sell (though the trend is changing!), fewer own canoes, and only a handful have taken a lengthy wilderness trip in one. They will, however, appear very knowledgeable, especially when you are about to part with your money. So canoe selection is pretty much up to the buyer, and the old economic adage *caveat emptor* ("let the buyer beware") really applies here, for there are some really bad canoes on the market. Evidently ignorance begets ignorance, for even if you make a bad choice, the high demand for canoes will prevent you from getting hurt very much. Even the worst of the commercial canoes can probably be sold for sixty percent of its original purchase price five years later -- providing, of course, it has been well kept. There is an antithesis here. Most people are so ignorant about canoes that if you invest in a *really* good one you may find the resale potential extremely limited.

For example, in 1973 I organized a trip to James Bay, Ontario. One of my canoes, a whitewater model, was too specialized for the trip, and the other, a fiberglass Sawyer Cruiser, was too small for the big rapids and heavy loads we would be carrying. So I decided to trade the $275 Sawyer on a more suitable wilderness canoe. The best offer I could get from a marina was $125; I was advised that people didn't want "cheap plastic canoes." I pointed out that my Sawyer was not a cheap plastic canoe but a sophisticated cruiser with racing aspirations. "No matter," was the reply, "fiberglass is fiberglass." Ultimately, I advertised the canoe in *HUT*, the official publication of the Minnesota Canoe Association. The Sawyer went at $220 to a knowledgeable canoeist in less than a week after the ad appeared!

Contrary to popular belief (and the claims of some manufacturers), there is no such thing as a "perfect" canoe -- or even an "all-round" canoe. No single watercraft, regardless of its design, materials, or quality of construction, can do everything well.

It's unrealistic to expect a single canoe to win flatwater races on Saturday, clean house in whitewater slalom on Sunday, and confidently truck the family and 150 pounds of camping gear on a two week stint across wilderness waters. It's equally absurd to expect that same canoe to weigh in at forty pounds and hang together when it's wrapped around a mid-stream boulder. Even if such a canoe existed, its high price would put it out of reach of even the most discriminating paddler. Canoes, like cars, have distinct personalities -- a major reason why serious canoeists often own several canoes.

Since I can't put you into the "perfect" canoe -- or even the best one for your needs -- I'll instead offer some guidelines to help you make intelligent buying decisions. But first, you need to know some basic terminology.

CANOE TERMINOLOGY

Aft: Toward the stern (back) end of the canoe.

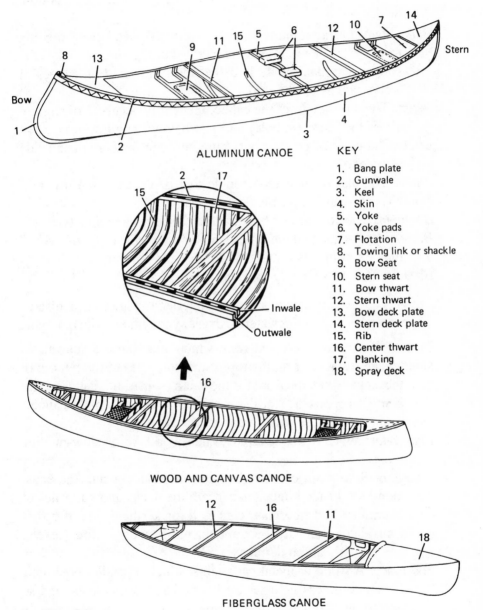

Bow

Stern

8 13

11 15 5 6 12 10 7 14

9

1

2

3 4

ALUMINUM CANOE

15 2 17

Inwale

Outwale

16

WOOD AND CANVAS CANOE

12 16 11 18

FIBERGLASS CANOE

KEY

1. Bang plate
2. Gunwale
3. Keel
4. Skin
5. Yoke
6. Yoke pads
7. Flotation
8. Towing link or shackle
9. Bow Seat
10. Stern seat
11. Bow thwart
12. Stern thwart
13. Bow deck plate
14. Stern deck plate
15. Rib
16. Center thwart
17. Planking
18. Spray deck

Figure 2-1

Amidships: The center or middle of the canoe.

Bailer: A scoop (Usually made from an empty bleach jug by cutting off the bottom) for dipping accumulated water from the bottom of the canoe.

Bang plate: On aluminum canoes. A curved metal plate running from deck to keel. Holds the metal skin together and takes the bangs. The bang plate is called the *stem band* on canoes of wood-canvas construction.

Beam: The widest part of the canoe. Generally occurs at or slightly aft of the waist (middle) and just below the gunwales.

Bilge: The point of greatest curvature between the bottom and side of a canoe.

Blade: The part of the canoe paddle that is placed in the water.

Bow: The forward (front) end of the canoe.

Bowman: The forward or bow paddler (whether male or female).

Broadside: A canoe which is perpendicular to the current of a river, thus exposing its broad side to obstacles in the water.

Broach: To turn suddenly into the wind.

Carry: To carry a canoe and gear overland, either to a distant watershed or to safer water. *Carry* is synonymous with *portage*.

Deck: Panels at the bow and stern which attach to the gunwales.

Depth: The distance from the top of the gunwales to the bottom of the canoe when measured at the beam (sometimes called *center depth*, as opposed to the depth at the extreme ends of the canoe).

Draft: The amount of water a canoe draws.

Flat water: Water without rapids, such as a lake or slow-moving river.

Flotation: Styrofoam or other buoyant material set into the ends, along the inside bilges, or beneath the decks and gunwales of aluminum and fiberglass canoes to make them float if upset. Can also mean any buoyant material, such as life jackets, beach balls, and innertubes.

Footbrace: A wood or metal bar against which a paddler braces his feet. Footbraces help secure the paddler in the canoe and so add to the efficiency of his strokes.

Fore (forward): Toward the front end (bow) of the canoe.

Freeboard: The distance from the water line to the top of the gun-wales at their lowest point. The greater the freeboard, the greater the ability of the canoe to handle rough water, assuming the canoe is well designed.

Grab loop: A loop of rope which passes through the hole or painter ring at each end of the canoe. Gives you something to "grab" when you capsize.

Grip: The top end of the shaft of a canoe paddle, where you grip it.

Gunwales (pronounced "gunnels"): The upper rails of the canoe.

Hogged: A canoe with a bent-in keel.

Inwale: That part of the gunwale that protrudes into the inside of the canoe.

Keel: A strip of wood or aluminum which runs along the center bottom of the canoe. Keels prevent lateral slippage in winds and protect the bottoms of canoes from damage in rocky areas. However, their main purpose is to stiffen the bottom of a canoe (see KEELS -- FRIEND OR FIEND on page 13 for the complete low-down). There are two types of keels in common use:

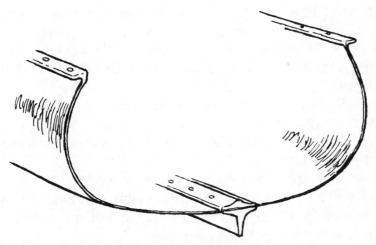

Figure 2-2   Standard or tee keel for use on windy lakes only.

STANDARD, FIN, OR TEE KEEL

A deep keel which extends up to an inch or more into the water. An ideal choice where travel will be *limited* to large, windy lakes.

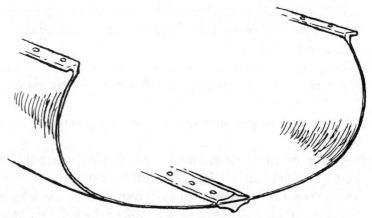

Figure 2-3   Canoes with shoe (white-water) keels are more maneuverable and are less likely to catch on subsurface rocks than similar models with standard keels.

SHOE (WHITE-WATER) KEEL
A rounded or flat strip of metal or wood designed to protect the bottom of a canoe from damage. The smooth contours of shoe keels allow water to flow over them with little resistance. Hence they permit quick turns in rapids.

Leeward: A sheltered or protected place out of the wind. In nautical terms, *leeward* is the direction toward which the wind is blowing.

Line: Rope used to tie up a canoe or pull it around obstacles in the water. Also refers to working a canoe downstream around obstacles in the water with the aid of ropes (lines) attached to the bow and stern.

Outwale: The part of the gunwale that protrudes over the outside of the canoe hull. Outwales are desirable for canoes that will be used in whitewater, as they help deflect spray when the bow of the canoe plunges in rapids.

Painters: Lines attached to the bow and stern of a canoe.

Planking: Lightweight boards nailed to the ribs on wood-canvas canoes. Planking runs perpendicular to the ribs of a canoe. Its main purpose is to support the canvas.

Portage: see *carry.*

Ribs: The lateral supports which run at right angles to the keel on the inside of a canoe. Ribs provide hull rigidity and structural strength, and are necessary on aluminum and wood-canvas canoes. The trend is away from ribs in canoes of modern construction, as the new synthetics are very strong and do not require cross-bracing for support.

Rocker: An upward curve of the keel line of a canoe. When placed on a level surface a canoe with rocker will, like a rocking chair, rock up and down (fore and aft). Canoes with rocker turn more easily than those without rocker.

Rock garden: A shallow place in a river that has many scattered rocks.

Seats: Generally, there are two seats in a canoe. They many be made of wood, fiberglass, plastic, or aluminum. Wood-framed seats which are strung with cane or nylon webbing and tractor-type molded fiberglass seats are most comfortable. Aluminum seats are least comfortable and get cold in cool weather. For greatest warmth (and comfort), cover aluminum seats with waterproof foam and secure the foam to the seats with waterproof tape. You spend long hours sitting in a canoe; consequently, more than passing consideration should be given to the seats.

Sliding seat: A canoe seat which can be moved forward or aft to adjust trim. Most of the best canoes now feature sliding bow seats as a standard or optional accessory.

Skid plate: A piece of thick Kevlar that is glued to the bottom ends of Royalex canoes. Prevents abrasion of the vinyl skin of the canoe. Skid plates are a desirable additon to Royalex canoes that will be used in shallow rocky rivers.

Skin: The outer covering of the canoe. May be wood, canvas, aluminum, or other material.

Splash cover: A fitted cover designed to keep water out of a canoe. Splash covers are useful in rough rapids and big waves. Even small, sporty canoes are suitable for wilderness use if they are covered.

Spray deck: An extra-long deck equipped with a cowling to deflect water which comes over the ends of a canoe.

Spray skirt: A waterproof fabric sleeve which is attached to the splash cover at one end and is secured around a paddler's waist by means of elastic shock cord at the other end.

Thwart: A cross-brace which runs from gunwale to gunwale.

Thwarts give strength and rigidity to the hull.

Toe blocks: A feature of whitewater canoes. Wood or foam blocks glued to the canoe's bottom support the paddler's feet and keep him from sliding around in the boat while maneuvering.

Thigh straps: A feature of whitewater canoes: A webbing harness which runs from the gunwale or seat frame through a ring on the canoe's bottom. The paddler pushes his knees tight against the straps to "lock" them in place -- a very secure arrangement, especially when combined with "toe blocks".

Tracking: Working a canoe upstream, against the current, with the aid of ropes (lines) attached to the bow and stern.

Trim: The difference in the draft at the bow from that at the stern of a canoe. A properly trimmed canoe will sit dead level in the water. Trim can be adjusted by weighting the bow or the stern.

Tumblehome: The inward curve of the sides of a canoe above the waterline.

Tumpline: A strap which is secured just above a person's forehead to help support a pack or canoe.

Waist: The middle of the canoe.

Water line: The place to which the water comes on the hull of the canoe when it is set in the water.

White water: Foamy (air-filled), turbulent water.

Yoke: A special crossbar equipped with shoulder pads for portaging the canoe.

SELECTING THE WILDERNESS CANOE

Wilderness canoes should be longer and deeper than those used for daytripping. Long canoes are faster (and thus easier to paddle) than short canoes, and deep hulls provide a margin of safety on wind-lashed lakes and thrashing rapids. Choose a canoe at least 17 feet long; 18 or 18½ feet is better. The width (beam) should be at least 34 inches, and the center depth not less than 13½ inches. The bows should have increasing flare so they will have sufficient buoyancy to climb up over big waves without knifing dangerously through them.

Because a canoe's ability to rise and fall easily with waves depends upon its hull design and not the height of its ends, high bows and sterns serve little purpose other than to add weight to the canoe. Generally, ends should not be higher than the center depth of the canoe plus 10 inches. Thus, a canoe with a 13-inch depth should have a *maximum* end height of 23 inches. Ends that are too high act as sails, making canoe-handling on windblown lakes difficult.

KEELS -- FRIEND OR FIEND?

An external keel will make any canoe track (hold its course) better. However, it will also act as a cow-catcher in rapids; it'll hang up on rocks and cause upsets. There's smug satisfaction in watching your friends spill when the keel of their canoe catches on the same rock that your "keel-less" canoe slid easily over just moments before. Later, when your friends have dried out you'll swear that your superiority in rapids is due to your impeccable paddling skill rather than a smooth bottom canoe!

Let's not mince words. External keels are generally the sign of an inferior canoe design. A canoe which requires an after-thought tacked on below to make it paddle straight belongs back on the re-drawing board. Good tracking may be achieved simply by combining a round or Vee bottom, narrow ends, a straight keel line (see the section on "Rocker" below) and somewhat squarish stems (ends). Aluminum canoes are formed in two halves, so they need a keel to hold the halves together. But even here, the keel could be mounted on the inside of the hull rather than the outside.

The *real* reason for keels is to stiffen a floppy bottom. The biggest, flattest canoe bottom can be strengthened considerably by hanging a piece of angle aluminum or one-by-two along its length. Throw in a bunch of ribs and maybe a vertical strut or three -- and the most shapeless hull will become rigid.

My recommendation: *Avoid canoes with keels. Exception -- aluminum canoes which don't come any other way. Some aluminum canoe makers offer shallow draft "shoe" keels on their heavyweight whitewater models. Shoe keels make a lot more sense than the standard T-grip rock grabbers.*

ROCKER

The fore and aft upward curve of the keel-line of a canoe is called "rocker". A canoe with lots of rocker (anything over one and one-half inches is a lot) will turn easily in rapids and rise

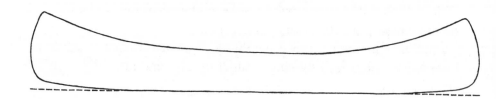

Figure 2-4   ROCKER: The fore and aft upward curve of the keel-line of a canoe is called "rocker." Rockered canoes turn more easily (and rise to the waves more easily) than those without rocker.

quickly to oncoming waves. But it will track poorly and be somewhat slower on the flats than a similar hull with no rocker.

Racers like a canoe with zero rocker -- perhaps a hint of lift in the ends, but that's all. Whitewater canoes should have severe rocker -- three or more inches is not uncommon. A wilderness tripper might fall somewhere in between -- about one to one and one-half inches. The important thing to consider is *how* the boat will be used. A canoe that tracks like a mountain cat when near empty will turn with impudence when heavily loaded. A heavy load forces a canoe down into the water (acts like a keel) and so improves tracking. Wilderness canoes ordinarily are heavily loaded and therefore require some rocker. Conversely, it makes little sense to have lots of rocker in a minimally loaded day cruiser.

When I first became interested in whitewater canoeing, I traded my standard keeled aluminum canoe for a very responsive keel-less Royalex model with a great deal of rocker. I took my wife on her first wilderness trip in this canoe. All went well until we encountered some very heavy wind-driven waves. I told Sharon it was unsafe to continue, but she insisted on reaching a certain distant campsite whose virtues I had extolled. To keep water out of the canoe, I began striking the waves at a slight angle, but my strength was not enough to hold the skittish canoe on course. We swung broadside, gulping several inches of water. Luckily I brought the canoe around in time to avoid another large wave. Sluggishly, we paddled to an island to dump the accumulated water. Sharon blamed the entire episode on me; I, of course, blamed the canoe!

The *amount* of rocker a canoe needs depends largely on its length and hull configuration. Short hulls need less rocker than long ones, and flat bottom canoes turn more easily than round bottom ones. Very short canoes -- 14½ feet or less (solo boats) -- with no rocker may be turned easily with minimal paddle effort by leaning them in the *opposite* direction you wish to turn (you use the rocker in the side-wall). A rocker of more than one and one-half inches is ridiculous in a true solo canoe, unless of course it's a flat-out whitewater slalom boat.

My advice: *Use a tape measure to determine the amount of rocker in a canoe before you buy it. Figure on zero rocker for a racer, maybe a half-inch for a day cruiser, and up to one-and-one-half inches for a wilderness tripper. For all out whitewater use, the more rocker the merrier.*

TUMBLEHOME

The inward curve of the sides of a canoe *above the waterline* is called "tumblehome". Some canoes have lots of tumblehome, others have none at all, Tumblehome is used for these reasons:

• The craft can be made wide at the waterline for stability and narrow at the gunwales for ease-of-paddling (you don't have to reach so far over the side).

Figure 2-5   The inward curve of the sides of the canoe above the waterline, is called "tumblehome" (canoe "a"). Canoe "b" has flared sides, which are much more seaworthy. Note that the maximum beam (c-d) is the same for both canoes.

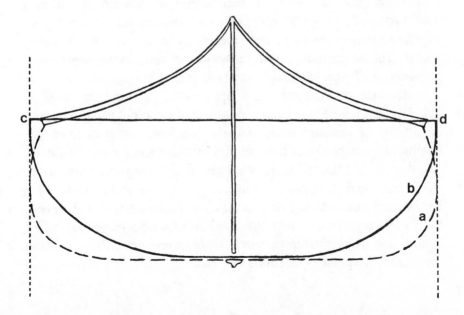

• Curved side-walls are more rigid than broad flat areas, thus a canoe with lots of tumblehome will be stiffer and require less bracing than a gently arched or radically flared boat.

The most seaworthy configuration of *any* watercraft consists of sides which flare boldly right to the gunwales as exemplified in a wild river dory. Nonetheless, most of the best tripping canoes necessarily feature some tumblehome to maintain sidewall stiffness and reduce gunwale width. Given a choice, I'd choose a canoe with no tumblehome whatsoever. Unfortunately, a lot of very good canoes don't come this way. Moral? Moderation in all things. It couldn't be more true for that ol' debbil tumblehome!

FLAT OR ROUND BOTTOM?

Virtually every text on wilderness canoeing recommends flat-bottom canoes over round-bottom ones, on the assumption that round-bottom hulls lack stability. Yet the fact remains that accomplished canoeists prefer round- or vee-bottom canoes for use on *every* type of water, from placid lakes to thundering rapids.

As far as stability is concerned, when it is loaded a round-bottom canoe feels nearly as stable as a flat-bottom one, and in reality the round hull is far more stable in rough water because you can control the canoe with your body. The responsiveness of the round hull permits you to make small balance adjustments easily. You can ride the waves and rapids and feel every movement of the canoe -- like a jockey on a well-trained racehorse. Should you broach (turn broadside to the waves), you can immediately transfer your weight to expose more of the side of the canoe to the oncoming waves. The sluggishness of a flat-bottom canoe, on the other hand, prevents much real control except for steering.

Because of their curved shape, round bottoms are stronger than flat bottoms. Thus, round-bottom canoes do not usually require the additional reinforcement of keels. Keelless, flat-bottom canoes commonly suffer from lack of hull rigidity and have difficulty retaining their bottom shape when paddled through the water.

Additionally, round-bottom hulls are considerably faster than flat-bottom ones. Although you may not be concerned with speed, the time may come when you will need to paddle many miles against the wind on a large lake. At this time you will be grateful for whatever speed your canoe possesses.

Perhaps the biggest objection to round-bottom canoes is their lack of carrying capacity when compared to flat-bottom craft of the same length. This was a valid objection several decades ago, when most round-hulled canoes were narrow, shallow models with racing pedigrees. Today, however, there are many large, round-bottom canoes available -- at reasonable prices. If carrying capacity is a problem, merely choose a bigger canoe.

SELECTING A STORE-BOUGHT CANOE

Since you usually can't take a new canoe out and try it before you buy, here are some things to look for and some tests to perform right in the store.

1. Use a tape measure to determine length, width, and depth. Don't believe the manufacturer's specifications. Is the canoe big enough for rough water?

2. Place the canoe on grass, a carpet, or the showroom floor. Climb in. Can you kneel beneath each seat? This is important because kneeling increases stability, and you'll often find it necessary to kneel in the rough water of rapids: Exception -- some fine-lined canoes are so narrow in the bow that kneeling is impractical (you can't spread your knees wide for stability). In these boats, it's better to have a *low-mounted* seat and to brace your feet solidly against the bow flotation tank or an improvised foot-brace of some sort.

3. Manufacturer's listed canoe weights are almost always five to fifteen percent overoptimistic (I have never owned a canoe which weighed *less* than its advertised weight). Even identical canoe models from the same manufacturer vary considerably in weight (aluminum canoes are an exception). Take a bathroom scale with you when you go canoe-shopping!

4. Climb out of the canoe and spin it around on the ground. If the canoe spins easily and is a keelless model, it probably has a fair amount of rocker. You can also look at the hull at ground level to see how much dead rise there is at the ends, or you can measure it precisely. But the spin test will provide a fair indication of the craft's maneuverability. (It's important to realize that the spin test provides only a very rough estimate of a canoe's turning ability. To use this test effectively you should try several canoe models

and compare them. Remember, you want a canoe that turns reasonably well when loaded.)

5. You will probably carry a wilderness canoe almost as much as you will paddle it. The carrying yoke or center thwart should be installed almost at the exact center of the canoe. Have the salesperson help you place the canoe on your shoulders (just let the center thwart rest on your neck). Is the canoe balanced, or is one end much heavier than the other? If the canoe is out of balance, can the center thwart be easily moved?

6. A wilderness canoe must be equipped with *painters*, or end lines. Ideally, the attachment point for these lines (the towing link) should be located as close to the water line as possible. Where lines are secured to the deck of a canoe, the force of the water acting on the canoe is so distant from the point of attachment of the painters that a quick pull of a rope can, in some rapids or currents, overturn the canoe. I nearly lost my life once when a canoe in which I was paddling upset while being lined down a difficult rapid. I made two errors which I will never repeat; lining a canoe with a person in it (me), and tying a rope to the deck plate, which is much too high.

7. Gunwales should be aluminum or wood so that holes can be drilled or brackets attached to function as *tie points* for ropes. In rough water you will want to secure your gear in the canoe, and it is nice to have attachment points along the gunwales. Some kinds of plastic crack under stress and don't stand up to extreme temperature changes.

8. Canoes built of nonbuoyant materials must have built-in flotation. Usually this consists of styrofoam blocks placed in sealed compartments at each end of the canoe. Make sure flotation does not interfere with front legroom.

9. To prevent bottom wobble, flat-bottom canoes should have an inner or outer keel, or they should have their bottoms reinforced with additional material.

As you look around for the ideal wilderness canoe, remember that most novice canoeists buy small, short canoes because they are light and easy to handle and store. As a result, many manufacturers design their small canoes for an inexperienced market, with high bows and sterns, plastic gunwales, flotation under the seats, big keels, and so on. Experienced canoeists usually select the longest and deepest canoes they can carry; hence, big canoes are usually designed to meet the needs of more knowledgeable paddlers. Most canoes 17½ to 18½ feet long will meet many of the wilderness design requirements. This is not to say that shorter canoes have no place in the wilderness. There are some very suitable 16- and 17-foot models available -- but you will have to know where to look for them.

THE CASE FOR THE SHORT CANOE

If your canoeing will be limited to the near wilderness of small streams and rivers, a small, light canoe may be right for you. If you plan to do a lot of rock dodging in shallow rapids or to twist your way down narrow, mountain-fed streams like the ones in North Carolina, Vermont, and West Virginia, a 16-foot deep-hulled canoe would be a good choice. Short canoes generally turn quickly and are light and easy to handle on portages.

Carrying long canoes through brushy areas, between trees, and up and down steep banks can be very frustrating. It is in these areas that the short canoe excels. And if you prefer to paddle alone (see Chapter 4, Solo Canoeing is Different) you will find a lightly loaded, narrow, 14 to 16 foot canoe to be fast, responsive, and easily maneuvered.

Tandem (two person) canoes which are shorter than 16 feet, however, respond sluggishly to the paddle and have poor directional stability. With the exception of specialized whitewater craft, such canoes are better adapted to portaging than paddling. There is little sense in buying, paddling, or carrying more canoe than you need. However, to attempt a rough-water voyage with a canoe that is too small is to invite disaster!

NEW CANOE DESIGNS

One of the most exciting improvements in canoe design has been the appearance of the asymmetric hull. Basically this consists of a long, narrow, somewhat flared bow with a fairly uniform taper and a fat, buoyant stern. The stern is made fuller than the bow (below the water line) because when a canoe is paddled through water it tends to create turbulence (a wake) at its tail end. The foamy nature of this turbulent water reduces the buoyancy of the canoe at the stern. The faster the craft is paddled, the less the buoyancy of the stern. At a speed of about six miles per hour the

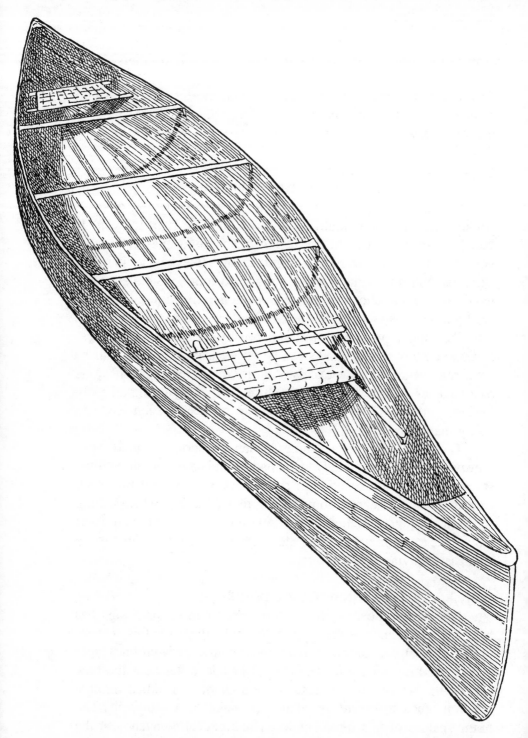

Figure 2-6   An Asymmetric Canoe: There's no denying the advantages of asymmetry for straight ahead running, but asymmetric canoes are often unpredictable in tricky currents.

stern sinks sufficiently to make it appear that the canoe is being paddled uphill. To correct for this the stern is built wider (more buoyant) than the bow. The resulting canoe is easier to paddle, hence faster than conventionally designed craft (especially in water which is less than two or three feet deep).

Virtually all competitive racing canoes are asymmetric, as are many of the best high-performance cruisers. I've owned a number of asymmetric canoes and have been alternately pleased and displeased with their performance. There's no denying the advantages of asymmetry for straight-ahead running, even in big brawny rapids. But asymmetric hulls -- especially those which are *very* asymmetric -- are often fickle (unpredictable) in tricky currents and when performing precise slalom maneuvers which require strong leans. For this reason, I prefer symmetrical boats for all-around wilderness travel where a variety of water conditions will be encountered.

Fortunately, canoe builders are toning down the bizarre asymmetry of their earlier designs with the result that "total" canoe performance is improved. Some of the best big water tripping and whitewater racing canoes now feature only a trace of asymmetry below the waterline.

In the hands of experienced crews, high volume asymmetric canoes are ideal for extended trips on all types of water, except perhaps the trickiest rapids. Being experts' canoes, they require some finesse, as they feel quite tippy until you get used to them. When loaded, however, they firm right up and are very stable.

FREEBOARD

Even if you never take a far northern or arctic trip, you will be happiest with a big canoe, because it has adequate freeboard to weather out rough water. Some of the most popular canoe areas, like the Quetico-Superior wilderness of Minnesota-Canada and the Allagash wilderness waterway of Maine, are now so heavily traveled that finding unoccupied campsites has become a problem. The dense foliage and/or rocky nature of these areas prevents camping just anywhere, and camping areas are restricted for environmental reasons. I have been caught in a big *Norwester* (fierce wind out of the northwest) on an overpopulated lake more than once, with no suitable landing place in sight. At such times I was grateful for every inch of freeboard my canoe possessed.

I'll never forget the first day I paddled Yellowstone Lake in Yellowstone National Park, Wyoming. A strange combination of sea and mountain breezes suddenly caused the lake to turn on edge in midafternoon. What began as a pleasant morning paddle on quiet water finished as a mad dash to shore in 4-foot rollers. My 18-foot aluminum canoe barely made it to shore without swamping. (Since these conditions occur almost daily on Yellowstone Lake, canoeists should paddle in the early morning hours and camp by one or two P.M.)

While some experts recommend a minimum of 6 inches of freeboard, no serious canoeist I know would think of using any canoe so heavily loaded on any but a mirror-calm lake. My own preference is a 9-inch minimum. A deep-hulled 18-foot canoe will easily ride that high if moderately loaded.

WEIGHT

Most people can comfortably carry canoes weighing up to seventy-five pounds. Beyond this weight canoes seem to get very heavy very fast. I know of few individuals who can tolerate more than eighty-five pounds for any great distance. There are a few big men who take pride in carrying heavy canoes. Some people select them because they are tougher than similar lightweight models. Whether the extra strength of a heavy canoe will save it from a pounding in heavy rapids is debatable, but one thing is evident -- you will certainly be reluctant to carry a heavy canoe very far. In fact, many lightweight canoes have successfully negotiated wilderness waterways. I am slight of build and weigh only 135 pounds, and I can carry up to seventy-five pounds for about half a mile without stopping. If the weight increases or the distance is longer, my frame simply mashes down and refuses to move; hence I favor a lightweight canoe. Just as a good hunter can use a smaller caliber rifle because he is proficient in placing the shot, so, too, can an accomplished canoeist get by with a lighter weight canoe. There are limits, of course. No wilderness canoe can be fragile (although the birch-bark models certainly were), but it doesn't have to be built like a tank, either. Proficient canoeists seldom hit rocks directly or at high speeds. Their biggest problem in rough-water canoeing is usually swamping in heavy rapids. Under such conditions even a strong, well-built canoe can be broken in half or wrapped around a rock like a pretzel. Where the choice lies between a light, big canoe, and a heavy, strong, smaller model, choose the big canoe. It is important that you select a canoe that you can carry. Portaging in the wilderness is the rule, not the exception.

BUILDING MATERIALS

ALUMINUM

Aluminum canoes have achieved great popularity, and for good reason. They are inexpensive, incredibly strong, reasonably light, and virtually maintenance free. Most of the canoes used by professional outfitters are aluminum as are the majority you'll find in summer camps. Two decades ago, aluminum was pre-eminent for whitewater and wilderness travel. Now, canoes built of Royalex and fiberglass/Kevlar are justifiably more popular.

Some manufacturers build lightweight aluminum canoes. The weight difference is in the thickness of the metal skin which averages .050 inches for the standard models and .035 inches or less for the lightweights. Generally, the thicker the skin, the tougher the boat.

Since the machinery which produces aluminum canoes is very expensive, there have been few design innovations. Most aluminum canoe designs are decades old; some date back to the 1940's. Few are very good. Fortunately, state-of-the-art designs constructed from ultralight aircraft alloys are beginning to appear. These boats lack the high upturned ends and bulbous bows of their 1940's predecessors and so are considered ugly by traditional standards. But they are fast, fun to paddle, and much less expensive than similar canoes built of other materials.

In buying an aluminum canoe, look for closely spaced, flush rivets. This is a sign of a properly tempered hull and is indicative of quality construction. Despite manufacturers' claims that spot welding is as strong as riveting, welded canoes seem to suffer greater damage on rocky whitewater streams. A canoe which pulls its rivets in rough water can usually be repaired to its former strength by inserting oversize rivets. This repair can often be completed in the field with a minimum of tools and time. When spot welds separate, however, you must return the canoe to the factory to effect an acceptable repair. In essence, canoes with riveted hulls and fittings can be repaired by almost anybody; welded canoes cannot!

Almost any aluminum canoe seventeen feet or more long is suitable for wilderness tripping, as the flared ends, flat bottoms, and high sides make for great carrying capacity. (There are so many design factors which affect the determination of carrying capacity that manufacturers' recommendations are generally unreliable. The *real* carrying capacity of a canoe is almost always considerably less than that advertised.) Because of their stability, aluminum canoes are ideal for touring with young children who refuse to stay put for very long.

For all its advantages, aluminum has a few drawbacks, the greatest of which is its tendency to cling to subsurface rocks. If an aluminum canoe strikes a rock below the water line, it will often be stopped completely. You may have no recourse but to get out of the canoe and push off the rock. The problem of sticking can be somewhat reduced by applying a good coat of paste wax to the bottom of the hull. For best results apply at least two coats of wax and buff each to silky smoothness. This is much less of a problem with canoes built of other materials.

Aluminum also dents, and try as you may, you will never remove the dents completely. Old aluminum canoes gradually take on the appearance of a high school shop ballpeen hammer project as they acquire dent upon dent.

FIBERGLASS CANOES

Note: All the best fiberglass canoes are selectively reinforced with Kevlar 49. See the section on KEVLAR for a description of this popular fabric.

Now here's a canoe building material you can get excited about! It's very strong, acceptably light, relatively inexpensive...and the easiest of all canoe building materials to repair. No, it's not as durable as heavy heat-treated aluminum or polyethylene. So what? If you need more strength than that obtainable in a well-built fiberglass canoe, then you're either willfully abusing your craft or you don't know how to paddle! Fact is, *good* fiberglass canoes are plenty strong enough for use in any type of water. Granted, the strength advantages of Kevlar over fiberglass are real, but not real enough to justify the hundreds (!) of extra dollars all-Kevlar construction commands. Buy Kevlar to save weight, not to gain strength!

All the best fiberglass canoes now utilize some Kevlar (scrap) in their construction -- mostly to reinforce delicate canoe stems and areas which are most subject to abrasion. Today's "fiberglass composite" canoes are light and strong -- a far cry from those available a decade ago.

CONSTRUCTION METHODS

There are so many ways to build fiberglass composite canoes that it would require a full chapter to outline them all. To understand the most commonly used procedures, you should know some terminology.

Fiberglass cloth: "Cloth" is composed of twisted strands of fiberglass which are woven at right angles to one another. Cloth yields the highest glass to resin ratio (about 1:1) of all the fiberglass fabrics and therefore has the greatest tensile strength. Most of the best "all-fiberglass" canoes are built of "all-cloth" laminates.

Fiberglass matt: Composed of chopped crosslinked glass fibers which are held together with a dried resin binder. Matt has a glass to resin ratio of about 1:3, which means it's only about one-third as strong as woven cloth. Its main use is as a stiffening agent in canoe bilges and other places where extreme rigidity is desirable. Canoe hulls can also be stiffened with "cloth" (some are), but this is more expensive, both in terms of labor and material costs.

Roving: A much coarser weave than cloth. Its glass to resin ratio is slightly less than that of cloth but its impact resistance is greater. Also used to help stiffen a hull.

Gel-coat: An abrasion resistant waterproof resin used on the outside of a fiberglass canoe. Color is in the thin layer of gel-coat which "scratches white" when you hit rocks. To save a few pounds, some canoes are built without gel-coat (called "skin-coat" construction). However, skin-coat canoes are more subject to damage from abrasion than are those with gel-coat. A tripping canoe should have a gel-coat finish.

RESINS

There are polyester, vinylester, and epoxy resins -- and dozens of formulations for each.

Polyester resin: Least strong, least expensive, and standard of the canoe-building industry.

Vinylester resin: May be the best compromise between cost and strength. Vinylester has low toxicity and it's relatively easy to work with. Most of the best Kevlar canoes are now being built with this resin.

Epoxy resin: Epoxy is the strongest of all resins. It is also expensive, difficult to work with, and frequently, more toxic than polyester or vinylester. Epoxy is used on a regular basis by only a small number of custom canoe builders. Whether it has enough advantages over vinylester to warrant its higher cost is debatable.

HOW THEY'RE BUILT

Chopper-gun layup: Chopped strands of fiberglass mixed with polyester resin is sprayed into a mold. The resulting canoe is very heavy, not very strong, and cheap. All the worst canoes are built this way. The tell-tale matrix of chopped fibers is visible on the inner walls of the craft. Chopper-gun canoes are no bargain at any price.

Hand layup: Glass cloth, and possibly roving and matt, is laid into a mold by hand then saturated with resin and squeegeed out. "All-cloth" canoes are the toughest and most resilient of the breed and are also the most expensive. You can tell hand layup at a glance, as you can see the crisp outline of the glass weave in the inside of the hull.

Vacuum-bagging: A plastic "vacuum bag" is placed into the mold and the air is pumped out. This compresses the resin-soaked laminate and evenly distributes the resin, thus giving you the highest glass/Kevlar to resin ratio possible -- all of which translates into a very light, very strong canoe. All the competitive racing canoes are built this way.

Foam cores: A canoe bottom that flexes due to water pressure won't maintain its shape and paddling efficiency. For this reason, performance-minded canoeists prefer hulls which are as stiff as possible. The lightest, strongest way to stiffen a canoe is to sandwich a layer of closed cell foam between the Kevlar or fiberglass laminates. Often, foam ribs are added to increase the torsional stiffness of the side-walls. The entire boat is then vacuum-bagged to eliminate as much resin (and weight) as possible.

Vacuum-bagged foam core hulls are *extremely* light. Some Kevlar racing models weigh under 25 pounds, and tripping boats of 45 pounds are a reality. On the surface, you can make a very good case for this type of construction. However, the light stiff hulls preferred by racers often break when they hit rocks. You need some flex in a wilderness canoe, even if it means sacrificing paddling performance. And because there's less fabric (fiberglass and/or Kevlar) in a foam-cored boat than in an all-cloth one, the hull is more easily damaged. Once the foam-core is cut through, cosmetic repairs become difficult. Replacing large sections of damaged foam has been described as similar to performing a lobotomy. Canoes with foam cores are ideal for racing, lazy waterways, or folks who can afford to repair or replace them when they become damaged.

Color: Canoe color is a personal thing, though dark colors add weight to the gel-coat. That's because it takes more color agent to get a dark green or red color than a clear (colorless) or white one. Generally, the darker the color, the heavier the finished canoe will be.

As you probably guessed, my favorite color is "white." White canoes "scratch white" and so hide surface damage. White is also the easiest color to match when making cosmetic repairs -- something every canoeist has to do at least once a year.

KEVLAR 49

Kevlar is a honey-gold colored fabric manufactured by the Dupont Company. It looks much like fiberglass cloth (and it is used in the same way) only its properties and price (!) are much different. Kevlar 49 composites have a tensile strength about 40 percent higher than epoxy-fiberglass and a specific gravity of 1.45 grams per cubic centimeter, versus 2.55 for glass. This means that canoes built of Kevlar are much stronger and lighter than equivalent glass models. Kevlar is widely used as a tire cord fiber and as bullet-proof material in flak vests -- testimony to its incredible strength. Unfortunately, the fabric is very expensive and difficult to work with, so "all-Kevlar" canoes typically cost 300 to 600 dollars more than identical fiberglass models.

According to extensive tests performed by Dupont, some types of construction have resulted in a 33 percent weight savings over comparable glass canoes. In conventional construction, by using Kevlar five to ten pounds can easily be cut from a 75 pound canoe while *adding* durability.

Unlike fiberglass, Kevlar cannot be sanded. It just frizzes up like cotton candy -- the canoe looks like it needs a haircut! Bash enough rocks with a Kevlar canoe and you're certain to expose the "hairy" fibers of the cloth. Repairing the mess requires painting on resin (epoxy, polyester, or vinylester) and cutting off the fibers while the resin is "green". The alternative is to cover the damaged area with a fiberglass patch which can be sanded (the recommended procedure). In short, cosmetic repairs are at best, "difficult!"

For this reason, it's best to avoid all-Kevlar construction unless you absolutely positively want the lightest boat possible. A composite layup with S-glass (an abrasion resistant form of fiberglass) as the outer layer will be more durable, easier to patch, nearly as strong, and less expensive than all-Kevlar construction. Many of the best canoe makers are already building canoes like this. Those that aren't may do so if you request it. Right now, American canoeists are enamored with light weight canoes, much to the detriment of long term durability...and repairability.

My preference? A vinylester, *all-cloth* Kevlar canoe with an S-glass outer layer in an all-hand or vacuum-bagged layup. Color?

White, of course. My 18½-foot Mad River TW Special is built this way and it weighs an honest 73 pounds.

POLYETHYLENE

When the first polyethylene kayaks appeared more than a decade ago, they received mixed reviews. Granted, they were strong -- you could wrap one around a boulder and later retrieve it intact. But the boats were heavy, and state-of-the-art designs simply didn't exist.

Now, that's old hat. Some of the best whitewater kayaks are now rotationally molded from cross-linked polyethylene.

Given the success of polyethylene kayaks, it was only a matter of time before canoe companies got into the act. The first real success was the Coleman canoe -- a less than daring buff-bowed design with a network of interior aluminum tubes for stiffening. At the outset, Coleman discovered that unsupported polyethylene sheet simply wouldn't hold its shape unless it was given a helping hand, via internal struts, ribs and keel. But the same metal framework which held the plastic in shape also kept it from giving when the boat smashed headlong into a rock. The result was that these canoes performed better on paper than in the maelstrom of a rocky rapid.

The problem is academic: How do you stiffen a polyethylene canoe without resorting to internal struts and ribs?

Old Town Canoe Company may have found an answer. In 1985 they announced a new use of polyethylene. They sandwiched an expanded polyethylene core between two layers of rotationally-molded cross-linked polyethylene. The result was a tough and rigid boat -- one whose properties were similar to that of a sandwiched Royalex hull. And because of the stiffness imparted by the foam core, no internal bracing was necessary. At this writing, Old Town offers only a single model built by this method -- a 17'4" cruising/ tripping canoe called the "Discovery." If this method of fabrication proves profitable (and it should), other models from this and other companies are sure to follow.

The attractiveness of cored cross-linked polyethylene centers around its strength, resistance to abrasion, stiffness, and relatively low cost. The finished canoe is still rather heavy and the aesthetics of wood or fiberglass simply aren't there. Nevertheless, if you want a good tough canoe at an attractive price, this may be the route to go.

ABS (ACRYLONITRILE BUTADIENE STYRENE) AND ABS ROYALEX

Ribbed ABS plastic canoes appeared on the market in the 1960's with high hopes. Within two decades they disappeared without a trace. Good! These boats were neither light nor inexpensive and their designs were just short of dreadful. Even their strength was uncertain. In fact, commercial outfitters who tried conventional ABS canoes in the livery trade found they literally came apart at the seams! Their one redeeming character was good resistance to abrasion. No canoeist I know will mourn their passing.

However, when expanded to a foam (Royalex, made by Uniroyal), ABS is an exceptional canoe-building material. Royalex differs from ordinary ABS plastic in that it is laminated and vacuum-formed under intense heat and pressure so that its central core contains many tiny air pockets. The resulting product, called a *thermoplastic laminate*, is very strong, naturally buoyant, acceptably light, and fairly expensive.

Royalex canoes are very tough indeed. They are nearly impossible to puncture and they "snick" over subsurface rocks so easily that even a mediocre canoeist has little difficulty making it through a twisting "rock garden" -- while paddlers of aluminum canoes are still pushing off rocks, Royalex owners are hundreds of feet downstream. Unfortunately, unless the bottom of a Royalex canoe is reinforced with extra layers of material or is well-rounded, it will ripple or "oil-can" in rough water, which detracts from the canoe's speed. In fact, the bottoms of most Royalex hulls will "hog" in water unless they are held firm by a load of heavy camping gear. And, Royalex is difficult to form into tight curves, which means that fine entry lines and other features which contribute to "high performance" are impossible to obtain.

Although canoes built of other materials are often lighter and faster, Royalex models have enjoyed much success in rocky whitewater races, mainly due to their ability to wobble over rocks. Once you get over your initial fear of the jellylike bottom, the fact that ABS Royalex canoes are almost indestructible and as maintenance-free as aluminum ones may attract you to them. For paddling the unforgiving waterways of the far north -- where you can't afford to have a canoe fail -- Royalex is the premiere material!

CEDAR STRIP CANOES -- THE ONES THAT WIN RACES

Many of the canoes that win long-distance flat-water races are hand-built of cedar or redwood strips, nailed to a form, glued together, and covered with fiberglass cloth and polyester or epoxy resin (the nails are removed prior to glassing). The result is a very beautiful, very light canoe. Since construction is all done by hand, the few companies that produce this style canoe command high prices (one thousand dollars and up). Strip canoes, however, are easily built by anyone with power tools, basic woodworking know-how, and patience! They are very inexpensive to make. Easy-to-follow plans for the construction of several excellent canoe models are available at low cost from the Minnesota Canoe Association, P.O. Box 14177, University Station, Minneapolis, Minnesota 55401; and the U.S. Canoe Association, 617 South 94th St., Milwaukee, Wisconsin 53214.

It is interesting to note the greatest cross-continent canoe safari of the twentieth century was completed in a canoe built of Sitka spruce strips and fiberglass. In April, 1971 Verlen Kruger of De-Witt, Michigan, and Clint Waddell of Saint Paul, Minnesota, launched a hand-built twenty-one-foot strip canoe at Montreal's Lachine docks on the Saint Lawrence River. The two men paddled 6500 miles across some of the roughest waterways in North America, and terminated their trip at the Bering Sea in Alaska just. five months later. Vital canoe statistics were:

LENGTH: 21 feet
WIDTH MEASURED 3 INCHES OFF THE BOTTOM: 27 inches;
AT THE CENTER THWART: 34 inches
DEPTH: 18 inches at the bow; 12½ inches rest of length
WEIGHT: 85 pounds
SEATS: Sawyer molded fiberglass, bucket-type
YOKES: Form-fitted center yoke for one-man carry, and a pad and yoke at each end for two-man carry

COVER: 8-ounce waterproof nylon snap-on for complete protection from spray.

Experienced paddlers will recognize Kruger's hand-built canoe as a lengthened version of the standard Canadian racer. The Waddell-Kruger expedition to the Bering Sea is one of the most fantastic canoe voyages of our time -- perhaps of any time. The fact that this trip was safely completed in a modern canoe of revolutionary design should do much to dispel the myth that canoes have changed little since the time of the Indian birch barks.

WOOD-CANVAS CANOES

Wood-canvas canoes are a dying breed. The Chestnut canoe company, which a decade ago produced dozens of canoe models, recently closed their doors in Canada. And Old Town, granddaddy of them all, offers only a few wood-ribbed models (on special order) -- all of which are covered with fiberglass not the traditional canvas.

There are a handful of custom builders scattered around the country who still eke out a living by the manufacture of wood-canvas canoes, but these are small shops; prices are high and the waiting period is long. Relics or not, well-built wood-canvas canoes are much tougher than most people think. They have quite a lot of flex in their hulls, and like fiberglass and Royalex canoes, they slide over rocks easily. A good wood-canvas canoe will probably weigh about the same as an all-cloth fiberglass one, and be nearly as strong. Unfortunately, canvas canoes absorb water unless they're kept well-sealed. Overall weight may increase by ten percent or more after only a few weeks of exposure to water.

Nonetheless, if you're strong enough to carry a water-soaked canoe of wood and cloth, and you can afford one, the annual chore of patching, sanding, and painting will be more than made up for by the pride of ownership. There are many canoeists who feel that absolutely nothing paddles as pleasantly as a traditional wood-canvas canoe. Certainly, few other canoes are as beautiful.

EASE OF REPAIR

If you use your canoe hard in rocky whitewater, you'll ultimately need to repair it. Canoes built of fiberglass and Kevlar are easiest to repair; a properly applied patch is hardly noticeable. Wood-strip canoes mend nicely, as do wood-canvas ones. It's possible to fix a Royalex/ABS or aluminum canoe but the patch will be a glaring reminder of the rock you hit. From an aesthetic viewpoint, polyethylene hulls cannot be repaired.

Despite what some canoe manufacturers say, no canoe-building material is "indestructible". So consider the merits of a less durable canoe that is easily patched over a more durable one that is not!

THE TOUGHNESS MYTH

Regardless of the material a canoe is built of, manufacturers will tell you that their canoes are the toughest afloat. Fiberglass canoe builders take pride in reporting how many times stronger than aluminum their canoe models are. Consider this: Many of the synthetics may take more abuse in direct impact than heavy, heat-treated aluminum, but they are subject to considerably more damage from abrasion. If you will be grinding your canoe against rocks, dragging it over sand bars, or treating it in other abusive ways, then get an aluminum canoe. It will outlast several other canoes of different materials. However, if you baby your canoe in areas where abrasion is a problem, you may get better service, performance, and enjoyment from a nonaluminum canoe.

ON BUYING A USED CANOE

Now that you are familiar with canoe design and construction, you should have a pretty good idea of what you want in a canoe. The following guidelines will help you get the best deal on a good used canoe:

1. Know the retail value of the canoe *before* you talk to the owner. Figure on paying up to eighty percent of the current retail price for well-cared-for, top-line aluminum canoes, and around fifty percent for lesser known aluminum, fiberglass, and ABS cheapies. Quality-built fiberglass, Kevlar, and Royalex canoes generally command sixty to seventy-five percent of their *new* retail cost, if they have been well kept.

2. If you are trying to save money, purchase a canoe with a hole in it. Contrary to popular belief, canoes are easily patched (see Chapter 9 -- Canoe Rescue and Repair). Check with commercial outfitters, who often sell damaged canoes cheaply (shoddy equipment is bad for their image). With ingenuity and the proper repair materials, you can often restore a canoe to nearly new condition.

3. If you select a used fiberglass canoe, choose one with adequate size and depth. Fiberglass canoes will generally ride about two to four inches lower in the water than aluminum models of the same size, so their carrying capacity will be reduced.

4. Turn used canoes upside down and sight along the keel. Don't buy a canoe with a ''hogged'' (bent-in) keel. Once a keel is bent, it is almost impossible to straighten it properly.

5. Carefully sight along each gunwale. It is very difficult to straighten heat-treated aluminum gunwales, although a hammer and piece of two-by-four can be used to improve aesthetics somewhat. Plastic and wood gunwales which are cracked or broken must be completely replaced.

6. On aluminum canoes, check for stressed or pulled rivets which could cause leakage.

7. Check fiberglass canoes for signs of hull delamination. Home-built and factory prefabricated kit models especially should be carefully examined, as the quality of these canoes depends entirely upon the skill of the builder. This doesn't mean that hand-built canoes are bad. On the contrary, many canoe clubs own their own molds, and club members produce superb canoes at a fraction of the cost (and weight) of factory-built models. A well constructed club-built canoe may be an excellent investment. Occasionally a racing enthusiast will offer a nearly new canoe for sale at little more than the original cost of the building materials, simply because he or she is displeased with the canoe's performance. Canoe clubs and canoe races are good places to frequent if you are looking for a good, inexpensive canoe.

In summary, select a canoe of adequate size and depth. Be certain that the keel line of the canoe is straight, and check for damaged fittings. Eliminate from consideration any fiberglass or Kevlar canoe which shows signs of hull delamination, and be knowledgeable of the canoe's value before you buy. Lastly, join a canoe club. Club membership will bring you into contact with skilled paddlers and canoe builders and will increase your chances of locating a good used canoe at a reasonable price.

3.
Low Cost Ways to Improve the Performance of Your Canoe

If you want to learn the fine points of canoeing, attend a competitive race event. Flatwater, downriver, or whitewater slalom -- makes no difference. In every case the name of the game is "winning". And that -- or losing -- is often a matter of seconds or tenths of seconds. At the highest levels of competition, the performance edge is as much due to the "right" equipment as to the capabilities of the paddlers.

Between races, check out the boats. But look beyond the basics of brand names and hull design. Examine instead how the canoes are tricked out -- how they're "tuned". Study the seating arrangement: height and support of seats, type of sliding mechanism (if any), location of knee pads, toe blocks, thigh straps, etc. What about safety accessories like grab loops and flotation? It won't take you long to discover that these customized race machines are a far cry from what you can buy in the stores.

After the race, engage in some friendly banter with the competitors. Artfully turn the subject from racing to fast touring and wilderness tripping. Do your new friends own cruising canoes? If so, what modifications have been performed to make them safer and more comfortable to paddle? Listen intently and bring a note pad. You'll discover a wealth of honestly useful ideas.

Here are some tips you may learn from your conversations with the masters. Emphasis is on low cost modifications you can perform on your own canoe.

CARRYING YOKE

Canoes are usually carried by one person, with the aid of a padded carrying yoke (an extra-cost item). Aluminum yokes are channeled to fit over the existing center thwart (an exception is the excellent Alumacraft yoke, which is supplied as standard equipment in lieu of a center thwart), while wooden yokes replace the thwart completely. Most manufacturers install the center thwart or yoke in a location determined by a formula, which is often subject to some error. For example, the yoke on one of my canoes was misplaced by four inches, making the craft so tail-heavy that it was impossible to carry.

The most satisfactory method of balancing a canoe is to try it on your shoulders. I like just enough weight in the tail so that the bow will rise very slowly when the canoe is shouldered. I consider a canoe out of balance if more than gentle pressure is required to

Figure 3-1   The Yoke should be made with hardwood. The fabric is stretched over the foam and fastened with staples to a 4 x 8 inch wood block. Drainage holes should be drilled through this block as illustrated in the photo inset.

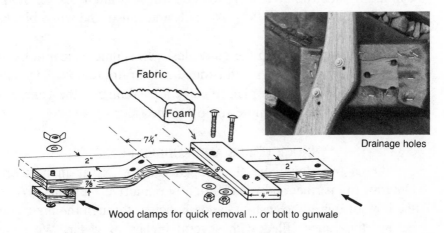

Fabric

Foam

Drainage holes

Wood clamps for quick removal ... or bolt to gunwale

bring it back to a horizontal position. A friend of mine, on the other hand, likes his canoe perfectly balanced, as he prefers to walk with his hands in his pockets. You can easily change the balance on your canoe by reinstalling the yoke in a new set of mounting holes drilled in the gunwales.

If you are very broad-shouldered you will like the spacing of factory-made yoke pads, but if you're of average build you will need to move the pads closer together and to change their angle somewhat. Most people prefer pads mounted at right angles to the yoke bar, with a distance of 7-7½ inches between them.

If you do much portaging you'll want a wooden yoke. The springiness and warmth of wood against your neck makes for more comfort than the inflexibility and coldness of aluminum. Make your yoke from a good hardwood (ash or oak is best) and finish to a 3/4 to 7/8 -inch thickness (Figure 3-1). Completed width should be two to two-and-one-half inches to insure adequate strength. Cut two 8-by-4 inch yoke pad blocks from ½-inch pine and pile polyurethane foam on each block (use pillow padding available at any discount store). Compress each pad to about two-and-one-half inches and cover with a *light-colored* naugahide to reflect heat (I found the difference in surface temperature between a black and white pad in strong sunlight to be 35 degrees!) Staple naugahide into place and finish with upholstery tacks. Then drill a few quarter or three-eighths inch diameter holes through the face of each yoke pad block so that water which accumulates in the foam (when you capsize) will drain out. Commercial yokes don't have drain holes, so moisture becomes trapped in the yoke pads and causes the wood blocks to rot.

Secure your yoke to the gunwales with stainless steel bolts or use the simple clamp device illustrated. Clamp-in, removable yokes are the way to go if you plan to carry a passenger -- the yoke can be removed to provide more room for the rider.

SHOCK CORDS AND RUBBER ROPES

On a trip down the flooded Groundhog River in northern Ontario, my partner and I inadvertently ran a five-foot falls. When the bow of our eighteen-foot canoe punched through the big roller below, the canoe filled with several inches of water. We spun

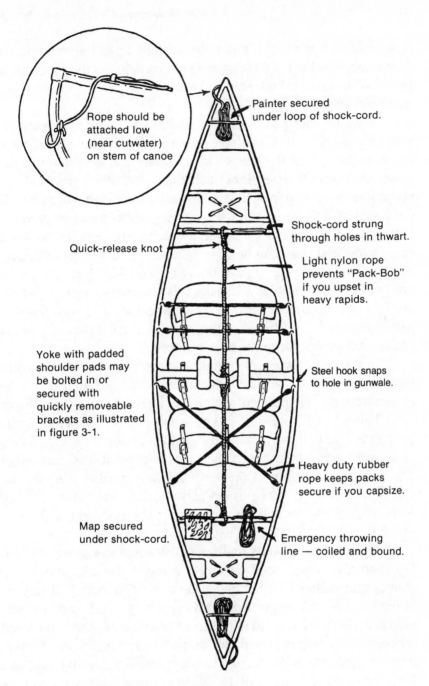

Rope should be attached low (near cutwater) on stem of canoe

Painter secured under loop of shock-cord.

Shock-cord strung through holes in thwart.

Quick-release knot

Light nylon rope prevents "Pack-Bob" if you upset in heavy rapids.

Yoke with padded shoulder pads may be bolted in or secured with quickly removeable brackets as illustrated in figure 3-1.

Steel hook snaps to hole in gunwale.

Heavy duty rubber rope keeps packs secure if you capsize.

Map secured under shock-cord.

Emergency throwing line — coiled and bound.

Figure 3-2   A "customized" canoe protects your valuables.

broadside in the rapids, swamping completely. Fortunately, our four watertight Duluth packs stayed put throughout the run, providing us with sufficient buoyancy to keep afloat. We retained enough freeboard to paddle cautiously ashore.

In whitewater you need the additional flotation provided by water-tight packs, and you can only utilize this flotation if packs are well secured in the canoe. If your canoe is aluminum, drill a series of holes, three-eighths inch diameter, along the gunwales about four inches apart. These holes will provide anchor points for cords and steel hooks to which heavy-duty rubber ropes are attached. If the gunwales of your canoe have water-drain slots (as on wood-canvas models), you can hook your cords or rubber ropes directly to them. The solid rails of most fiberglass and ABS boats, however, present more of a problem. Usually it is possible to drill small holes through the inwale or just below the gunwale. Short loops of parachute cord can then be run through these holes to provide attachment points for your security ropes.

Run at least two rubber ropes across each pack, and where very heavy rapids will be encountered add a length of nylon parachute cord. Tie the cord with a quick release knot (see Chapter 11 -- Tying It All Together) so you won't have difficulty salvaging your gear if you overturn. You can stuff your bailing sponge, fishing gear, and loose articles under the ropes to prevent loss in an upset. The parachute cords will prevent *pack-bob* (packs rising up in a water-filled canoe). Rubber ropes permit quick removal and replacement of packs when making portages. It is a real pain in the neck to constantly tie and untie a network of ropes.

Drill holes in thwarts and deck plates and install lightweight, fabric-covered shock cord (Figure 3-2 shows the procedure). Wet clothes and oddities placed under the corded thwarts will stay put in high winds and on portages. An especially good place for your map is under a shock-corded thwart. The loss of a map can be very serious on a wilderness trip, for unlike backpacking, there are no trails to guide the way. A friend once traded a thirty-five cent map for several dollars worth of fishing lures to a party who had lost theirs when they overturned in a set of rapids. You should carry an extra map on all wilderness trips, but the one in use should always be well secured in the canoe.

PAINTERS

As previously stated, end lines or painters should be attached as close to the water-line of a canoe as possible. A hole can usually be drilled below the deck plate and a hollow plastic tube epoxied into place. The tube will keep water from leaking into the canoe when the bow plunges in rapids. Make sure the plastic tube is of sufficient size to allow passage of a ¼ inch diameter painter. It is important that end lines be available when you need them; they should not be tied into place or left hanging loose to entangle a swimmer in the event of an upset. Once on a northern Canadian trip a canoe got away while it was being unloaded in an eddy above a bouldery falls. When we retrieved it at the base of the falls, one deck plate had been torn off. A painter, which was attached to the deck plate and left lying loose in the canoe's bottom, had streamed out and caught between two rocks.

The best solution for keeping painters immediately available *and* out of the way is to coil and stuff them under a loop of shock cord attached to the deck. Thus stored, they can be released by a simple tug of the end. They will not stream out independently if you overturn, and will remain in place while portaging. Use bright-colored ¼ inch polypropylene rope for painters. Poly rope is very light and won't absorb water; you will be able to find it more easily should you capsize in foamy rapids.

GRAB LOOPS

Attach a loop of polyethylene rope to each end of your canoe. Should you swamp in rapids, you can quickly grab the loop, which may be more accessible than a painter. Grab loops are also convenient handholds for lifting the canoe.

GLARE REDUCTION

Glare from the deck plate of an aluminum canoe can be hazardous if you are in a set of rapids requiring complex maneuvering. An easy solution is to paint each deck plate flat black. The person in the bow will appreciate this small bit of forethought, and you will damage your canoe less if the forward paddler can see better.

CANOE POCKETS

Verlen Kruger, who recently completed a three year cross-continent canoe odyssey of some 28,000 (!) miles was the probable inventor of "canoe pockets." On an early safari of 7,000 miles (Montreal to the Bering Sea), Verlen installed small plastic bicycle baskets in his canoe and used them to store sunglasses, bug dope and such. The baskets provided no security for valuables in a capsize, but they were handy nonetheless.

A better solution is to sew up an envelope style bag from waterproof nylon and tie it to a canoe thwart or gunwale. Or, puchase an "Otter Bag" from California Rivers, or a "Thwart Bag" from Blackhawk Outfitters.* The Otter Bag has a Velcro closure and enough room for a light lunch and a host of sundries. The Thwart Bag is a bit larger. Both products keep contents in place on portages and in rough water upsets.

CANOE TUMPLINES

A tumpline consists of a wide leather or canvas strap secured to a pack or bundle. The packer places this strap just above his forehead, grabs the tumpline near his head, leans forward into the trace, and takes off down the trail. The early voyageurs carried 180 pounds and more across rugged portages using only this rig. If tumplines have a major failing, it is that they exert tremendous pressure on neck muscles, and most modern voyageurs just don't have strong enough necks to tolerate this for very long. Consequently, many canoeists use a combination of tumpline and straps on their packs. By distributing the weight between tumpline and straps, you can carry very heavy loads for short distances in relative comfort.

For years canoeists have been trying to install tumplines on their canoes to make carrying easier. Unfortunately, conventional tumplines are too rigid. When the canoe bounces up, the tump comes off your head and wraps around your neck. And when the canoe comes down, your head receives the full impact of the weight. Ten years ago I began to experiment earnestly with canoe tumplines. At the time I was anticipating an arctic canoe trip with a thirteen-mile portage. Although I was excited about the trip, I began to have nightmares about carrying my 75-pound canoe across that portage.

*California Rivers, Inc. P.O. Box 468, Geyserville, CA 95441
Blackhawk Outfitters, 937 North Washington St., Janesville, WI 53545

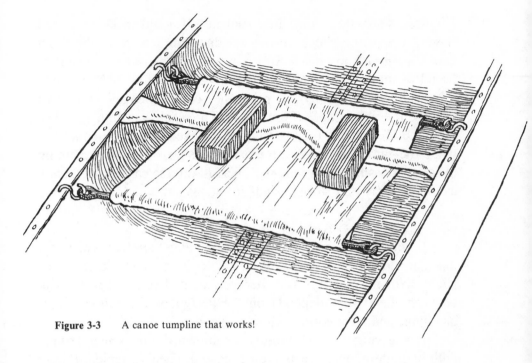

Figure 3-3   A canoe tumpline that works!

Figure 3-4   Ken Saelens models his ingeniously designed tumpline.

I figured that with a tumpline, somehow I could make it. I tried rigging one using shock cords, but that didn't work -- the thing kept slipping off my head. So I posed the problem to an inventive friend of mine, Ken Saelens. Ken thought a while, then attached a 24-inch length of canvas beneath the yoke of the canoe with two heavy-duty rubber ropes (Figure 3-4). The result was dramatic. The tumpline took about fifty percent of the weight off my shoulders while the canvas eliminated the dangerous possibility of it coming loose and possibly strangling me. In addition, the canvas was handy as a lunch tray and storage shelf for small items.

FOOTBRACES AND/OR KNEE PADS

If you're familiar with the recent canoeing literature, you know that the modern way to paddle a canoe is to *sit* not kneel in it. Right? Not necessarily! Whether you sit or kneel -- or alternate between the two -- depends on the design of the canoe you're paddling, and how you "prefer" to paddle.

If you've got a high volume Grumman or Old Town Tripper with its high mounted seats, you'll *have* to kneel in rapids. Purely a matter of getting the CG (center of gravity) low enough for stability in the rough stuff. However, kneeling is practical only if the canoe you're piloting is wide enough at the bow to permit a comfortable kneeling stance (knees spread wide against the bilges). If it isn't -- and most fine-lined cruisers are not! -- then you're best off to maintain your position on the low mounted seat* and brace your feet firmly against a bow flotation tank or improvised brace.

If footbraces are important in the bow of a skinny cruiser, they're even more important in the stern. The simplest brace consists of a pair of wood rails glassed to the floor or sidewalls of the boat. An aluminum tube, flattened at the ends, is screwed to the rails.

On the other hand, if your canoe is spacious enough up front for comfortable kneeling, you'll want to raise the seats to a comfortable 10-12 inch height (if they're not already set there) and install knee pads. You can purchase self-sticking neoprene pads from the Blue Hole Canoe Company** or make your own from a closed-cell

---

*Modern fast cruising canoes generally have seats set 7-9 inches off the floor. Seats in tripping and whitewater canoes are set much higher -- 10-13 inches. The higher the seat, the more comfortable -- and tippy -- the canoe.
**Blue Hole Canoe Co., Sunbright, TN 38373.

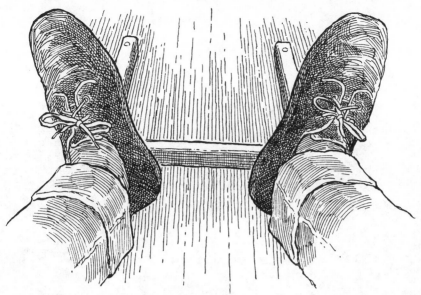

Figure 3-5   Footbraces "lock" you firmly into the canoe when you paddle from a sitting position. The simplest brace consists of a pair of wood rails glassed to the floor of the canoe. An aluminum tube, fastened at the ends, is screwed to the rails.

foam trail mattress. Glue knee pads into the hull with contact cement.

Most big tripping canoes provide for both sitting and kneeling options. You may want to install knee pads *and* footbraces in these boats.

SEAT HEIGHT AND PLACEMENT

I have yet to own a canoe whose seats were placed where I wanted them. Seats on fine-lined cruisers are generally mounted low for stability rather than high for efficiency and all day comfort.

Many of the best canoes now come with sliding seats, which solves the trim problem when paddlers of different weights are aboard. But seat height is another matter. Most canoeists simply refuse to raise or lower their seats to a height which suits them, falsely believing it's wrong to tamper with what was obviously ordained by God.

If you don't like the location of your canoe seats, change them, even if it means drilling new holes through the sidewalls of an expensive canoe!

CANOE COVER

Canoe covers are usually home-built affairs. They're constructed of waterproof nylon and have holes (skirts) for the paddlers.

Figure 3-6   A three-piece canoe cover designed by the author. This model features a "belly" section which expands or shrinks as the load height changes, and end caps which can be "reefed" while portaging.

They attach to the canoe by snaps, Velcro, or stainless steel cable.

Some folks swear by canoe covers (I'm one of them). Others swear at them! There's no denying that they cut wind (as much as fifty percent!), keep out rain and whitewater and extend the versatility of low-volume canoes -- you can use a small canoe in rough water if it is covered. However, covers can be extremely dangerous, especially if they come off in a capsize and entrap you, or if the spray-skirt does not permit an easy exit.

Canoeists who paddle covered boats have a tendency to get very bold -- they think they can run anything. When you're paddling with an experienced whitewater crowd and are properly clad in a life jacket, wet-suit and helmet, you can afford to take some chances. In the wilderness -- or alone on *any* river -- you can't! Nonetheless, nearly all racing canoes occasionally wear covers, as do those which challenge the unforgiving waters of the far north. And once you've "gone covered" in a solo canoe, you won't have it any other way, even if your trips are limited to sheltered waters.

At this writing, there are no commercial covers which are versatile enough for extended canoe tripping. All are one-piece designs which won't fit if packs rise above the gunwales. The best set-up I've used is a three-piece model of my own design. It has a "belly" section which expands or shrinks as the load height changes. The end caps can be rolled and tied -- and may remain on the canoe -- while portaging. For solo canoeing, I prefer a two piece cover which I also engineered. Step-by-step instructions for building both these designs can be found in my book, CANOEING WILD RIVERS.

I've outlined but a small number of "tuning" tips you'll discover when you probe the minds of expert canoeists. If you want to learn more, attend paddling clinics and tripping seminars. And don't neglect your studies. *Canoe* magazine, *Small Boat Journal*, *Boat Pennsylvania*, *River Runner*, and other fine publications will keep you abreast of the latest developments and provide continuing food for thought. Finally, don't be afraid to question the ways of others or to assign worthy value to your own methods. After all, no one has a monopoly on good ideas!

4.
Solo Canoeing
is Different

Sunrise on any river, U.S.A. A damp morning mist, warmed by the day's beginning, rises reluctantly above the cool green water. Beneath the slowly burning fog, an ever-growing ribbon of gold expands confidently across the horizon.

In awesome silence, you slip your trim light solo canoe into the awaiting riffles, while nearby, friends in a tandem canoe follow suit. A gentle push of the paddle sets you free and in harmony with the determined current.

For awhile you paddle powerfully, each stroke crisp and well-timed. The quick canoe responds eagerly and glides whisper quiet at what seems to be incredible speed. Round a bend, a great blue heron curiously looks your way. In awkward slow motion he stretches his wings and with casual assuredness, begins to fly. The muffled hiss of your wake has broken the spell!

The sun is in full posture now and the day is flooded with its warmth and light. Everywhere, the sights and sounds of the river entice you to linger, so you rest your paddle, laze back, and wait

49

for your friends to catch up. Above, puffy clouds of hushed white whisk quietly by, and for a time, you are left alone with your dreams and the delights of the river.

Then you hear it -- the hollow drone of rushing water. Falls? The shock of realization brings you bolt-upright. Your eyes search knowingly for the danger signs -- a broken tree line or crest of dancing white. Then you see it -- a narrow band of discontinuous water which stretches entirely across your path.

Ledge! You call loudly to your friends behind. But no panic; you're in control. A few well-placed backstrokes bring the little canoe swiftly to shore.

The falls, a sheer six foot drop over sharp granite, is not negotiable. And neither is the rapid below. You'll have to take the half mile portage that's indicated on your map. Singlehandedly, you shoulder your 35 pound canoe while a few yards away your friends struggle with their tandem craft of twice the weight. A smug smile flashes briefly as you jubilantly strike off down the trail. You're beginning to discover the joys of the solo canoe!

Part way through the portage you ascend a long steep hill, at the top of which stands a well-worn canoe rest. But the little boat is no burden, so you unhesitatingly continue on. Seconds later, you hear the hollow clunk of a canoe being set upon the wooden brace you just passed -- a reminder that your tandem friends don't share your unencumbered feeling. The smile returns!

Now the trail descends quickly and you move along at a furious pace. A glint of white suddenly appears among the blanketing foliage and you know the river is near.

You set the little canoe at the water's edge and stare unbelievingly at the river. You've canoed in low water before, but this is ridiculous! A shallow rock fan stretches well into the next bend, perhaps a quarter mile. Three, maybe four inches of water lie between the water's surface and its pebble bottom. And everywhere, huge round rocks protrude like polished marbles on an earthen field. No way can the big canoe get through there without grinding, scraping...breaking.

But you can!

As you gingerly board your solo canoe for the slalom run, you watch amusedly as your friends put on their wading shoes. "It's gonna be a long walk," you tease. "Sure glad I can ride!"

Once under way, the little canoe comes alive. It leans when you lean, goes forward, backward, sideways on command. There's no argument from a partner, your spouse, or your mother-in-law. A screw-up is a screw-up and you have no one to blame but yourself.

You discover that the tightest turns are possible if you brace far out on your paddle and lean the canoe until its gunwale barely touches the water. Ahead, are a cluster of rocks with a two foot channel in between. No problem; you tilt the canoe to one side and scoot cleanly through.

Now you're both bow and stern -- sweeping, drawing, prying, bracing.* Occasionally, the muffled screech of fiberglass impacting rock rewards your indecision and carelessness. But no matter; these surface scratches do much more harm to your ego than your canoe.

Within minutes it's over and you find yourself drifting aimlessly in the deep still water below the rapid. A few lazy backstrokes bring you to shore, where you get out and stretch...and wait for your friends to finish lining their canoe through the rock garden you just paddled!

These then, are the joys of the solo canoe -- joys that become more intense as the years creep by and suddenly you discover that you're not as athletic as you used to be. Small-framed men and women need no introduction to the pleasures of soloing for they, more than anyone else, "understand" what it means to be always last on the portage trail and forever chained to the bow seat of a tandem canoe. Tough day at the office? Perhaps an hour's play on a park pond will provide the relaxation you need. Got a canoe trip planned and can't find a partner? Great; take your solo canoe! Extended wilderness tripping? You bet! A well designed "little boat" can carry at least 300 pounds -- nearly half the weight of an average tandem canoe. Unless you plan to bring along the kitchen sink, you'll have more space than you can possibly use.

"But I'm a family person," you say. "How can I take the kids along if I paddle alone?" Well, you can't, of course. But wouldn't it be nice if the children could paddle *their own* canoe, rather than ride in yours? Easy enough if you outfit your solo canoe with seats fore and aft. Now, your teenie-boppers can experience the joy of canoeing in a boat that's suited to their dimensions.

* See Chapter 7, PADDLE POWER for a discussion of these and other strokes.

Figure 4-1 "Got a trip planned and can't find a Partner? Great; take your solo canoe! Unless you plan to bring along the kitchen sink, you'll have more space than you can possibly use."

Meanwhile, the grownups can tag along behind in a big canoe. *Two* canoes -- one tandem, one solo -- per family, is not extravagance; it's common sense...and a delightfully good time!

Whitewater, flatwater, local streams or the deep wilderness. The solo canoe will go anywhere a tandem canoe will go -- a bit more slowly perhaps, but with a grace, style and elegance that is unmatched by the most sophisticated large canoe.

Solo canoes *are* different, and many of the procedures and equipment used to paddle and portage them also are different.

EQUIPMENT

Paddles: You must have two paddles in the event one breaks. Paddle length is determined by the reach of your arms and the style boat you paddle (see Chapter 7 for the specifics). Flat-water racing canoes require short paddles -- 50 to 53 inches long, preferably with angled blades. Whitewater slalom and traditionally styled touring canoes are more compatible with longer paddles -- 54 to 60 inches.

Some canoeists prefer to use a double paddle for some or all of their paddling. A well-designed solo canoe will dance across the water when powered by twin blades. However, the standard kayak paddle is too short; you need a length of 8½ or 9 feet (not commonly available), which means you'll have to make your own. Be sure the paddle breaks apart at the center for storage between uses.

Double paddles are considered "gauche" in fashionable canoeing circles. To many (myself included), soloing is an art form -- one which necessarily demands efficient use of the single blade. Nonetheless, don't let me or anyone else spoil your pleasure. Double paddles *are* efficient. If you like them, use them!

Portage yoke: The traditional way to carry a lightweight solo canoe is with a gunwale perched on one shoulder. Though this is acceptable for short carries, it can be terribly painful if you have to walk very far. So, for trips with frequent portages, you'll need a fitted wood yoke like the one illustrated in the last chapter.

The yoke *must* be removable (unlike those used on tandem canoes) so it won't interfere with paddling (you sit or kneel in the middle of the canoe, remember?) The best arrangement is to attach the yoke to the gunwales with hardwood clamps and wingnuts, or buy a pair of indestructible aluminum yoke brackets from Old Town or Mad River Canoe companies.

It takes only a few seconds to install or remove a clamp-mounted yoke. Keep the yoke tied to a thwart or gunwale when you're not using it to avoid loss if you capsize. Some canoeists clamp their yoke to the gunwale (at an angle) behind the seat so it can't possibly be lost in an upset.

Knee pads: The advantage of solo canoes over kayaks is versatility. You can sit or kneel (or even stand) if you wish. In rough water, kneeling is an "option" in big steady tandem canoes; in "tender" solo canoes, it is an absolute must! Glue knee pads into the bottom of your canoe for the ultimate in comfort.

Packs: For day trips, a small nylon pack is fine -- as long as it's not too heavy. A solo canoe is sensitive to proper trim (the difference between the draft at each end). A few misplaced pounds, fore or aft of dead center, may unbalance it and adversely affect performance. Consequently, it's unwise to place "all of your eggs in one basket", even if they will all fit. It's better to use two packs -- a large "soft" (no frame) tripping pack of some sort, and a medium size day pack.

I place food, sleeping gear, tent and cooking items into the large pack and set it in front of my feet. The small pack, which contains extra clothes, rain gear, sweater and other frequently used essentials, goes behind the seat (some canoeists reverse the position of these packs). By moving the packs forward or back, I can balance the canoe perfectly.

An annoying characteristic of all open solo canoes is that they are always wet inside. Every time you change sides with your paddle ("HUT"), which you do often to steer and rest muscles, water drips off the blade and into the canoe. Keep a large sponge secured beneath a loop of shock cord tied around the side of your seat frame. Sponging out accumulated water is a never-ending process!

A wet canoe bottom means wet packs, so be sure to waterproof everything completely, according to the directions in Chapter 12 (THE NECESSITIES). The procedure for packing tandem canoes is to set packs upright in the bottom of the canoe -- preventing water which accumulates in the canoe's bottom from getting into the pack through its mouth. But any pack which rises above the gunwales of a solo canoe becomes a sail when the wind is up. So you'll have to set packs flat and waterproof their contents *thoroughly*.

For a week trip your solo canoe will easily carry more cargo than you'll ever want to bring along. Nevertheless, that's no excuse to bring too much. The price of gluttony is a sluggish canoe, or at best an unspirited one. If you choose items carefully, your heaviest pack should weigh less than 50 pounds; your light pack around 15 pounds. (See Chapter 12 for a discussion of the things you *really* need.) Carry the heavy pack, paddles, life vest and camera over the portage first. Second trip, take the canoe and small day pack. This works out to about 55 pounds per trip.

Touring the wilds in a solo canoe is easier if you travel in the company of other canoes since you can share the weight of community essentials -- tent, cookset, axe, saw, etc. I recently completed a ten day canoe trip on an Ontario river along with three other solo friends. My share of the outfit (including food and personal gear) was 60 pounds -- less than I commonly carry on tandem canoe trips of the same length.

It's important to fit all your camping gear into two packs so you can complete the portages in three trips (one round trip plus the return leg). A third pack means *two* additional portage crossings, so plan wisely and "go light".

Map and Compass: You are your own partner in a solo canoe; there's no time to fumble for navigational aids when you're fighting waves on a wind-tossed lake. A few moments of distraction and you may find yourself lost...or upside down!

For these reasons it's essential to secure your map under a loop of shock-cord strung through holes drilled in the front thwart, as suggested in the last chapter. Also, I carry *two* compasses -- a small but highly accurate Silva Huntsman (for plotting the course from the map), and a Silva wrist model (for easy reference while paddling). The Huntsman rests in my shirt pocket, protected against loss by a lanyard attached to a buttonhole. I keep the wrist compass strapped to the forward thwart. With this set-up, my map and compass are always visible, regardless of how actively I paddle.

PADDLING ALONE

There is but one seat in a solo canoe so you have little option where to sit. The lone paddler must have complete control over both ends of the canoe, possible only when he or she is seated near the center.

If you don't own a solo canoe it is possible to paddle a big canoe alone. However, you must assume a position just aft of center by rigging up some sort of kneeling thwart or seat here. Many people prefer to paddle a tandem canoe alone from the stern seat because the canoe is so narrow at this point. But this practice is extremely dangerous since it knocks the canoe way out of trim. The bow rides high in the air while the stern sinks low. The effect is that of paddling a seven-foot canoe with a ten-foot overhang. The slightest breeze will capsize you instantly. Also, any degree of control or speed is impossible.

Some canoeists recommend that you solo a tandem canoe from the stern and weight the bow with logs or duffle. Again, a mistake. You can't control the bow of a canoe if you're located fifteen feet away, at the opposite end of the lever arm.

An acceptable practice when soloing tandem canoes is to sit in the front seat facing the stern. This location gets the mass (you) closer to center. It's still an inefficient position, but it's much safer than controlling the boat from the stern.

Occupy a position at or near the center of a tandem canoe when you're paddling alone. All other positions diminish control and safety! If you find it difficult to reach the water from your centralized position, scoot to port or starboard and place both knees close together in the bilge of the canoe. This is a very comfortable position on quiet water. When a rough sea threatens, spread your knees wide and re-center your weight.

As you gain solo experience, you'll develop a repertoire of special strokes -- the "C", "Draw," "Cross-draw," "Low Brace," and others outlined in Chapter 7, will soon come naturally. But you don't need all these to use and enjoy your solo canoe. In fact, the most efficient way to paddle alone is to simply switch sides whenever the boat begins to waver off course. This generally works out to about three strokes per side. Though some people consider the practice boring, it is very powerful and state-of-the-art for racing!

Some paddlers prefer a hybrid style of paddling; they use a double-paddle on open water and change to a short single blade and racing switch-stroke on the river. In rapids they select a long single paddle and twist their way between obstacles with a variety of hard-to-define sophisticated strokes. That is the beauty of soloing; you are free to chase your star in your own way at your own pace.

DANGERS

The only real danger unique to paddling a solo craft is capsizing on open water. If other canoes are near, they will come to your aid. But if you're alone you will have to swim your outfit to shore -- no easy task if you're not wearing a life jacket. So get the best life vest you can find and *always* wear it, no matter how peaceful the waterway.

Also, be sure your canoe has sufficient flotation to keep it from sinking while you're towing it ashore. All canoes are not so equipped. Flotation material commonly adds three or four pounds to a typical solo canoe, one reason why it is not found on some of the best lightweight racing canoes.

Also unique to the solo canoe is the extra strength and skill needed to make these small boats perform at their best. A solo craft has but one engine, so you must work constantly and efficiently to keep it humming along. In rapids, control and decision making rest in your hands alone. Hence, you must be a stronger and more skillful paddler to solo than to go with a partner.

WHERE TO GO?

The wonderful thing about solo canoes is that they're at home on any waterway. You don't need to take a lengthy wilderness trip to enjoy them.

Not far from my home is a 20-acre spring-fed lake -- a playground for herons, mink and muskrat. Occasionally I see a beaver or buck deer in velvet. The only access is a rough and usually muddy road, so there are few people. Once a week or so during the ice-free season I sneak down to that small lake, solo canoe atop my shoulders; not for serious paddling you understand, just a chance to get away from the city for awhile.

When I first found this spot ten years ago, I was alone. Then my friends discovered the fun I was having and wanted to share it. Now there are five of us, each with his/her own solo canoe. Fun? As much as before. After all, no rule says that "going solo" has to mean "alone"!

CHOOSING A SOLO CANOE

A decade ago it was nearly impossible to find a pure bred solo canoe. If you wanted to paddle alone you tricked out a fifteen or sixteen foot tandem canoe with a center seat and learned to live with the wide (thirty-two inch plus) beam and high wind-susceptible ends.

Today, a variety of true solo canoes are available. They range from short joyful play boats to long efficient racers. In between are a variety of cruisers, pack boats, and wilderness trippers. Getting what you want in a solo craft is easy once you've identified your own tripping requirements.

DESIGN CONSIDERATIONS

Solo canoes are generally narrower, shallower, and finer-lined than double canoes. Thirty inches at the rails is the *maximum* for a true solo canoe, while a center depth of eleven, or at most twelve inches provides ample seaworthiness in all but the most menacing rapids.

The soloist is located at the craft's middle (fulcrum) which permits the near weightless ends of the boat to rise and fall willingly with waves. For this reason, even the tiniest solo canoes are much more seaworthy than their small size suggests. Large buoyant bows and high ends are out-of-place on all but full-blown whitewater slalom canoes.

Other things being equal, the longer the canoe, the faster it will run. But the price you pay for speed is decreased maneuverability. Solo canoes much longer than 15½ feet generally don't turn worth a hoot -- exactly what you don't want if your game is flittering about beaver ponds or negotiating twisty creeks. Very short (under 14 feet) solo canoes, on the other hand, usually don't track well or maintain a smooth glide. They quit running as soon as you let up on the power. However, these little canoes provide a "personal feel" that is unmatched by bigger boats.

The foregoing is of course a gross over-simplification of the facts, for dozens of complex variables combine to determine a solo canoe's overall performance. It's quite possible for a sophisticated 13½ footer to out-run, out-turn, and generally out-class a much longer less thoughtfully designed canoe. Nonetheless, the relationship holds true enough for boats of equal breeding.

So if you want to race, get the longest canoe you can find. Seventeen feet is not unmanageable. For playing in shallow creeks and snag-filled waters, consider the merits of a 12 to 14 footer. Fifteen feet maximizes most variables and is therefore ideal for a variety of uses -- day cruising, wilderness touring, moderate whitewater, etc.

SOLO CANOE ROUNDUP

The solo canoe is a specialized beast. There are models for just about every purpose and paddling style. All you need to do is match your dreams to your pocketbook. Here's what's available:

UTILITY CANOES

These canoes are wide (34-36 inches), flat-bottomed, and emminently stable. Most are 10 to 12 feet long and are constructed of fiberglass or Royalex. Utility canoes are terribly slow, noisy, and not much fun to paddle. Their one attribute is that they make wonderfully stable platforms from which to fish and photograph -- the reason why so many people buy them.

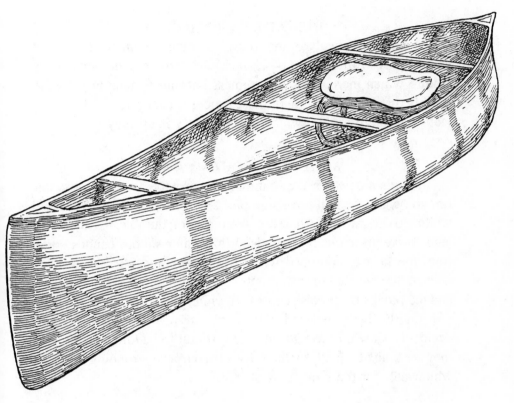

Figure 4-2   Solo Racing Canoe: Note asymmetric shape and severe tumblehome at middle. Some racing canoes feature sliding "tractor" seats to keep the paddler centered in the canoe.

FLATWATER RACING CANOES

Length averages 16 to 18 feet, width at the gunwales, around 24 inches, depth 12 inches, and weight, under 30 pounds. All have extreme tumblehome to make paddling easier, which seriously detracts from their seaworthiness. They come equipped with sliding bucket seats and footbraces and are best propelled with bent-shaft paddles of 52 inches or so.* These canoes are built exclusively of fiberglass, Kevlar, or an exotic combination of these and other high-tech materials. They feel surprisingly stable when you get in

* See Chapter 7, Paddle Power, for a discussion of paddle lengths and types.)

them but they'll unhorse you instantly in rough water if you don't understand their ways. Flatwater racing canoes are wickedly fast high performance boats for experts only.

WHITEWATER RACING CANOES

Nearly identical to the flatwater racing canoes mentioned above, only with higher (14-15 inch) sides to keep out splash -- a feature which increases seaworthiness but makes handling in wind terribly difficult. The forté of these canoes is charging hell-bent-for-leather through rapids, which unfortunately is all they do well.

WHITEWATER SLALOM CANOES

Here's a new breed of cat that will provide all the whitewater fun you want. Length hovers around 13½ feet, depth 14-15 inches, width 30-32 inches. All are constructed of durable Royalex and tend to weigh about 50 pounds. Whitewater slalom canoes come from the factory equipped with thwarts fore and aft, but no seat. Owners are advised to install optional ethafoam saddles, knee pads and toe blocks for precise control in whitewater. These canoes have a distinctly lively feel and will literally turn on a dime. They are decidedly slow on the flats and are difficult to paddle straight. But they are king of the hill for their intended purpose -- running complex whitewater for the pure sport of it.

FLATWATER PLAY BOATS

These intensely beautiful canoes are designed for the gentle art of messing around on quiet water. They'll twist down a beaver stream, pirouette around lily pads, or run a bleach jug obstacle course with precision and flair. They run 11 to 13½ feet long, 11 to 12 inches deep, and 26-30 inches wide at the rails. All are built of fiberglass, Kevlar, or wood. Construction is impeccable! In the hands of a practiced paddler, they'll cruise along with a mediocre team in an average tandem canoe and will safely negotiate waves and rapids which most people would consider dangerous. They are much more seaworthy than their small size suggests and are suitable for canoe trips of up to a week if you pack light and paddle well. For dynamic performance and stability, you *kneel* in these canoes!

Figure 4-3   Wilderness Cruising/Fast Touring Canoe: These are comfortable boats which can be paddled sitting or kneeling with equal assurance.

WILDERNESS CRUISING/FAST TOURING CANOES

These are best described as "high performance do everything" canoes. They're fast on the flats, though not blistering so; they'll handle a wind-tossed lake or scary rapid with reasonable aplomb, and they'll twist though a rock garden with the grace and confidence of a pure-bred slalom hull. They're decidedly lively on all types of water, yet surprisingly forgiving when pushed to their limits. These are "comfortable" boats which can be paddled sitting or kneeling with equal assurance.

Because these canoes do so many things well, they are the most popular of all pure-bred solo designs. Specifications average: Length, 14-16 feet; width, 24-30 inches; depth, 11-12 inches. Materials are fiberglass, Kevlar, or a high-tech composite.

That's the basic line-up. There are some special designs which bridge the gap between categories, so I could nit-pick and split the classifications still further. But that might only confuse and frustrate you. Besides, most salespeople in the best canoe shops are sufficiently knowledgeable in canoe design and construction to recommend the right canoe for you if you can accurately describe your needs. I warn you, through; soloing is addictive. No single canoe will do everything well, so your first boat may simply whet your appetite for more. Right now I have three solo canoes...and a fourth is on the way!

5.
Portaging
the Canoe

Every canoe trip includes some sort of portage -- be it the innocent task of loading the canoe onto the family station wagon, carrying it to and from the launching site, or lifting it over fallen trees, dams and other obstacles in a local stream. And if you're off to the wilds of Canada, portaging is part of the daily routine!

Although canoes, equipment, and paddling methods have changed considerably during the past century, the technique of portaging has remained the same. I say "technique" because portaging is as much an art as a feat of physical strength. I've seen 90 pound girls lift 75 pound canoes single-handed and carry them nonstop over very rough trails for more than a quarter of a mile. And I've known 200 pound men who could not carry the same canoe more than 200 feet without profanely dropping it on the nearest boulder! A canoe on land is out of its native habitat, and in the hands of a careless person may suffer great damage.

Outfitters in the Quetico-Superior wilderness of Minnesota and the Allagash of Maine, seldom get more than six good years of service out of their rental canoes. It's not the obstacles in water that cause the damage; it's the thoughtless abuse on land. Consequently, many youth camps have initiated the "wet-foot" policy, which simply means that canoes *must* be loaded, unloaded, picked up and set down in a *minimum* of 12 inches of water. Since wet-footing eliminates all land injuries, organizations practicing this procedure often boast more than 20 years of good service from their canoes (for example the Charles Sommers Canoe Base, in Ely, Minnesota, maintains a fleet of dent-free, aluminum canoes, some of which were purchased in the 1950's).

I am not an advocate of the wet-foot policy. Spending several hours a day with wet, shriveled-up feet is not my idea of a good time. With care it is perfectly possible to stand on land, or in a few inches of water, and load and unload the most fragile canoe without damaging it. Virtually all land damage occurs while picking a canoe up or setting it down. For this reason a thorough understanding of portaging techniques is essential to a dent and gouge-free canoe trip.

The trickiest part of portaging is getting the canoe from the ground to your shoulders. Even old timers who've sweated under the yoke for more miles than they can recall, appreciate a helping hand here. Nonetheless, with a bit of practice, shouldering a 75 pound canoe is easy. In fact, once you get the mechanics down pat, you may prefer to loft it yourself rather than trust the outcome to a well-meaning friend who's not familiar with the process.

Surprisingly, it's almost always easier to carry a canoe alone than with a friend. That's because partners can rarely coordinate their movements. When one person "bounces", the other "jounces" -- all of which makes for a terribly awkward and painful experience. Two person carries are only efficient on groomed trails, and then only when the canoe is outfitted with a yoke at *each* end!

Except in wind, a healthy adult can usually manage a canoe of reasonable weight (up to 85 pounds) without help if he or she has a good yoke and knows the proven lift-and-carry procedures.

ONE PERSON LIFT AND CARRY

On wilderness trips I seldom pick up a canoe by myself. It just takes too much effort, and I would rather save my energy for the portage trail. There will, however, be many times when you will need to lift a canoe to your shoulders alone, so you should become proficient in the one-person lift-and-carry.

If you're right-handed, stand at the center left side of the canoe, facing it. Pull the canoe up by the near gunwale and grasp the center of the yoke with your right hand (Figure 5-1). Keeping your legs well apart, flip the canoe onto your thighs with a quick pull of the right arm. As the canoe comes up, grab the far gunwale with your left hand just forward of the yoke (the canoe should now be almost wholly supported by your thighs). Next, transfer your right hand to a position just back of the yoke on the gunwale (Figure 5-2). Thus your left hand is forward of the yoke on the top gunwale, and your right hand is just behind it on the bottom gunwale.

The next part is the hardest. With a quick upward push from your right knee, snap the canoe up and around, over your head (Figure 5-3), and settle the yoke pads on your shoulders (Figure 5-4). Many beginners have difficulty here because they are fearful of getting their necks twisted up in the yoke. In reality, this almost never occurs. It's sort of like closing both eyes and touching your nose with a fist. Just as you always seem to successfully locate your nose, so too will you always find the portage yoke when the canoe comes up. The key to lifting the canoe is determination and a quick snap. You would have to be very strong to pick up even a light canoe slowly, whereas a person of small stature will have little difficulty raising canoes weighing up to ninety pounds if he or she is snappy about it. Although the one-person lift requires some practice to perfect, it is important to learn it properly, for there are many times when you will need to use this skill. When teaching this lift to new canoeists, I often tell them to remember the words *right, left, right* to insure that their hands will be properly positioned during the pick-up sequence. Thus:

1. *Right* hand grasps yoke center and canoe is spun to thighs.
2. *Left* hand grasps top gunwale forward of yoke.
3. *Right* hand grasps lower gunwale just back of yoke and canoe is snapped to shoulders.

Figure 5-1 One Person Lift: Step 1. *Right* hand grasps yoke center and canoe is spun to thighs.

Figure 5-2 Step 2. *Left* hand grasps top gunwales forward of the yoke and canoe is balanced on thighs. Note location of right hand.

Figure 5-3   Step 3. With a quick upward push from your right knee, snap the canoe up and around, over your head.

Figure 5-4   Step 4. Settle the yoke pads on your shoulders and . . . relax!

Beginners often have trouble carrying the canoe once they have it in position. The key to carrying a canoe is not strength at all; rather, it is learning to relax under the portage yoke. In order to accomplish this successfully, it is best that you have one or two friends help you position the canoe on your shoulders. When the yoke pads settle into place, stand perfectly straight and reach forward with your hands to grasp the gunwales. Place your fingers on the shelflike lip of the gunwales and your thumbs on the opposite side. If the canoe is properly balanced (slightly tail-heavy), light pressure from your fingers will bring the bow down to a horizontal position. The canoe is now ready for portaging. To get used to the yoke, stand in place and drop your left arm to your side. Most of the canoe's weight will now rest on your right shoulder. Repeat, dropping the other arm. You will become less tired on portages if you continually change the weight from shoulder to shoulder. When you feel confident under the yoke, you are ready for your first short hike. Walk about two hundred feet and set the canoe down. Rest up a while and try again -- only this time go twice as far. If you feel good after this second session, you probably have the mechanics down pat. Your shoulder muscles may hurt somewhat, but if you feel a stabbing pain the canoe is not properly positioned. Most likely you are hunching in fear under the yoke instead of standing straight. Several short practice sessions will teach you the technique of portaging much better than further discussion.

TWO-OR THREE-PERSON LIFT, ONE-PERSON CARRY

Even if you are capable of handling a canoe alone, you should enlist help in lifting it to your shoulders. The two-person lift is identical to the one-person lift, except that your helper stands next to you, behind the yoke, and you stand slightly in front of it. The canoe should be supported on the thighs of both you and your partner prior to raising it into position. Your hands will be forward of the yoke and your partner's will be behind it. At a mutually agreed upon signal, flip the canoe, with the help of your partner, up onto your shoulders.

For a completely effortless pickup, try the three-person lift. This is identical to the two-person lift, except you have an additional person. Position yourself at the yoke and have one helper stand at the bow thwart and another helper at the stern thwart. Again, you should all be on the same side of the canoe. All lift together. Nothing could be simpler.

END LIFT

The end lift is an easy way for one or two people to get a heavy canoe up.

PROCEDURE

Stand at the right rear of the canoe, facing the stern. Reach across with your right hand and grasp the left gunwale near the stern seat. Grab the right gunwale with your left hand (Figure 5-5). Now just roll the canoe over on its front end (Figure 5-6) and lift the tail in the air (Figure 5-7). While holding the canoe high, bow on the ground, shuffle yourself forward into the yoke. If you have a helper, let him or her hold the canoe up while you snuggle into the yoke.

The end pickup is popular with persons who for one reason or another don't feel confident using the standard side lift. Although lifting a canoe by one end is accepted practice, it is not good canoeing technique, mainly because the end in contact with the ground gets chewed up. Use this method on grass if you like, but avoid it in rocky areas -- unless, of course, you want to fit a new deck plate to your canoe after every few trips.

TWO-PERSON CARRIES
RACING CARRY

Each paddler places his or her end of the canoe (usually, right side up) on a shoulder and cradles an arm around it for support. Once the canoe is in position, racers take off at a run and make very good time over short distances. You will like the racing carry if you have a very light, keelless canoe (keels gouge shoulders miserably, rendering this method too painful for canoes with keels).

SEAT CARRY

Turn the canoe over and place the front edge of a seat on the back of your neck. Your partner should follow suit, using the other seat. You should both wear life jackets to help pad your necks. This method works reasonably well if the distance is short and the life jackets used are the inexpensive orange horse-collar type. The

Figure 5-5   The End Lift: Step 1.

Figure 5-6   Step 2.

Figure 5-7   Step 3.

newer style vest preservers don't have enough padding, and your neck suffers accordingly. The canoe used by Kruger and Waddell on their Alaskan canoe safari was equipped with a portage yoke at each end to facilitate this style of carry. While some veteran canoeists scoff at two-person carries, they are ideal under some conditions -- and you don't have to impress anyone but yourself on a wilderness trip!

WHERE'S THE PORTAGE?

Much of North America's canoe country consists of a maze of lakes connected by waterfalls, rapids, and meandering streams. In some cases you can run the rapids or walk the streams. Often you will have no recourse but to pack your canoe and gear over rugged portage trails. One of the great challenges of the wilderness is locating the proper portage. Usually this is easy enough, especially on small lakes. On large lakes with a multitude of islands, channels, and bays, good maps, a reliable compass, and a high degree of resourcefulness will be required (see Chapter 14 -- Wilderness Navigation, for a complete discussion of route finding). In isolated areas a portage may be marked by a blazed tree, a jutting pole, a piece of discarded wearing apparel hanging from a tree limb, or a small opening in the forest. One portage, located along the Granite River on the United States-Canadian border, requires carrying your canoe up over a steep, sheer rock face. Except for a small faded *P* painted on the rock some years ago, the portage is impossible to spot.

Locating routes around dangerous rapids and waterfalls on large rivers can be a matter of survival. On my early wilderness river trips, I was always afraid that I would miss a portage and paddle over a falls. Such fear, though common in beginners, is unfounded. Your ears quickly become attuned to the roar of perilous rapids and the gurgle of safe fast water. Usually (though not always) rapids can be heard for great distances. I especially remember the Grand Rapids on the Mattagami River in northern Ontario. I could hear those rapids nearly ten miles away when the wind was right. As the wind lessened in force, so did the sound, and when the wind blew harder the noise became louder. This waning and waxing of sound haunted me throughout the night and provided ample opportunity for me to exaggerate the size and fury of the rapids. When our party finally reached Grand Rapids, we found it to be nothing spectacular, although it was perhaps two miles long and a quarter of a mile wide. The tremendous thundering we heard was due to the great number of rapids, not their size. Your ears are a most valuable tool for detecting the dangers ahead. For this reason white-water helmets always have holes or cutouts for the ears.

On isolated northern rivers there may be nothing to mark portage trails, yet a route around impassable water often exists. Most portages are trampled into place by large animals like moose and bear, who, like you, need to get around rapids and falls. It remains for you to find these trails. Sometimes this can be difficult, as the only evidence of them may be a few broken twigs and bushes near the water's edge. Portages are most often located on the inside curves of rivers, and this is the place you should look first. When you hear the roar of rapids and see the white plumes of dancing horse-tails leaping high into the air, immediately get to the inside bend and paddle ashore. Then get out of your canoe and start looking. Walk the rapids to see if they are safe to run. If you can find no portage and the rapids look safe, proceed cautiously downstream. Sometimes a single hidden ledge can make a rapid unnavigable, and you may not be able to see the ledge until it is too late.

The absence of a portage does not mean the rapid is safe to run. Unusually high water may flood existing portages, making them impossible to find, and very low water can change channel characteristics so completely that you may paddle right by the portage without seeing it.

In some areas, especially those near James and Hudson bays, portages are so overgrown with vegetation that you may have to hack your way through a maze of brush to reach safer water at the end of the trail. Cutting paths through the bush is not in keeping with the modern wilderness ethic (leave only footprints, take only pictures), but occasionally, for reasons of safety, you may have no choice. Fortunately for the environment, the scrubby trees you destroy will grow back quickly.

Never underestimate the power of rapids, especially if the water is high. The rule of thumb in the wilderness is, If in doubt, portage! Develop your whitewater skills at home, not on an isolated canoe trip where a single error can be fatal.

6.
The Art of
Car-Topping

Somewhere among the pages of every introductory canoeing text, there's an obscure and generally useless paragraph devoted to the art of car-topping a canoe. I say ''art'' because it takes considerable skill to quickly and neatly secure one or more canoes to the overhead racks of a car so they'll stay put in gale force winds yet come unbridled instantly at your command.

Given enough rope -- and time, anyone can tie down a canoe so it won't blow off a car. The fun comes when you've got several boats to haul, or when the wind whips to impressive speeds. Then you'd better know what you're doing or you may have an airborne missile on your hands.

After years of transporting canoes atop all sorts of vehicles, I've learned that it pays to buy the best carrying racks available. A good many people buy inexpensive suction-cup carriers, strap their canoes on, and take to the road without a second thought to the safety of their craft. The canoe owner who successfully uses these types of carriers for many years without an accident is either exceptionally cautious, unusually lucky, or a very slow driver!

Get canoe racks that bolt directly to the car's drip eaves. Avoid models that put pressure on the roof. In some cases you can buy individual mounting brackets and attach them to two-by-fours to make racks. Most avid canoeists prefer this type of arrangement. The wide weight-bearing surface of the two-by-fours keeps canoes from sliding around, and the large size of the wood cross-bars makes for very sturdy racks. If you buy separate brackets and make your own car-top carriers, make the cross-bars about 82 inches long. This length will enable you to carry two canoes comfortably. Even if you never plan to buy a second canoe, you will often need to shuttle more than one, especially if you paddle with a club. A common mistake is to make double racks about 78 inches long. Although you can easily fit two canoes on them, the sides will nearly touch; on a long drive, regardless of the care you take, the canoe hulls will come into contact. The resulting friction may remove enough material to cause serious damage to one or both canoes. This is a very real problem, especially when canoes are built of different materials -- for example, aluminum and fiberglass.

As an added precaution, canoes carried in pairs should have a 12-by-24 inch piece of carpet placed between them. This pad should be well secured to one of the canoes with light rope. It is also a good idea to carpet cross-bars. Sew the carpeting around the bars with heavy waxed thread. Virtually every canoe I have owned has suffered some damage from being transported on noncarpeted racks. You especially need carpeting if your canoe has wood or plastic gunwales. When you are selecting a car-top carrier, don't be misled by the gaudy appearance of chrome-plated models. Canoe racks are wet much of the time, and even good quality plated steel fittings will rust. Look for cast or machined aluminum parts. The cost will be much higher, but the service will be considerably better. For the past ten years I have been using a set of all-aluminum carriers by Quick 'N Easy and I have found these to be ideal.

FOR SAFETY'S SAKE, TIE 'EM DOWN

Most canoeists give only casual thought to securing their canoes to car-top carriers. A properly tied down canoe should show little, if any, movement, even in high winds at speeds well in excess of those legally posted. As a rule of thumb, each canoe carried should be tied down separately. This will eliminate many embarrassing problems at highway speeds. Attach a stout ¼ inch nylon rope to each car rack. Run the lines over the belly of the canoe and secure them to the other side of the rack. Tie each as close as possible to the gunwales of the canoe to prevent wind-shift. The power-cinch (see Chapter 11 -- Tying It All Together) is the most suitable knot and is the only one that should be used for tying down canoes. Additionally, tie two ropes to *each* end of the canoe and attach the free ends of these lines to their respective bumpers, as far apart as possible. Again, use a power-cinch. Make up a special set of nylon ropes with S-hooks at each end, or install steel eye-bolts in the bumpers. It is very difficult to attach naked ropes to bumpers properly. The sharp bumper edges can easily cut thick rope on a long auto trip if sufficient friction is generated by high winds. Caution: Avoid use of rubber truck tie-downs. Although they are quite popular, they have too much stretch and can cause problems if the canoe is buffeted by wind. Some canoeists use them because they are easy to get on and off. For safety's sake, I prefer to tie 'em down. Lastly, if you cartop two canoes on one car, use a *separate* belly rope for each canoe. This is in keeping with the aforementioned rule of thumb, and will also help keep paired canoes from rubbing.

HOW DO YOU CARRY THREE CANOES
ON A CAR RACK BUILT FOR TWO?

To carry a third canoe on a two car rack, mount two boats on the carriers as described, then place two five foot long carpeted one by two's across the belly of each canoe. Center the third craft on top of these wooden supports and tie it to the metal crossbars *and* car bumpers. On a long trip it's a good idea to tie the ends of the one by two's to the steel carriers.

Canoe clubs frequently trek to the river with a half dozen or more canoes and kayaks piled high on a vehicle. (I think the record -- established at a national whitewater event -- is ten boats!) Such displays of civil engineering are impressive, but not necessarily safe. Most canoeists would agree that you're tempting fate whenever you carry more than three boats at a time on the overhead racks of a car. If you need to haul more than three canoes, use a trailer -- it's much safer.

CARRYING CANOES ON CARS THAT DON'T HAVE RAIN-GUTTERS

The safest way to carry a canoe on a car that does not have rain gutters on which to mount car-top carriers, is to leave the car at home and portage the canoe on your back! A more realistic solution is to transport it on ethafoam gunwale blocks which are available in kit form at most marinas. Nylon straps furnished with the kit clip to the window moldings of the car. The ends of the craft are cinched to the bumpers with the ropes provided.

The system doesn't sound very secure, and it isn't. It's adequate for a single canoe in moderate winds, but carrying two canoes this way *in any wind* is out of the question. In really severe weather your best bet is to replace the nylon straps with ropes and run them *through the windows* (under the roof) of the car. This will lock the canoe so firmly to the car that it can't possibly blow off.

If you plan to carry more than one canoe on a car without rain gutters, you're well advised to install a stainless-steel luggage rack on the roof and bolt wooden crossbars to it.

At this writing, one manufacturer (*Yakima*) now offers a sophisticated car-top carrier designed for use on cars with airplane style doors. The new Yakima racks are expensive, but worth it.

TRAILERING

Best way to carry large numbers of canoes is aboard a trailer built especially for the purpose. Be sure the trailer has good size fenders so it won't throw dirt and gravel into the canoes, and a high enough "tree" so the ends of the bottom canoes won't bottom-out on rutted roads. As always, use good nylon line, not rubber ropes, to secure the canoes to the trailer.

Caution: Well tied-down canoes stiffen a trailer tree considerably. However, when the canoes are removed and the trailer is run empty over rough roads, substantial strain is placed on the unsupported tree. After a few years (or less!) of bouncing around, the cross bars usually give way and require re-welding. A number of methods have been used to stiffen the crossbars but the best is a vertical strut (see Figure 6-1) which spans two bars. The strut bolts in place with wing-nuts and swings aside to load and unload

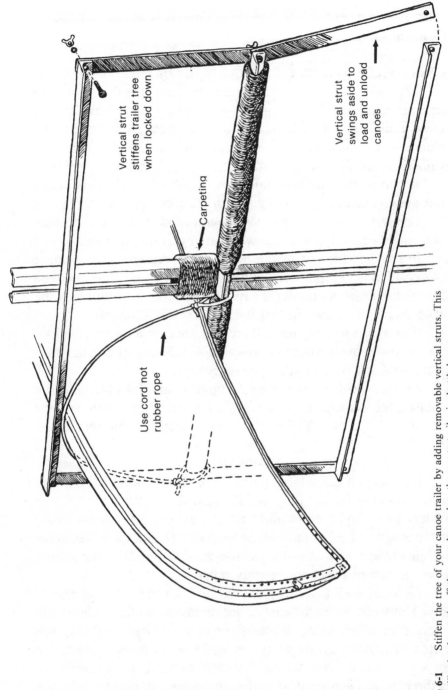

Vertical strut stiffens trailer tree when locked down

Vertical strut swings aside to load and unload canoes

← Carpeting

Use cord not rubber rope

Figure 6-1 Stiffen the tree of your canoe trailer by adding removable vertical struts. This brace will take the strain off the cross-bars when the empty trailer is shuttled.

the canoes. This set-up virtually eliminates stress...and trailer break-down.

PROCEDURES FOR CARRYING FRAGILE CANOES

Ultralight fiberglass, Kevlar, and woodstrip canoes should be handled with a loving touch. They should be carried on padded cross-bars or foam gunwale pads only, and tied with clean, large diameter (quarter to three-eighths-inch) ropes which won't gall their delicate skin.

You can break the spine of a lightweight canoe if you snug its ends too tightly, so it's preferable to tie *only* the bow to the front bumper. If you cinch down the tail you may bow the hull and damage it.

If you're hauling two canoes on a double rack, place the fragile canoe on the right side (passenger side) of the carriers. This will allow the sturdier (and more rigidly tied) craft on the driver's side to take the abuse of high winds generated by passing trucks. If you cartop three canoes, put the most fragile one on top.

Some cartop carriers come with aluminum "gunwale clamps" which attach to the crossbars and lock the inwale (inside gunwale) of the inverted canoe to the racks. *Don't use gunwale clamps!* They abrade the underside of the inwale and they're not compatible with carpeted crossbars. Gunwale clamps are fine for topping an aluminum fishing boat (or aluminum canoe) but they're out-of-place on a well built canoe with wood or vinyl gunwales. Use nylon ropes and learn to tie the "power cinch" and you won't have trouble with canoes sliding around on your car racks.

SPECIAL CONSIDERATIONS WHEN TRAVELING IN VERY HIGH WINDS

In very high winds you may want to rig a bridle around the bow (windshield end) of your car-topped canoe. To make the bridle, tie a length of rope tightly around the hull near the seat (loop it through the seat supports) and secure it to the bumper (Figure 6-2). The bridle will absorb wind stress and take the load off brass and plastic fittings which may break or bend under stress.

Is it safe to carry a long canoe on a small car? You bet! Canoe racers do it all the time. The determining factor is the length of your car's *roofline*. The longer the roof, the farther apart you can

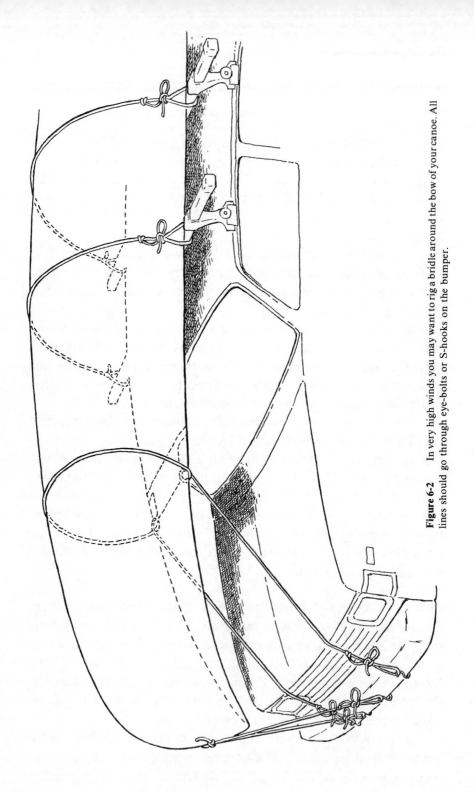

Figure 6-2   In very high winds you may want to rig a bridle around the bow of your canoe. All lines should go through eye-bolts or S-hooks on the bumper.

mount your car-top carriers. Generally, the best stability (for the canoe) results when racks are spaced at least three feet apart.

If your canoe overhangs the ends of your car by a considerable margin, you may want to rig bridles at the bow and stern so that lines will extend outward (parallel to the windshield) to reach the bumper, rather than inward. However, this procedure should be necessary only in gale-force winds.

CAR-TOPPING COVERED BOATS

Covered boats (slalom canoes and kayaks) have round narrow hulls which don't ride well on standard carpeted crossbars. One solution is to wedge sponge rubber around them so they won't roll around on the carriers. Another answer is to buy a special set of "kayak racks" which are designed expressly for carrying these skittish craft.*

It's common practice to carry covered boats on their sides, stacked one upon another (with padding in between) like a deck of cards set on edge. Four boats can usually be hauled safely this way on a set of 80-inch long crossbars. As always, each boat should be *individually* tied to the carriers and bumpers.

You can always tell a serious canoeist by the outfit he uses to haul his canoe to the river. Gaudy carriers that ride on over-size suction cups, twisted ropes which are knotted around sharp bumper edges, naked metal crossbars, and paired canoes whose sides grind together -- all spell potential damage to canoes, cars, and passers-by.

Safe car-topping means taking the time to tie down each canoe properly and to check the tightness of ropes at every opportunity. Ropes *will* loosen on a long haul and will have to be snugged up periodically. This is especially true after a rain (nylon rope stretches considerably when it gets wet).

No one wants to lose a canoe in a high wind, at worst maiming or killing the occupants of another car. The equipment I've suggested is proven and the skills for using it are easy to learn. Take time to "do it right". The rewards are obvious!

---

*These unique carriers have a curved padded metal sling which conforms to the rounded contours of the hull. Generally, you'll find "kayak racks" only at canoe/kayak specialty shops.

7.
Paddle Power!

Although paddling a canoe today is much the same as it was a century ago, better equipment and techniques have made it possible for canoeists of limited experience to successfully negotiate rapids which two decades ago were considered impossible. Modern canoeists use paddle strokes which are more powerful, efficient, and less demanding of energy than those used by less scientific paddlers of the past. As a result, a whole new style of canoeing has evolved -- a style geared to the superbly designed responsive canoes and ultralight equipment of today.

Some of our best competitors in both white- and flat-water events have been paddling for only a few years, yet they would put a professional northwoods guide to shame. While experience is still the best teacher, you can gain a great deal from good books and watching others. It may surprise you to know that whitewater canoeists often learn their basic skills in swimming pools. In fact, some very good scores in slalom competition have been posted by first-year paddlers who never saw a river before their first event.

This is not to say that experience on wilderness waterways is not valuable. But you can learn to handle your canoe efficiently on the calm lakes and rivers near your home. First, however, you will have to forget much of what you learned from traditional books of the past.

EQUIPMENT FIRST -- THE CANOE PADDLE

Not long ago I received a call from a canoeist who wanted to know how to repair an aluminum canoe. It seems his canoe turned broadside to the current, upset, and wrapped around a rock. Total damage included a bent keel, two bent ribs, and several pulled rivets. "How did it happen?" I asked. "Well," he replied, "We were approaching Dragon's Tooth, doing just fine, when I broke my paddle. Before I could get to the spare, she spun around and ... well, it was all I could do to get out of there."

As you can see, being up a creek without a paddle is considerably less dangerous than being caught in the middle of a raging river without one. In either case, a cheap, poorly constructed paddle is usually at fault; good paddles seldom fail.

There are reasons besides safety to buy a quality-built paddle. You can't play a good game of hockey without skates that fit properly, and you can't make a canoe respond to your whims without a decently designed, comfortable paddle. Good paddles are not cheap, but as the case in point illustrates, this is one place where you should not try to save money. Older canoe books often gave detailed instructions on how to make a paddle. Today we have little use for such information, for the age of technology has produced a wide variety of unbelievably strong, nearly break-proof paddles.

FIRST CONSIDERATION -- THE RIGHT LENGTH

Nearly every text on canoeing offers these time-worn formulas for selecting the proper length paddle.

1. Nose to toes -- the grip should reach your nose when the paddle is stood upright.

2. Chest span -- stretch out your arms; the length of the span equals the length of the paddle.

3. A bowman should use a paddle which comes to his nose;

a sternman should select one which comes to his eyes or the top of his head.

Nonsense! Any recipe for length *must* take into account the kind of canoe you're paddling, the height of the seats, the length of your torso, the reach of your arms, your own strength, and how you "prefer" to paddle (dynamic racing/switch style or slow paced northwoods J-stroke -- see the paddling section which follows).

As you can see, picking the correct paddle length depends on a number of variables, all of which are interrelated. For this reason, experienced canoeists often own a shedful of paddles, each designed for a specific purpose and paddling style.

Let's dissect the variables which affect paddle length:

SEAT HEIGHT
Seats on the typical high volume aluminum or Royalex canoe are set relatively high (11 to 13 inches off the floor) for comfort, while those on the modern fine-lined cruiser are slung low (7 to 9 inches) for stability. The higher you sit, the longer the paddle and vice versa. What works best in one style canoe may be terribly awkward in another.

LENGTH OF ARMS AND TORSO, AND STRENGTH
The length of your torso and reach of your arms affects paddle length too. Long-armed folk who sit tall in the saddle can comfortably wield long paddles; short folk with short arms should do the opposite. Strength is an important factor too: A strong person can naturally handle a long lever arm (long paddle) more easily than a weak person. Figure 7-1 on page 84 will give you a good starting point for length, without resorting to scientific measurements.

Here's the procedure if you want to get technical:

1. Set your canoe in the water and climb aboard.
2. Measure the distance from your nose (height of the top grip) to the water. That's the *shaft* length. To this add the length of the blade (20-25 inches, depending on paddle style). That's the correct paddle length for you. Note that the overall length of the paddle is in part programmed by the blade length.

SUGGESTED STRAIGHT PADDLE LENGTHS FOR USE IN THE FOLLOWING CANOES*

PERSONS WITH...	TANDEM CANOES		SOLO CANOES	
	Stock aluminum and Royalex canoes (Grumman, Old Town Tripper, Mad River Explorer, etc.)	High performance cruisers (Sawyer Cruiser, We-no-nah Jensen's, etc.)	Racers and fast cruisers (Sawyer Summersong, We-no-nah Advantage, etc.)	Freestyle and white-water canoes (Mad River Ladyslipper, Galt Dandy, Blue Hole Sunburst, etc.)
Short torsos/ short arms	54 inches	52 inches	52 inches	56 inches
Average length torso and arms	56 inches	54 inches	54 inches	58 inches
Long torsos/ long arms	58 inches	55 inches	55 inches	62 inches

*NOTE: These are "guidelines." They *are not* engraved in stone! Bent-shaft paddles (see discussion on page 85) should be about two inches shorter.

Figure 7-1

If you want to get more scientific, you can add in another variable -- the weight of your tripping outfit. The more gear you pile into the hull, the lower it will sit in the water, and the shorter your paddle must be.

Nonetheless, unless you're a masochist with figures, your original estimate -- or the suggested length I've listed -- will get you around in fine style.

STRAIGHT OR BENT PADDLE?

As its name implies, bent paddles have their blades off-set at an angle. Bends of five to seventeen degrees are available, though fourteen degrees is most popular.

Here's why the bent shaft is more efficient: When you complete a forward stroke with a straight paddle, the blade is in a "climbing" position upon recovery -- it *lifts* water and consequently slows the canoe. But the forward bend of the angle paddle puts the blade perpendicular to the water at the end of the stroke, so no water is lifted and no speed is lost. All energy is transmitted into forward motion!

Bent paddles *are* more efficient than straight paddles, and that's why every canoe racer and performance-minded cruiser uses them. However, they are not ideal for all types of canoeing. They're a bit awkward in rapids and they don't lend themselves to the powerful steering strokes of northwoods style (J-stroke) paddling. They're simply not as versatile as straight paddles.

Should you buy a bent paddle? That depends on the type of canoe you paddle, how you "prefer" to paddle, and with whom you paddle. There's little advantage in using a bent shaft in a typical wide-bowed aluminum or Royalex canoe. Reaching far over the wide gunwales of these boats tends to diminish the effectiveness of the "push down with your shoulders" racing stroke. Angle paddles may not be the best choice for beginners. Only after you've learned to maneuver with a straight paddle, should you invest in a bent shaft -- and then only if you prefer the dynamic power-paddling technique (see POWER PADDLING on page 106) favored by today's racers. If your preference is gliding silently among the lily pads, casting a lure into quiet waters, then forget about bent paddles. Likewise, if your partner prefers the straight shaft. Mixing bent and straight paddle technique in the same canoe isn't the best idea.

If you do choose a bent paddle (after you've gained some experience, you'll probably want one), specify a length that's about *two inches shorter* than your favorite straight shaft. For the utmost power, select a 14 or 15 degree bend; for the greatest control, opt for a 10 degree bend. Some manufacturers offer paddles with five degree bends, but these offer no advantages over models with straight shafts.

BLADE STYLE

There are dozens of blade styles, but all are variations of the basic shapes outlined in Figure 7-2. Some canoeing texts suggest that blade shape is unimportant, but that's not quite correct. Paddles, like canoes, are designed for specific purposes and each blade style has its place. The four shapes outlined in Figure 7-2 pretty much cover the gamut of canoeing possibilities.

A. *Cruising paddle.*

The modern laminated cruising paddle has straight sides, a squared-off tip, and fairly abrupt shoulders. The seven and one-half to eight-inch wide blade provides plenty of surface area for making time in aerated water, yet the blade is narrow enough for effective control. Long-bladed paddles are best suited to use in deep lakes; short-bladed ones are the choice for shallow rivers.

B. *Racing paddle.*

The wide tip provides plenty of surface area in shallow rivers (where you can't submerge the whole blade) and the tapered shoulders allow you to bring the blade very close to the canoe for greater power and less frequent directional correction. The short blade also means less weight, hence faster recovery at the end of the stroke.

C. *Beavertail.*

Most ancient of the blade shapes, the beavertail took its form as the most efficient shape which could be cut from a single six-inch wide board. When good waterproof glues were developed, the modern laminated paddle evolved and all but replaced the venerable beavertail.

However, beavertail paddles are making a mild comeback among both traditional northwoods canoeists and those who favor the solo art. The long narrow, somewhat whippy blade of the beavertail makes subtle steering alá northwoods style (J-stroke)

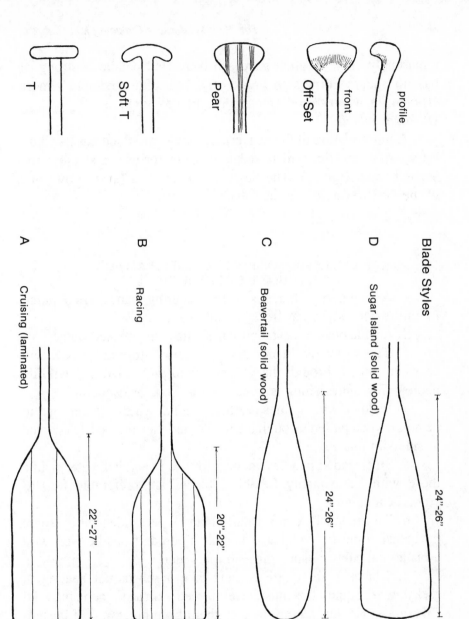

Figure 7-2 Blade Styles and Grips:

remarkably easy. A good solid ash beavertail paddle is strong (it has no square corners to break off), beautiful, and much more efficient than most modern canoeists like to admit.

D. *Sugar Island.*

A modification of the beavertail, the Sugar Island has its greatest width at the tip, which makes it better for use in shallow and aerated water (rapids). The Sugar Island style is favored by some of the best freestyle solo canoeists.

A SUMMARY OF FACTORS WHICH AFFECT
THE CHOICE OF BLADE SHAPE

1. A long narrow blade is best for steering maneuvers required in northwoods style and freestyle solo canoeing.

2. A wide blade is best for use in shallow and aerated water.

3. The wider the blade, the more awkward and noisy it will be when pulled through the water. Avoid wide blades if wildlife photography and fishing is your main reason for canoeing.

4. Paddles with splines (vertical ribs) down the center tend to be noisy when pulled through the water, and they are poorly adapted to side-slip maneuvers.

5. Stiff-bladed paddles are best for use in aerated water, while those with "reasonably flexible" blades are preferable for all-around canoeing.

6. Too much flex in a paddle blade -- as evidenced by some inexpensive plastic paddles -- is bad. You can't paddle well with a blade that rubber-bands through the water!

7. Blades with square corners take a substantial beating in rocky areas. Square tips must be reinforced with a synthetic material (fiberglass, Kevlar, Lexan) to keep them from breaking off in shallows.

8. Square-tip paddles exhibit rotational torque if they're not set into the water exactly perpendicular. For this reason, beginners should avoid them -- or round the corners on a wide radius. Choose the square tip only after you've mastered the fine points of paddle control!

WHICH SHAPE IS FOR YOU?

By now, you've probably developed some specific preferences for paddle shape. If not, I suggest you start with something that resembles a cross between paddles A and C -- eight inch wide blade, tapered edges, and rounded tip. This design will perform a multitude of tasks well.

GRIP STYLE

There are T-grips, pear grips, modified T's and off-set grips. What's best is a matter of preference, though there are some loose guidelines:

1. T-grips provide precise control of the blade angle -- a reason why nearly every serious whitewater canoeist chooses them.

2. There are "good" and bad pear grips. The best ones -- which are never found on cheap paddles -- come very close to complete perfection and are ideal for every use except perhaps the hairiest whitewater.

3. Off-set grips are best adapted to the bent paddle as they put the center of your hand in line with the force of the paddle blade. You'll also find off-set grips on some good straight paddles. Whether or not this is a good idea is debatable.

Most canoeists will probably be happiest with a generous pear or "soft" T-grip. The one place where a T-grip is out-of-place is in the modern freestyle canoe. Freestyle technique requires a number of unorthodox moves, many of which require a slightly rotated grip on the paddle.

WEIGHT

The lighter the paddle, the better. Period!

BALANCE

The best paddles balance just behind -- or within an inch or two -- of the blade and transmit a feeling of "unawareness of the blade" when you heft them.

CONSTRUCTION

You can get paddles of solid wood, laminated wood, Kevlar, plastic, fiberglass, aluminum, and composites -- wood with foam core blades, aluminum shaft with fiberglass blades, etc. Again, it's a matter of preference, though most canoeists would agree that, except for whitewater use, where paddles really take a beating, wood is still the premier material. Not only is it more pleasing to look at; it doesn't get as cold or as hot as synthetic materials. However, where areas are certain to be shallow and rocky, one of the glass-blade, aluminum-shaft models might be the best choice. Unfortunately, to create a really great paddle out of fiberglass and aluminum is expensive. The further one gets from sawing a simple paddle from a single board, the more expensive the process. For example, a cheap wood paddle has a shaft that is somewhat oval in cross-section, with the largest diameter of the oval in the same plane as the blade, because the paddle is cut from a single board. This flattened cross-section in the wrong direction makes these cheapies a pain to paddle with, and certainly doesn't do much for their strength. More expensive paddles have a round shaft, which requires more processing than the flattened shaft. This is a distinct improvement, but top-of-the-line models always have an oval shaft which runs at 90 degrees to the paddle blade, thus following the natural contours of the hand.

The final selection of a canoe paddle rests in your hands. No two "identical" paddles made by the same manufacturer will feel the same. So lift each paddle and swing it through the air. Check the flex of the blade -- except for tough whitewater use, there should be some. Do you like what you feel? Is the paddle durable enough to meet your needs? Can you afford the price? Good. Then buy it!

THE GREAT VARNISH MYTH

A varnished grip is supposed to give you blisters. Most racing paddles are dipped in or sprayed with a quality varnish. Racers paddle all day. Racers seldom get blisters. Racers don't wear gloves. Need I say more?

The key to a blisterless canoe trip rests in the quality and smoothness of the finish, rather than the type of finish applied. Whatever you use, sand and steelwool the final coat until the wood has a distinctly silky feel. This will protect both the paddle and your hands. However, if you feel the need to adhere to the ways of historic canoeists, the shaft and grip can be left unprotected. To many, a finishless or linseed oil-rubbed paddle is indicative of an expert canoeist.

CUSTOMIZING

In all my years of canoeing, I've owned only two paddles that felt "perfect" when I received them from the manufacturer. Every other paddle I've owned had to be customized. Either the grip or shaft didn't feel right or the blade shape was inappropriate. And I've never had a paddle whose finish I was completely satisfied with.

In short, don't expect miracles from even the best paddles. Human hands are very individualistic and so too must be the paddles that fit them. Don't be afraid to file and sand a new paddle until it fits right. After all, the only one you need to please is yourself. And, if pleasing yourself means spending 75 dollars for a really fine paddle, then go to it. Then later, when the icy grip of winter confines you to the warmth of your wood stove, take your paddle off its rack, swing it in proud defiance of the snows, and re-live the joys of running water and the magic of your canoe.

PADDLE STROKES

The following canoe strokes have been learned and perfected over the last 35 years. However, don't take that too seriously since up until a decade ago, according to an "efficient" canoe-paddling course I enrolled in, I did everything wrong -- in spite of the fact that I could paddle a canoe straight, turn effectively, and do a whole lot of other impressive things.

Experience is not always the best teacher. Now that I have seen the error of my ways, I'll pass on some of the things I have learned. If you're a canoeist from the old school, you may shake your head in disbelief and wonder at the new strokes. Nevertheless, they are much more powerful and efficient than the older variations.

Figure 7-3   Diagrams in this book will use this identification system.

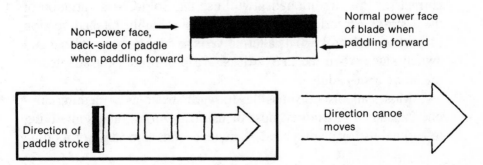

Non-power face, back-side of paddle when paddling forward

Normal power face of blade when paddling forward

Direction of paddle stroke

Direction canoe moves

THE BOW OR FORWARD STROKE

To make the forward stroke most effective, reach as far forward as you can, but don't lunge. Put the paddle into the water at least two feet in front of your body. At the start of the stroke, the top arm is bent and the lower arm is straight. At the end of the stroke the positions are reversed. Keep your top hand low -- below your eyes, and *push*. Most of the power in the stroke should come from pushing with the top hand, not from pulling with the bottom. The stroke is smooth and powerful, and the control is in the top hand. Paddle parallel to the keel, as close to the canoe as possible, and don't bring your lower hand beyond your hip. Bringing the paddle farther back than necessary wastes energy and power, and in fact actually *slows* the canoe down. This is because a paddle is not really pushed through water; rather, the canoe moves forward to the place where the stroke began. So if you bring your paddle back beyond the vertical (blade pulled upward in the water behind you), the canoe will be forced down in the water which will cause a drag on its forward motion. As mentioned, the major advantage of the bent paddle is that it eliminates this forward drag.

The most common mistake beginners make is to paddle across their bodies. It is important that the paddle shaft be perpendicular (or nearly so), not angled out from the canoe. To effect this, reach far across your body with your top hand and twist your shoulders into the stroke. For greatest power, paddle from a sitting position. Only when you are in heavy rapids or running waves should you kneel.

Solo adaptations: When straight-ahead power is applied to one side of a solo canoe, it will veer away from the paddling side. Two or three strokes (perhaps as many as four in a pure-bred solo racing canoe) is about maximum before the boat turns off course. To correct for this, traditionalists will use the Solo-C -- a variation of the J-stroke (described on page 112), or a highly pitched version of the forward stroke. The alternative is to simply power ahead and switch sides when the need arises -- a procedure best adapted to the short bent paddle.

Most canoeists dismiss the forward stroke as something anyone can do. The truth is most of us do it wrong, and some cling to bad habits for many years. A canoe spends almost all of its time

START OF FORWARD STROKE

FINISH OF
FORWARD STROKE

Figure 7-4   Forward Stroke: Put your paddle in the water at least two feet in front of your body. Keep your top hand low — below your eyes.

going forward; therefore greater effort should go into paddling it more efficiently.

THE BACK STROKE

Most canoeists pick up the back stroke out of necessity when a large rock looms ahead and they need to avoid it. Other names given to this stroke are help!, good grief!, and @##&**! It is the exact opposite of the forward stroke, and all comments made about that stroke apply here.

Start the stroke where the bow (forward) stroke ends, and end the stroke where the bow stroke starts. Confused? Well, this is one stroke that comes naturally.

There is an alternate form of the back stroke that is favored by some whitewater paddlers. Rotate your top hand and paddle shaft 180 degrees, so you are looking at your fingers rather than your knuckles. Power is thus provided by pushing your top hand back toward you rather than pulling it. Although not necessarily more powerful than the conventional back stroke, this variation allows you to turn your body and look backward in the direction you are paddling. It permits instant transfer to the very important *draw* stroke without sacrificing control (a must when executing the *back ferry* -- the canoeist's most useful river tactic. See Chapter 8 -- On the Water -- for a discussion of this technique).

Solo adaptations: Here again, the problem is keeping the solo canoe on course when power is applied to one side. Straight-line backing is best accomplished by using a "Reverse-C" (Figure 7-20) -- a slightly modified version of the J-stroke done in reverse. In tricky currents, an accomplished solo paddler will often alternate between this stroke and a diagonal draw (a conventional "draw" applied at a 45 degree angle to the canoe).

THE DRAW STROKE

The draw stroke is the most important turning stroke. A powerful draw makes the bow person an active navigator rather than just a horse-power machine (Figure 7-5). The draw stroke is perhaps the most important stroke in whitewater. Avoid the challenge of whitewater trips until you can perform this stroke quickly, powerfully, and precisely.

Solo Adaptation

Figure 7-5 Draw Stroke

For maximum power the draw should be executed from a kneeling position. Reach out as far from the gunwale as you can -- don't be afraid to lean the canoe. Keep your top hand high and draw the paddle quickly and powerfully toward you. When the paddle reaches within 6 inches of the canoe, slice it out and draw again.

It is important to realize that the force of the water under the canoe has a righting effect on the canoe, so you can lean way out on this stroke and apply power with your whole body. The canoe *will not* tip over. The righting effect ceases, however, when the paddle is no longer in motion, so you must recenter your weight the moment you take the power off the paddle. The modern trend of running rapids is to run them as slowly as possible, as this gives you time to respond correctly and results in less damage to your canoe if it strikes a rock. Rudder motions are useful for turning only if you have forward speed, which is why the draw is so important. Although commonly used by both paddlers, the draw is most effective in the bow. It is not uncommon on whitewater streams to hear, off in the distance, a desperate stern paddler screaming *"Draw . . . draw!"* to a frustrated partner.

Solo adaptation: Identical to the tandem "draw." Net movement of the canoe is sideways, in the direction of the stroke. By varying the angle of the draw (to the diagonal), a variety of intriguing moves are possible. This is an essential stroke for the solo canoeist -- one which must be mastered early. A lightweight "play" boat will literally dance sideways across the water with a few judicious flicks of the "draw."

THE PRYAWAY (PRY) STROKE

The pryaway is used for moving the canoe away from your paddling side. It can be used effectively by either paddler, but it is most often used in the stern. It is a modern version of the old "pushover" stroke, although considerably more powerful. Slice the paddle into the water as far under the canoe as possible. With a deft, powerful motion, pry the paddle over the top of the gunwale. After some practice you will find that it is easier and faster to use an underwater rather than an aerial recovery for your paddle. The mechanics of this will come naturally after a short time. Unlike the

Figure 7-6   The Pryaway

draw, the pryaway has no righting effect on the canoe; hence
it is important that you keep your weight well centered throughout
the stroke. Since the pryaway is very powerful, it should not be
used in shallow water where the paddle might catch on a rock and
overturn the canoe. In shallow water the bow person should use a
"cross draw."

Solo adaptations: The "pryaway" is best at home in heavy
water (powerful waves) where you need a quick lateral move plus
the stability (bracing action) of a paddle that's always in the water.
It is an essential stroke in the solo whitewater canoe.

However, the "pryaway" chews up paddle shafts and gunwales -- the reason why most solo canoeists avoid it. The alternative
is to switch sides and "draw," or to "cross-draw" with a strong

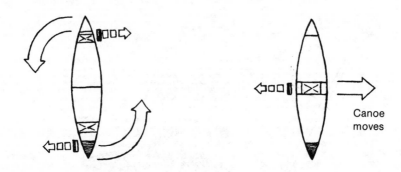

Figure 7-7   The Pryaway: Aerial view of the pryaway for both tandem and solo.

diagonal-draw component astern. For maneuvering in heavy white-water, the "pryaway" has no peer. Otherwise, the alternatives work as well and are easier on equipment.

THE CROSS-DRAW

The cross-draw, as the name implies, is a draw stroke crossed over to the other side of the canoe. It is used in water too shallow to effect a proper pryaway.

Pivot at the waist, swing the paddle over the bow (the stroke cannot be done in the stern) . . . and *draw!* Don't change your grip on the paddle. Angle the paddle forward so that it is nearly parallel to the water. Force water under and in front of the bow. As with the pryaway, keep your weight centered, as the cross draw has no stabilizing effect on the canoe.

A bow person who can correctly perform draw, cross-draw, and pryaway strokes is indispensable in whitewater. If you are paddling stern in fast water you will damage your canoe less if you trust your bow person's ability. The stern person is captain of the ship in calm water, but the bow paddler is the chief navigator and has the major responsibility in rapids.

Like many veteran canoeists, it was difficult for me to learn to trust my bow paddler. I, back in the stern, *always* made the route (not necessarily *right*) decisions. Then one day while the canoe was flipped over on its back I began to look at the number

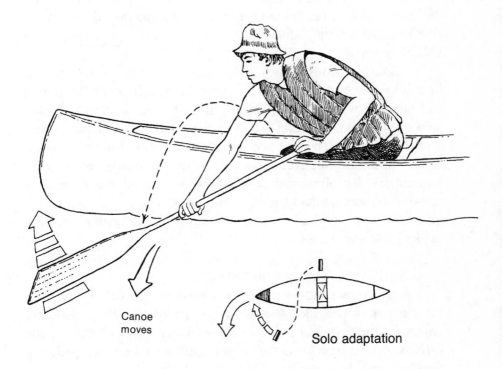

Canoe
moves

Solo adaptation

Figure 7-8 Cross Draw: This is your most powerful stroke for turning to the off-side in a solo canoe.

and placement of dents which had accumulated over the years. Quite amazingly, almost all the dents were forward of the beam, and most of them were on the left side (my weaker side). On the next whitewater trip I paddled bow and put my neophyte partner in the stern. Amazingly, the canoe struck only a few rocks, mostly with the tail, although I must admit that directional control from the back was at times somewhat lacking. The moral, of course, is, first train your bow paddler -- then trust him or her. The rewards will be many.

Solo adaptations: This is THE stroke for turning to the off-side in a solo canoe. It is extremely powerful and if properly applied and coupled with a strong lean, will snap even a straight-keeled solo canoe around quicker'n a cat's wink. Older canoe books recommend the "sweep" stroke for off-side turns, but the "cross-draw" is more effective, especially when the canoe has forward motion. Even professional canoe racers who *never* use cross-over maneuvers, occasionally cheat and "cross-draw". As you may guess, the "cross-draw" is one of my favorite strokes in both tandem and solo canoe.

THE J-STROKE

A canoe moving forward has a tendency to veer away from the side on which the stern person is paddling. When paddling backward the reverse is true. The J-stroke is used to keep a canoe on a straight course. It is the stern person's stroke when paddling forward, and a reverse form of it (the "reverse-J") is used by the bow paddler when moving backward. Begin the "J" like a typical forward stroke, but shortly after the paddle enters the water, start changing its pitch ever so slightly by turning the thumb of your top hand down and away from your body. As the paddle is pushed forward through the water, continue to increase the pitch progressively. At the completion of the stroke, the thumb of the top hand should be pointing straight down, placing the paddle in a rudder position. If at the end of the stroke additional correction is needed, force the paddle out from the canoe in a prying fashion. If no further correction is necessary, take the paddle out of the water and repeat the stroke.

There are many variations of the *J-stroke*, and each canoeist develops a style that suits him or her best. Many very good paddlers

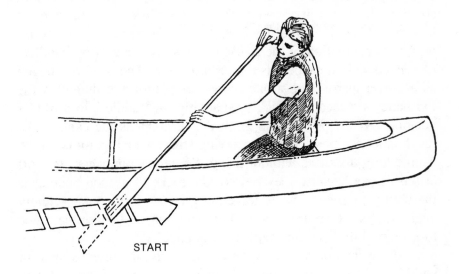

START

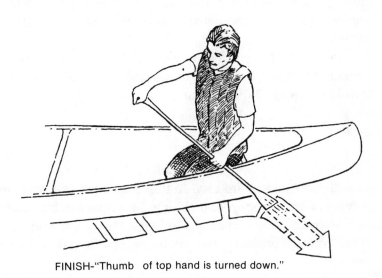

FINISH-"Thumb of top hand is turned down."

Figure 7-9 The J-Stroke

finish the stroke by prying the paddle shaft off the gunwales or their thighs. Completing the stroke with a pry is frowned upon in some circles, since it abuses paddles (and gunwales). However, it is a very efficient form of the J, and most whitewater canoeists use it. Another variation of the J, used almost exclusively by paddlers of decked slalom canoes, is the *thumbs-up J.* This stroke is begun as a powerful forward stroke; upon completion the thumb of the top hand is turned up quickly, snapping the paddle into a rudder position. A fast pry off the gunwales straightens the canoe. The result is a very powerful and relaxing stroke which permits you to paddle long distances without tiring. Some veteran canoeists scoff at this stroke because they believe the mark of a good paddler is the ability to keep a canoe traveling on a straight course without veering. Both the thumbs-up and pry form of the J cause the canoe to veer slightly back and forth as it is paddled.

Many champion whitewater canoeists use the thumbs-up J for paddling their skittish, decked fiberglass boats. When gliding quietly among the lily pads, the traditional J is best. But in heavy rapids and waves the newer, more efficient variations are often better.

Solo adaptations: The traditional "J" doesn't provide enough leverage to keep a solo canoe on course. You'll have to use the "Solo-C" (Fig. 7-19) instead.

THE SWEEP STROKES

Sweep strokes are used to turn the canoe in a wide arc, either toward or away from your paddling side. Both the draw and pryaway are more efficient, especially in currents, and if you've mastered these you will probably reserve the sweeps for quiet-water maneuvers.

BOW SWEEP

Place your paddle in the water far forward, nearly touching the bow. Sweep the paddle outward in a wide arc and stop when it is perpendicular to the canoe. The "reverse sweep" is the exact opposite.

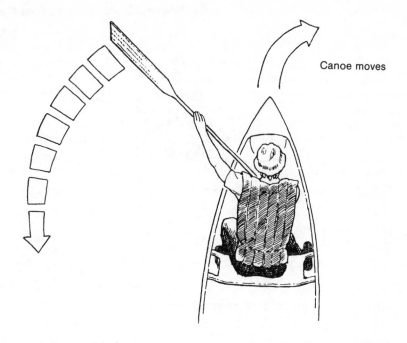

Figure 7-10   The Bow Sweep Stroke

Figure 7-11   The Solo Sweep: Canoe will pivot on its midpoint and turn clockwise.

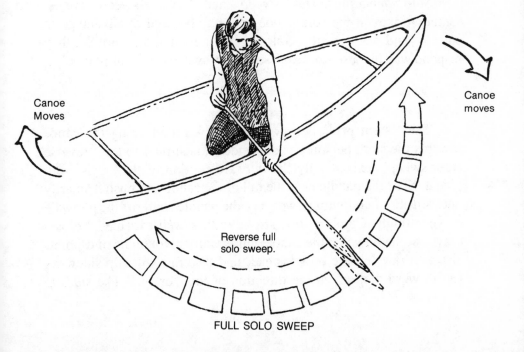

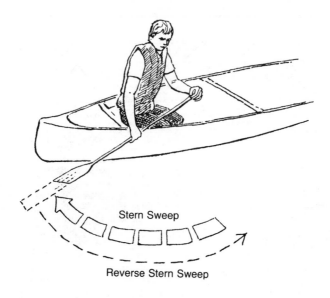

Stern Sweep

Reverse Stern Sweep

Figure 7-12   The Stern Sweep: Canoe will accelerate and turn towards paddler's left.

STERN SWEEP

Start the paddle at a right angle to the canoe. Sweep it in a wide arc all the way back to the stern. Go back to your starting point for the "reverse stern sweep."

Solo adaptations: The "sweep" and "reverse-sweep" are essential strokes in the solo canoe and may be used to advantage in currents and heavy water. Solo canoes are small and nimble; they respond well to these strokes. Use the *full* sweep in the solo canoe!

STERN PRY

The "stern pry" is a powerful stroke for turning the canoe towards the stern person's paddle side. It is similar to the "reverse stern sweep" except only the *outward* portion of the arc is completed. Start the paddle near the tail of the canoe and push it smartly outward. For maximum power, pry the paddle shaft off the gunwale or your thigh. Combine this stroke with a well-executed "cross-draw" at the bow and the canoe will literally pivot on its mid-point. Use a "draw" at the bow instead, and the craft will slip sideways (no forward motion) in the direction of the "draw." The *sideslip*

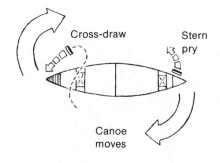

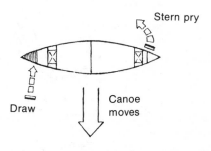

Similar to the reverse sweep except only the outward portion of the arc is completed.

Figure 7-13a   The Pivot

Figure 7-13b   The Side Slip

and *pivot* illustrated in Figures 7-13a/b are essential whitewater maneuvers.

Note: Because of its long lever arm, the "stern pry" is more powerful than the pryaway. It is also better in shallow water because the paddle can't catch on rocks and upset the canoe.

THE SCULLING DRAW

The sculling draw is an impressive-looking stroke. It is not one that you need to learn right away, as you can use the draw to perform the same function. However, it is a nice stroke in its place, and that place is in parallel landing to a shore line in water too shallow to get a good draw.

Place the paddle in the water in a draw position at a comfortable distance from the canoe. Turn the leading edge of the paddle about forty-five degrees away from the canoe, and while holding this

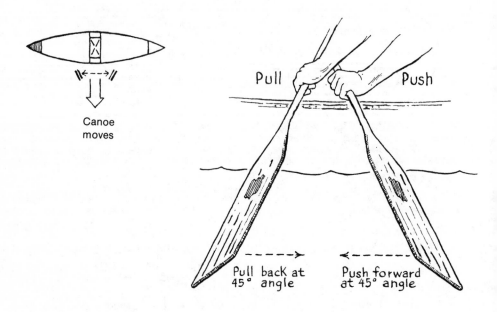

Canoe
moves

Pull

Push

Pull back at
45° angle

Push forward
at 45° angle

Figure 7-14   The Sculling Draw

blade angle pull the paddle backward through the water for a distance of about two feet. Then reverse the angle of the leading edge ninety degrees from the previous direction and, while holding this new blade angle, push the paddle forward about 2 feet to complete the stroke. The sculling draw is sometimes called the *figure 8* stroke because the paddle appears to describe an *8* in the water. This is not really accurate, however, since the paddle is pulled straight fore and aft, and only the blade angle is changed.

POWER PADDLING (the "MINNESOTA SWITCH")
The term "power-paddling" was coined by Harry Roberts, Vice President of Sawyer Canoe Company and former editor of **WILDERNESS CAMPING MAGAZINE.** The name aptly

describes this dynamic technique in which canoeists paddle power-
fully ahead, and on signal, switch sides to maintain a straight course.

Some early Indian tribes adopted an unorthodox but very efficient method of keeping a canoe on course. Both paddlers used
short, powerful forward strokes to propel the canoe, and when they
wanted to change direction they would merely flip their paddles
over the canoe and change paddle sides. This would give the stern
person leverage on the other side, so no correctional stroke (like
the J) was necessary. The net effect, of course, was that the canoe
traveled a somewhat erratic path in the water. The white man,
feeling that switching sides wasted energy and efficiency, adopted
the J-stroke, which is in common use today.

About forty years ago some professional Minnesota racers tried
the switching technique in competition. The results were dramatic.
Not only could a canoe be paddled faster by switching sides every
six strokes or so, but it could also be paddled farther, since the
paddlers became less tired. Over the years the "Minnesota switch"
grew in popularity, and today virtually all professional racers use
it instead of the J-stroke. Al Button, America's medal-winning
whitewater champion, used it at the whitewater world champion-
ships in 1975 to take a bronze medal. I asked Al if European
paddlers were showing any interest in the switching technique.
"When I took third place, they showed some interest," he replied.
"If I had been fortunate enough to take a first, everybody would
have been using it within a year!"

To an old-school canoeist the "Minnesota switch" is a prime
example of poor technique, mostly because the canoe does not
travel a straight-line course. But it *is* efficient, especially on wilderness trips when you want to make good time against big incoming
rollers on a windswept lake. Kruger and Waddell used the Minnesota
switch almost exclusively on their voyage to the Bering Sea. Their
cadence was approximately sixty strokes per minute, with a switch
after each six to eight strokes.

Procedure: Paddlers *sit* low in the canoe with feet braced (foot
braces are desirable) firmly ahead. After a half dozen or so strokes,
the stern paddler -- who can best see the course of the canoe --
shouts *HUT** or some other agreed upon signal. Paddlers then

---

*HUT is the traditional command for switching paddling sides. It is also the name of the official
magazine of the Minnesota Canoe Association.

Figure 7-15   As you gain solo experience, you'll develop a repertoire of special strokes. Here, Phil Sigglekow braces into a turn in his Pat Moore designed *Proem*. Photo credit: R. Hamilton Smith.

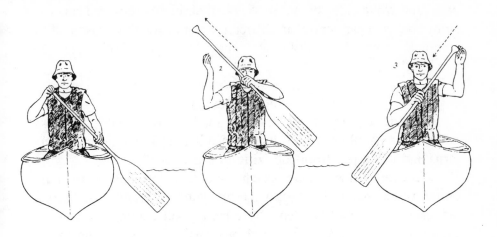

Figure 7-16 The Minnesota Switch: Switching sides is easy as 1, 2, 3. If correctly done only a split second is lost.

switch sides in unison (see Figure 7-16) and without missing a beat, continue to power-paddle ahead. This is a precise, snappy maneuver, one which requires more finesse and coordination than you might guess. If done correctly, only a split second is lost; if improperly executed in a strong current, a capsize is possible.

Experienced racing teams do *all* their paddling this way, invariably with bent-shaft paddles. To maneuver, they ''draw'' or switch sides and ''draw'' -- or the bowman uses a ''post,'' which is basically a ''high brace'' (Figure 7-18). As mentioned, racers occasionally ''cheat'' and cross-draw at the bow to effect turns. But mostly, they power-paddle ahead and switch sides to maneuver.

Some traditional canoeists maintain that you sacrifice canoe control when you adhere to power-paddling techniques. Until I paddled with the racers, I believed this too. But it simply isn't so. What onlookers often perceive as ''loss of control'' in tight turns is in reality the maneuvering limits of a racing canoe at speed. Race boats are straight-keeled; at best they turn poorly even when piloted by expert teams. It's doubtful that experienced whitewater folk could make these canoes sing any more beautifully on a twisting course.

However, there's no denying that kneeling paddlers who use long straight paddles (long paddles have more leverage than short ones) and whitewater slalom strokes in their highly rockered canoes enjoy the greatest control in difficult waters. For this reason, the complete canoeist should know -- and appreciate -- both styles of paddling!

THE BRACES

Low Brace: The "low brace" functions as an outrigger; it's not really a paddling stroke. Its purpose is to stabilize the canoe in turns and to keep it from capsizing in big waves.

To execute the stroke: Reach far out, paddle laid nearly flat on the water, palm of the top hand up. Put your weight solidly on the paddle -- a half-hearted effort isn't good enough. If you're capsizing, a powerful downward push will right you. The push should be lightning fast and smooth; don't "slap" the water with your paddle.

The "low brace" is essential for turning into or out of eddies (see Chapter 8, ON THE WATER), and any place the stern person

Figure 7-17   The Low Brace

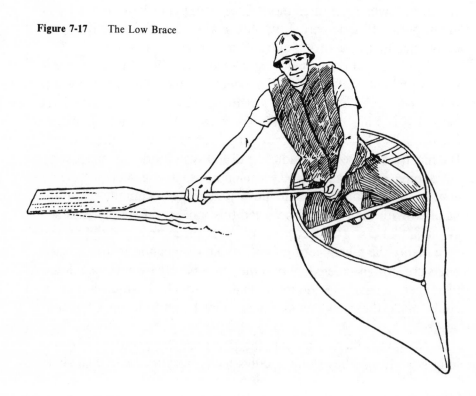

needs to check a strong inside turn. Canoe teams frequently run heavy waves in a "ready brace" or motionless outrigger position. Then, if an unusually high "haystack" (standing wave) threatens to unhorse them, the paddler on the "tipping side" can instantly brace to off-set the dangerous lean.

Solo adaptations: Solo canoes are skittish and they depend on strong leans and braces to keep them from capsizing in rough water. So learn this stroke early -- and master it -- if you plan to solo in anything more than a weak current.

You can use the low brace effectively on calm water too: Get up a full head of steam, reach back at about a 30 degree angle, and brace hard, power face of the paddle at a strong climbing angle to the water. The canoe will spin right around your paddle, in effect executing an inside wheelee or "static axle." Wahoo! Pure fun. The low brace is one of the most important (and spectacular) strokes for playing on quiet water.

High brace: There are times when you need a strong brace, a draw, and a canoe lean all at the same time. Enter the "high brace." Basically, the high brace is nothing more than a stationary draw with the power face of the paddle held against the current or at a

Figure 7-18   The High Brace

strong climbing angle to it. The success of the stroke depends on speed -- either paddling or current -- and a strong lean to offset the pull of the moving water. The high brace blends easily to the "draw" -- an essential stroke for pulling into an eddy and for making sharp turns. Both the high and low brace may be used effectively in both bow and stern of the tandem canoe. However, the high brace is more commonly used in the bow; the low brace in the stern.

Solo adaptations: When you find yourself capsizing to your off-side (side opposite your paddle), reach far out on a high brace and put your weight and trust on your paddle. The high brace is an essential stroke for the solo canoeist. You cannot do eddy turns or maintain stability in rough water without it. Learn this stroke early!

PADDLING ALONE

See Chapter 4, Solo Canoeing is Different, for what you need to know when paddling solo and tandem canoes alone.

PURE-BRED SOLO STROKES

As you've probably already discovered, all the typical tandem strokes can be used with varying success in the solo canoe. There are, however, a few strokes which are unique to the solo canoe. These are...

THE SOLO-C

The "Solo-C" is the lone paddler's J-stroke; it is the only way to keep a solo canoe on course without adopting the "Minnesota switch". In reality, the Solo-C (also called the "hook stroke") is nothing more than a refined J-stroke with a diagonal draw component added at the start.

Execution: Begin the stroke by reaching your paddle far forward, power face at a 30 to 45 degree angle to the canoe. Arc the blade powerfully inward, and continue pulling, parallel to the keel (blade *under* the bilge of the canoe) until you are three-fourths through the power phase. Finish with a gentle outward thrust (*not* the powerful kick used for completion of the J-stroke) for the final subtle correction of your course. If done correctly, the bow of your canoe will barely waver.

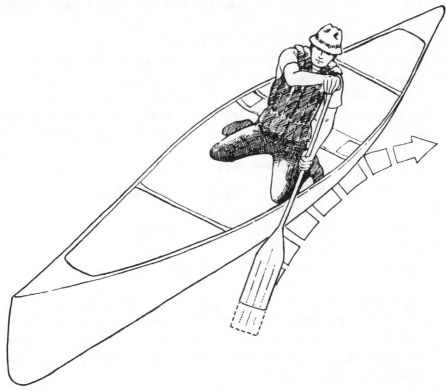

Figure 7-19   The Solo-C

Like the J-stroke, the top hand changes pitch progressively throughout the stroke; in the end the thumb is turned sharply down. Some of the best free-style (traditional) canoeists grasp the grip of the paddle at an angle to make the stroke more fluid. Some real die-hards even carve the top grip so that it can be only grasped one way, and by either the left or right hand. Switching paddling sides is actively discouraged. In fact, Mike Galt, high priest of the free-style solo art, once remarked that...''You should decide early in your paddling career on which side you want to paddle, then *never never* change!'' So much for elitism!

To watch an accomplished soloist C-stroking along, canoe running true and dead quiet, is a rare treat. The technique is beautiful to watch -- a true art form, difficult to master, and gloriously fun to perform. This is a stroke you must perfect if you want to derive the greatest satisfaction from a solo play or whitewater canoe. The Solo-C represents canoe technique at its highest pinnacle. It is not a stroke you can master in a single season!

THE REVERSE-C

The "Reverse-C" is used for backing the solo canoe in a straight line. Though it is basically the opposite of the forward-C, there is one real difference -- near the end of the stroke the paddle is given a sharp outward thrust (often it is pried off the gunwale) to straighten the canoe. Sometimes, the blade is momentarily left

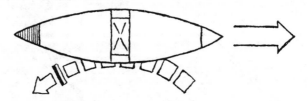

Figure 7-20   The Reverse "C": Done opposite of the forward "C", but . . .

in the water to provide ruddering action in the current. The timing of the outward thrust is critical: If executed too late in a strong current, it will be ineffectual. If done too early, it may unbalance and upset the canoe. The "Reverse-C" is one of the most important strokes in the solo repertoire!

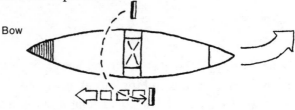

Figure 7-21   The Cross Backstroke

CROSS BACK-STROKE

Use this when you need a powerful backstroke and a turn at the same time. It is similar to the cross-draw, only much more severe. Rotate your shoulders and swing the paddle across the canoe. Then, paddle dynamically forward. By changing the angle of the paddle, you can back the canoe dead straight. Or, you can go into a cross-draw for a fast turn to the off-side.

OUTSIDE PIVOT

Best described as a "multiple outside turn", the "outside pivot" is part cross-draw and part sweep. It looks impressive but it's actually less efficient than two well done cross-draws which

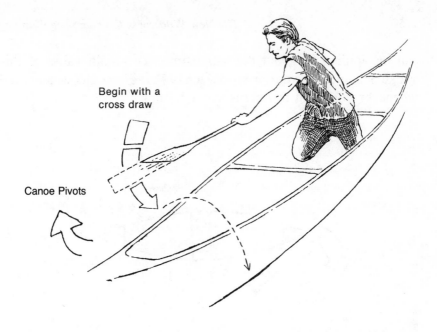

Begin with a
cross draw

Canoe Pivots

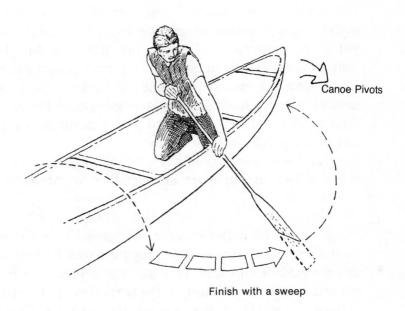

Canoe Pivots

Finish with a sweep

Figure 7-22 The Outside Pivot: Canoe pivots clockwise around its midpoint.

can be applied in about the same time. The main value of this stroke is in picking your way between obstacles in quiet water...and whenever you want to impress your friends.

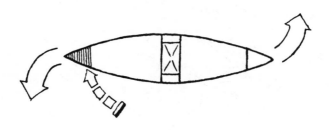

Figure 7-23   Acute, or Bow Draw:

ACUTE, OR BOW DRAW

Nothing more than the first part of a Solo-C stroke, only applied farther out and towards the bow. The "bow draw" is the fastest and most powerful way to turn the canoe sharply towards your paddle side. It is an essential stroke wherever tight maneuvers are the order of the day. Like the "C-stroke", the "bow draw" requires practice to master, mostly because of the awkward top hand position (the wrist is turned so the thumb is down -- power face of the paddle faces the canoe).

The "bow draw" is only effective if you throw your shoulders into it. This is an important and useful stroke. Master it early.

LEANING THE CANOE

It would be unfair to leave the subject of paddling without mentioning the technique of leaning the canoe to make a turn. To make a gradual turn *with the canoe under power*, lean the canoe (an inch or two is sufficient) to the *outside* of the turn (the reverse of what you would do on a bicycle). If you hold the lean the canoe will cut a nice arc in the *opposite* direction of the lean. Pro racers do much of their turning by this method and lone paddlers of decked slalom canoes often use a counter lean to help keep their skittish boats from turning away from their paddling side. Caution: Don't use this technique for quick turns in rapids -- you'll upset the canoe!

STANDING IN THE CANOE

The procedures discussed in this chapter naturally assume you will either sit or kneel in your canoe. But what about standing? Is it a viable position? Older canoe books suggest it is, while modern texts dismiss the idea with a simple snicker and an admonition that you should ''never stand'' in a canoe.

Hogwash! There are two times when you may want to stand in your canoe: 1) Just before entering a rapid -- to check the course from a higher vantage point, and 2) In calm water when you want to stretch your legs. Those who suggest that standing in a canoe is unsafe, simply don't know the limits of their craft. It is, in fact, possible to stand in almost any canoe -- even a skittish solo one, if you brace your feet wide apart and maintain your balance on the center line.

It is beyond the scope of this book to present a complete course in paddling. If you want to learn more, join a canoe club and get some firsthand instruction. Also, read the excellent books on technique listed in Appendix A.

8.
On the Water

Once, along the Hood River in the Northwest Territories of Canada, my partner and I entered what appeared to be a "relatively simple" rapid, only to discover that the waves and hydraulics were much worse than we had bargained for. It required all our strength and skill just to maintain alignment with the powerful current -- to keep from capsizing in the frothy water. The waves grew to monster proportions; ultimately, they completely engulfed the canoe and blotted my bowman from sight. But the tough nylon spray cover held and the big Royalex canoe plunged confidently on through.

The run was a long one, perhaps a quarter mile. There was no time to "question" the route, only to react. Finally, it was over and we drifted aimlessly into the pool of ice blue water below, our faces beaming with smiles, our bodies pumped high with the excitement of a successful run. Granted, we had stepped beyond safe bounds, but *we had made it*, and through it all we had retained perfect control of our craft (or so we thought). But our friends on shore had quite a different perspective. They laid into us with vociferous threats, unrepeatable expletives, and gave fair warning that we better *never never* pull a dumb stunt like that again! Repeated attempts to clear ourselves by suggesting that the run was "easy", was not enough. It was evident to everyone that God had directed our descent. We humbly apologized and vowed to show better judgment "next time".

As you have just observed, luck will occasionally get you through a difficult whitewater passage or across a dangerous running sea, but more often than not a lucky paddler is a good paddler. Unfortunately, in the process of becoming good, a spill or three is inevitable. Though competent canoeists question those who tip frequently, they wonder about those who have never tipped at all. Your safety on a canoe trip depends in large measure on your ability to respond correctly, and automatically, in dangerous situations. Proper responses can only be learned from practice. "Upsetting experiences" have educational value, and your survival in rapids may well depend on your whitewater education.

LOADING THE CANOE FOR ROUGH-WATER TRAVEL

Canoes should be loaded *in the water*, not on land. Standing in or placing heavy loads in canoes half out of water can bend aluminum and break wood and fiberglass bottoms. Admittedly, there are times when you may have to "bridge" your canoe while loading it. No problem: Even ultralight canoes are much tougher than most people think. Just be careful, and don't make a practice of this procedure.

A canoe almost always handles better when loaded dead level. Neither the bow nor the stern should be higher. If an uneven distribution of weight is unavoidable, the lesser of two evils is to lighten the bow. But a light bow will give you problems in a head wind -- you'll have difficulty keeping on course (the canoe will try to weather-vane into the wind). On the other hand, a weighted stern will provide better directional control in a following sea, though if the tail is too low, big waves may pour right in! In rapids, directional control will be reduced by burying one end. With the front end high you may successfully negotiate large standing waves, but you'll lose this advantage when you pile up on a rock because you can't maneuver. So whenever possible, load *dead level*, and keep the weight as close to the center and as low as possible in the canoe. This is one reason why Duluth packs (see Chapter 12 -- The Necessities) are preferred for wilderness tripping. A fully loaded Duluth pack comes only a few inches above the gunwales in a canoe of proper depth.

WAVES AND RUNNING SEAS

On most wilderness canoe trips high winds and large waves will be encountered. It is not always possible to put ashore when these conditions develop; you may have to remain at sea until a suitable landing place can be found. As waves grow in size, keeping water out of the canoe will become a problem, especially if the craft is heavily loaded. To prevent the canoe from swamping, the ends must be lightened. This is best accomplished by moving paddlers closer together, away from the bow and stern. If you stow your load close to the yoke, there will be ample space for the bow person to move back of the bow seat and the stern person to move forward of the stern seat. It is important to realize, however, that when paddlers move closer together directional control is reduced, because paddle leverage is decreased. Where a high degree of maneuverability is required, you would probably be wisest to stay on your seat (or kneel) and load as close to the center of the canoe as possible. Use a splash cover if you plan to run heavy rapids.

You can reduce the canoe's tendency to knife through incoming waves by paddling into them at about a thirty-degree angle. This technique, called "quartering," exposes more surface area of the canoe to the wave, thus giving the bow more lift.

However, it requires strength and experience to maintain a quartering course in a rough sea. It is not the simple task that canoeing books suggest. The penalty for sliding broadside off a giant wave face while attempting to quarter it, is a sure-fire capsize and an invigorating swim to shore. For this reason, beginners are probably wisest to lighten the ends of their canoe and power directly into the waves. Or, use a fabric splash cover. Better yet, go ashore and wait for more favorable conditions to paddle!

To maintain good forward speed when paddling into waves, you need a powerful stroke that transfers all your energy into forward motion; you cannot afford to waste power steering the canoe. When the wind is in your face and each succeeding roller dashes your canoe about, this is the time to use the "Minnesota Switch" (see

Chapter 7). *Both* partners must be well practiced in the switching technique. Playing dropsy with your paddle while negotiating four-foot waves or changing paddle sides at the wrong time is an invitation to disaster.

SEA ANCHOR

Older canoe books recommend that you rig a "sea anchor" (attach a large cooking pot to your twenty foot long stern painter, or to a harness rigged around the hull) to prevent broaching in a following sea. Quite honestly, in all my years of canoeing, I've never used a sea anchor on a canoe or observed one in use. My feeling is that if you can afford to take time to rig a sea anchor on a wind-blown lake you can take time to paddle ashore. And if you rig one in advance, suspecting that you'll need it when you "round the bend," then you have no business going out there to begin with. Certainly, a properly rigged sea anchor will keep you from broaching in a rough sea, but so will good paddling techniques. If you can't handle your craft on a wind-blown lake, then you had best remain ashore until the weather improves.

Some things work better in theory than in practice. Sea anchors are one of them!

SURFING

Surfing along the crest of a monster wave on a wind-tossed lake is one of the most exhilarating, if not dangerous, experiences in canoe-sport. Once your canoe begins to surf, there's little you can do other than "go with the flow" until the roller passes harmlessly by. Fortunately, loaded canoes don't surf very well or very long, so if you keep your wits about you, and the canoe running straight with the waves (keep paddling!), you'll probably come through with nothing more than white knuckles and a good shot of adrenalin.

There are two procedures for breaking a surf, neither of which works very well.

1. Backpaddle furiously: In all likelihood you'll broach and capsize or swamp.

2. Turn sharply into the wave; lean away from it to gain

freeboard. If you're lucky, you'll take some water over the rail. If not, you'll go swimming!

Usually, surfing is simply a good time. The exception is when you're running hell-bent-for-leather across a wave and just ahead is a rocky beach that threatens to grind your boat to bits. Now, you've got to act fast. First, execute procedure two. If you have enough skill, you may be able to turn into the wave without taking water. I've managed to accomplish this on several occasions and have always been amazed when it worked.

If you swamp when you broach the wave, jump quickly out of the canoe on the *windward* (wave) side. Keep a firm hold on the gunwales and try to work the canoe ashore. Some damage to the craft is inevitable. Some authorities suggest that you throw out your packs to lighten the load before you make the turn. Forget it! No way can you take your hands off the paddle in this situation.

As you can see, there's no sure recipe for taming a rough water surf!

LIGHTNING

There's a mistaken belief that non-metal canoes are safer in a lightning storm than metal ones. No way! In fact, it may be the other way around. Interestingly, sea-going ships are occasionally struck by lightning, with no ill effects. The current strikes the highest point on the ship (a steel arm or antenna or actual lightning rod) and is dissipated around the hull into the water. The occupants are not harmed. In a canoe, however, the paddlers *are* the lightning rods! No way can a human lightning rod survive the impact of one million volts of electricity!

The commonly quoted advice to "get off the water" when lightning is evident, is sound. It's also wasted rhetoric for only a fool continues to paddle during an electrical storm. Unfortunately, "getting off the water" isn't always as easy as it sounds. If the shore line is unforgiving, there may be simply no place to land.

Here's the procedure for safe passage: Continue to paddle along the shore line, perhaps fifty feet from land. There's a cone of protection which extends from the tallest trees (or land mass, as the case may be) about 45 degrees outward. Stay within this "safe zone" and far enough from land so that lightning can't jump from shore to you. Lightning may jump a dozen feet or more across the water, so keep this thought uppermost in your mind.

If you're caught outside the cone of protection and suddenly you feel electrical energy building (*dry* hair will stand on end!), you may still save the day by getting down *low* in the canoe (lay down!). This will reduce the human lightning rod effect and allow a strike to dissipate its energy from the canoe to the water.

Aluminum canoes are better electrical conductors than non-metal ones and so in theory, should more readily dissipate the current. This is all scientific speculation, you understand. In practice, you're best advised to get off the water -- and stay off it -- when lightning threatens!

TOWING

Accepting a tow from a passing motorboat is perhaps the biggest "faux pas" a canoeist can commit. It's sort of like eating garlic just before a visit to the dentist or giving your wife something for the house on her birthday. Being towed is a conscious admission that motorboats are better!

Fortunately, I've accepted a tow only once, on Wollaston Lake in Northwestern Saskatchewan. The idea was to run the 200 mile long Fond du Lac River in just seven days. To save time, we hired a tow to the mouth of the river, some thirty miles north.

I rigged a towing bridle (see instructions below) and tied the tow rope to a metal handle on the right side of the boat's transom. The twin outboards sprung into action and the operator opened the throttle. In a flash it was over -- my beautiful green Old Town canoe was swamped completely in the sidewash of the wake!

In the process of rescuing my gear, I discovered an important omission in the canoeing literature: Nowhere was it mentioned that the canoe must be towed in *dead center alignment with the motor*! The solution? Rig a Y-harness around the motor so the canoe would ride in the "vee" of the wake and not wander into the sidewash. Once this was accomplished, there were no further problems.

Towing a canoe presents no problem as long as you rig a towing bridle. This is most important, as the bow end of the canoe will submarine if you don't keep it up. Even if your tow rope can

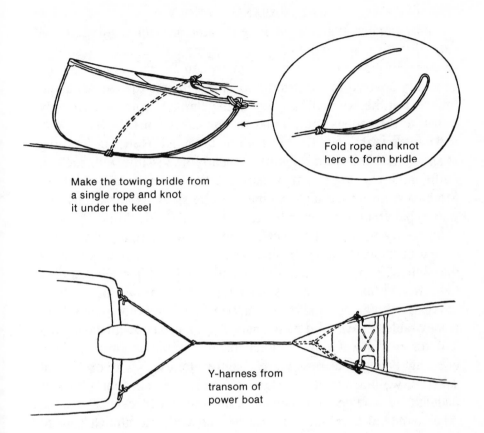

Make the towing bridle from
a single rope and knot
it under the keel

Fold rope and knot
here to form bridle

Y-harness from
transom of
power boat

Figure 8-1   Towing Bridle:

be attached close to the water line, a towing harness is best, as it takes the strain off the painter attachment ring or link.

To make a towing bridle tie your tow rope around the canoe's hull, winding it through the front seat supports as illustrated in Figure 8-1. Place the knot directly under the keel.* A properly rigged canoe can be towed at nearly full throttle (I've seen power-boats buzzing along at more than twenty-five miles an hour pulling harnessed canoes).

*I am indebted to Bill Mason, author of *PATH OF THE PADDLE*, for this simple method of rigging a harness.

CATAMARANED CANOES

For greater stability on rough water or while sailing, some authorities recommend that you "catamaran" a pair of similar canoes. To prevent water buildup between the two craft, you are generally advised to use strong poles to separate the canoes about four feet at the bow and six feet at the stern. If poles are securely lashed to the canoes and a large square sail is hoisted, the rig will make reasonably good time in a strong tail wind. However, running at an angle to the wind (tacking) is nearly impossible with such an outfit, and any degree of maneuverability is out of the question. Moreover, an important advantage of the single canoe over more stable, paired craft is its ability to roll with the side thrust of waves -- an ability which is completely negated by the rigid, unyielding design of the catamaran. In short, paired canoes respond poorly to the pitch of a rough sea, and consequently tend to ship water readily.

An additional concern is the danger of a rope lashing or wood crossbrace breaking, and if this happens in a good blow, a dunking is inevitable. I have used paired canoes for casual downwind sailing and for placid-water recreational paddling, but I consider them downright dangerous for general rough-water use -- with or without sails. A well-designed canoe will weather out six-foot waves if paddled by a team of experts. Catamaran-rigged canoes, on the other hand, even if securely braced and tied, are almost sure to break apart under these conditions.

When a sudden squall blows up and the waves grow to impressive heights, you will do best to put your faith in proper canoeing techniques. If this fails, hang onto your swamped canoe and trust your life jacket.

OUTBOARD MOTORS AND CANOES

Outboard motors have lost favor with modern wilderness canoeists. The noise and smell of gasoline just can't compete with the silence and grace of the paddle. Many of the more popular canoe areas are now completely closed to motor traffic, and each year additional acreage is placed into "paddle only" zones. Nevertheless, motors are still permitted on most wilderness waterways, and there is no doubt that, even with their additional weight, plus gas, they make a trip much easier.

You can put a motor on almost any canoe, but long canoes with big keels are best. Many of the new 1½ to 3 horsepower motors are extremely light and work very well when side-mounted on a typical two-ended canoe. There is little problem in using side-mounted motors; in fact, they are actually easier to use than transom-mounted models because you don't have to reach directly behind your body to operate the controls or to steer. The major failing of side mounts occurs in rapids and waves, where the out-of-balance canoe can flip over if the operator is not extremely careful to maintain control.

You can get along very nicely with a side mount if you use good judgment. However, if you plan to use a motor frequently, you should consider buying a special transom-equipped canoe designed especially for stern mounting. Select a model with a short transom above the water line and a completely formed stern below. Such a canoe will respond more positively to the motor than one with a chopped end, and will rise and fall more easily in large waves. Moreover, it will paddle almost as well as a conventional canoe. Caution: Should you upset with a motor-equipped canoe, your motor may drag the stern several feet below the water, leaving the lighter bow end perched high, like a half-surfaced torpedo. It may be very difficult for you to get a rig like this to shore by yourself, even on a moderately choppy lake. You will need all the flotation possible to increase the canoe's buoyancy; hence, you should have your watertight packs well secured in the canoe. You should also have at least one long line attached (a painter) to the canoe so that you can pull it behind you while you swim to shore. Two very good friends of mine nearly lost their lives on Minnesota's Namakan Lake when their motor-equipped canoe overturned. Fortunately they were in the water only about fifteen minutes before a passing fisherman came to their aid.

POLING THE CANOE

Although poling has long been part of the canoeist's art, it is seldom used by modern wilderness paddlers -- possibly because most are not familiar with its technique. Recently, however, there has been a revival of interest in canoe poling, and championship events are now held each year.

Poling is usually (though not always) done by one person. The poler assumes a standing position in a place that will trim the downstream end of the canoe slightly down -- forward of the center thwart when descending streams, and behind it when ascending them. Modern polers favor a strong, lightweight, aluminum pole about twelve feet long. Using quick, coordinated jabs, they can ascend streams with strong currents and shallow, moderate rapids; or they can carefully pick their way downstream, snubbing their poles to avoid obstacles.

Poling is a skill that requires coordination and much practice. An upstream pole in the morning followed by an afternoon downstream paddle or float is an ideal way to see the near wilderness without the necessity of organizing and running an auto shuttle. If you are interested in learning more about this interesting method of propelling a canoe, write to the A.C. Mackenzie River Company, P.O. Box 9301, Richmond Heights Station, Saint Louis, Missouri 63117. The Mackenzie River Company can provide you with a pole, a book, and even personalized on-the-river instruction.

CANOE SAILING

From the standpoint of sheer fun, few things rival a canoe under sail. Several companies manufacture excellent sail rigs which can be easily adapted to almost any canoe. A sail makes your canoe a multi-purpose boat, permitting you to enjoy it even on crowded, close-to-home lakes and reservoirs. Most wilderness canoeists just don't give enough thought to the values of a sail. The early voyageurs sailed their birch bark canoes quite regularly, and later wood-canvas freight canoes were commonly equipped with mast steps and bars for sails.

On a trip to James Bay, we fought wind and driving rain for ten straight days without a break. At one point in the trip, we covered only twelve miles in three days. On another day sixteen hours of strenuous, continuous paddling were required to cross twenty-mile long Mattagami Lake, just south of Smoky Falls, Ontario. When we finally entered the very large Moose River, we knew we would have to fight the prevailing north wind for more

Figure 8-2   Two paddles and a rain-fly or poncho is the easiest way to rig a sail.

than a hundred miles to reach James Bay. Then a miraculous change of weather occurred. The wind shifted completely to the south, providing us with a steady tail wind of perhaps twenty knots. We quicky fashioned sails and put to sea easily covering the hundred-mile distance to Moosonee in just fifteen hours! Shortly after we arrived at our destination, the wind reversed itself again. Our sail had given us the edge to play the weather odds and win.

The best and easiest way to rig a sail for a wilderness canoe is to use two paddles or poles and a rain-fly or poncho. Roll the fly or poncho around the paddles as you would a scroll (Figure 8-2). In practice, the bow person holds the rig against the gunwales and supports the paddle blades (or pole bases) with his thighs or feet. By opening and closing the scroll-like sail to catch the wind, you can control the speed of the canoe. You can also change the direction of the sail somewhat, allowing you to tack slightly.

It is not a good idea to tie makeshift sails in place on loaded wilderness canoes. A heavily loaded canoe can easily get out of control in a high wind and capsize, throwing you overboard while it keeps on plowing down the lake. You may find yourself not only in the water in a running sea, but canoeless as well. Hand-held sails work well enough for most situations. If you prefer a sturdier, more permanent arrangement, install a mast step and bar and do it right.

EVASIVE TACTICS

Assume you are canoeing on a river with a strong current. Directly in front of your canoe is a large rock. If you try to steer around the rock, you are likely to get caught broadside and possibly destroy your canoe. Back paddling is not the answer, for that will merely postpone the inevitable. You require a tactic that will slow the canoe down and move it sideways *at the same time*. You need a *back ferry*.

The back ferry makes use of two directional forces: the forward velocity of the river and the back-paddling speed of your canoe. In Figure 8-3 the stern person is paddling on the left and begins the back ferry with a powerful stern pry. The pry is repeated until the proper angle to the current (usually about thirty degrees) is attained. The stern paddler then joins the bow person in paddling

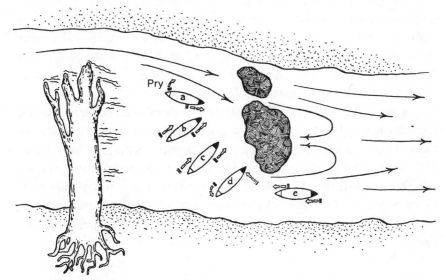

Figure 8-3   Back-Ferry To Safety (small arrows indicate direction of paddle movement).

vigorously backward. The net movement, as illustrated, will be nearly sideways. The faster the river speed, the smaller the ferry angle, and vice versa.* Only experience will tell you what angle is best. You can easily increase or decrease the ferry angle by drawing or prying as needed.

On powerful, fast-flowing rivers, getting to shore quickly can be important, especially if there is a bad rapid or bouldery falls ahead. Begin the back ferry by angling your stern in the direction you want to go. Maintain the proper angle and paddle backward until your stern barely touches the shore. Then pull the bow around (using a draw or pry, whichever is appropriate) until the canoe is parallel to the land.

---

*This relationship becomes *reversed* when the river speed exceeds your paddling speed. Although there is a definite trigonometric relationship between the speed of the current and the angle you should hold, in heavy rapids there is danger of swamping the canoe if you let your ferry angle get too large (greater than about forty degrees).

Landing stern first is a good habit to get into. In very swift currents bow landings can be dangerous, because a river is slowest near its edges and fastest near its center. When you nose into the slow water at the shore line, the faster main current grabs your stern and spins it downstream. If there is a sufficient current differential, you can be spun around so rapidly that you may lose your balance and possibly overturn the canoe.

Another evasive tactic based on the principle of vectors is the *forward ferry*. It is identical to the back ferry except that you spin the canoe 180 degrees and paddle forward instead of backward. This technique is used mostly by paddlers of kayaks and canoes which can turn quickly. Since the forward ferry is considerably more powerful than its backward counterpart, you can use a steeper angle to the current. You can also paddle longer distances without tiring.

Figure 8-4   Crossing a River Using a Forward Ferry (arrows indicate direction of paddle movement):

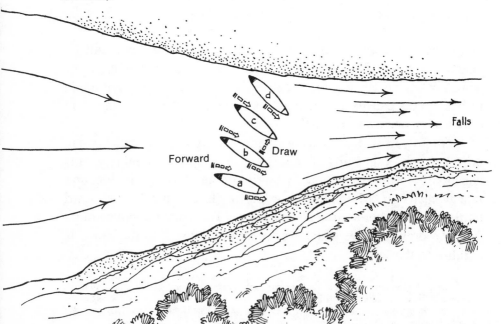

On a recent Canadian river trip, my partner and I put ashore just above a bouldery falls. After about an hour of scouting, we concluded that portaging was out of the question because a high rock bluff ran for several hundred yards along the river's edge. It was apparent that a portage, if one existed, was on the other bank of the hundred-yard-wide river. Somehow we would have to cross to the other side. We were within fifty feet of the falls, and the current was moving at perhaps five miles per hour. Paddling straight across was out of the question. We decided to use a very shallow angled forward ferry to test the current. Encountering no difficulty at the outset of our crossing, we steepened the angle considerably as we approached the center. We landed almost directly opposite our starting point on the other side of the river. I don't know what we would have done if this method had been unknown to us.

Although there are other whitewater techniques, wilderness canoes are usually heavily loaded and thus respond very sluggishly to the paddle. You can't effectively draw a heavy canoe sideways very far to avoid obstacles. Ferrying will be one of your most useful river tactics.

RIVER FEATURES
RIVER BENDS

Whenever possible, stay on the inside of all bends. Rivers run fastest and deepest at the outside bends, and because of this most of the debris usually piles up there. Should you overturn and get your life jacket or clothing caught in the branches of a half-submerged tree, it could be impossible to work your way free. You may be lucky to escape with your life! For this reason, you should seek the outside of a bend only when the water is very low or the current sluggish.

The safest way to negotiate bends is by ferrying. For crossing wide expanses of water, the forward ferry is preferred; otherwise, the back ferry is best. To begin the back ferry as you approach a curve, tuck your tail to the *inside* of the bend and back paddle. Although going around a bend sideways appears dangerous, it is in fact quite safe, for your canoe is almost perfectly aligned with the current. A slight pry or draw will quickly spin the bow downstream, putting you back on course. When you hear the thunder of rapids ahead but a curve prevents your seeing the telltale "hay-stacks," get to the inside of the bend and cautiously back ferry, keeping your stern just a few feet from shore. Should the rapid prove unrunnable, a few paddle strokes will bring you to the safety of the river bank.

In 1982, friends and I experienced a polar gale along the remote Hood River in Canada's Northwest Territories. For three days we were confined to our tents by 55 mile per hour winds and unrelenting rain. When the weather cleared, we were greeted by a silt-choked river in flood stage, the hydraulics of which were unbelievable. There were uprooted dwarf willows and debris everywhere in the river and they all piled up on the outside curves. The powerful current, which we estimated at more than ten miles an hour, produced man-sized waves at the outside of every bend. In many places, the river was more than a quarter mile wide!

Getting downstream that day was a matter of staying tight on the inside bends, away from the debris and engulfing whitewater.

Figure 8-5   Ferrying Around a Sharp Bend; Keep away from the outside of the bends, except in low water (arrows indicate direction of the paddle movement).

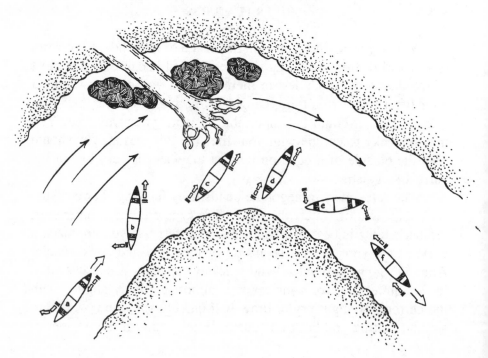

First, we'd ferry furiously to reach a right bank, only to ferry back across the channel when the river curved left. It was a continuous and exhaustive battle to stay on the inside curves. And it would have been impossible without our well-practiced ferries. Indeed, I doubt if we could have gotten downriver without them!

A final note on ferrying: Early in this chapter I emphatically suggested that canoes should always be loaded dead level. Ferrying is a good case in point, for it is very difficult to maintain the proper ferry angle in a strong current if the upstream end of the craft is trimmed down. Since it is impractical to lighten one end of the canoe before the start of a ferry, your best bet is to *always* load dead level. The rewards will be many!

EDDIES ARE A CANOEIST'S FRIEND

If you have ever thrown a stick just beyond a large rock or bridge piling in a river with a good current, you have probably observed that the stick floats back upstream in the lazy current below the obstacle. This is an eddy. Paddling long stretches of difficult rapids can be exceedingly nerve-racking. The quiet water of an eddy is a convenient stopping place to rest and collect your thoughts. Polers commonly travel upstream by hopping from eddy to eddy. If the water is sufficiently deep, paddlers, too, can success-fully use this technique.

Since the movement of water within an eddy is opposite to that of the river's flow, there is a current differential at the eddy's edge. This is the *eddy line*, and crossing it in strong currents can be dangerous if you are not prepared for the consequences. If you cautiously poke your bow into the slow upstream current, the main flow of the river will catch your stern and spin it quickly downstream. The result is a possible dunking. To enter an eddy bow first, you must drive powerfully forward across the eddy line. As the stern swings downstream, lean the canoe *upstream* to prevent upsetting. In the illustration (Figure 8-6), the bow person ''hangs on'' to the calm water of the eddy with a strong high brace and a severe lean, while the stern -- who has not yet crossed the eddy line -- also leans to the right to offset the centrifugal force of the current. As soon as the canoe completes the turn (which takes only a split second), the pair paddles forcefully up to the rock.

Figure 8-6 An Eddy Turn with a High-Brace in the Inside: Canoe must be leaned *upstream* when the bow crosses the eddy line.

Figure 8-7 An Eddy Turn with a Low Brace on the Inside: Bow person may use a pry, as illustrated (preferred), or a crossdraw to turn the canoe into the eddy.

If, however, the bow person were paddling on the left (Figure 8-7) and the stern on the right, the roles -- but not the canoe lean -- would be reversed. Both paddles would drive the canoe forward until it crossed the eddy line; then, at that moment, the stern would lean far out on a "low brace" while the bow sliced forward into the eddy, completing the maneuver with a pry and a forward drive. Whew!

Whenever possible, I prefer to "eddy-in" with the bow paddler on the *inside* of the turn as illustrated in Figure 8-6. The procedure is less tricky and seems to result in greater control due to the powerful stabilizing effect of the high brace up front.

Any eddy turn from a fast current is exciting and sure to produce a dumping if you aren't well-practiced in the technique. The most common error is failure to apply a strong *upstream* lean as the eddy line is crossed. Another mistake is that of judgment -- entering the eddy too late. It won't take you long to discover that you'll miss the eddy by a wide margin unless you enter it just below the rock. The current carries you *downstream*, remember?

All this talk about bow-first eddy turns is academic, for the sluggish response of heavily laden touring canoes generally precludes effective use of the technique, except in weak or moderate currents. The safest way to enter an eddy is by back ferrying. Begin the ferry as you approach the eddy line. Set the stern into the quiet water and back paddle to safety. When you have rested sufficiently, leave the eddy at its weak lower end. If the upstream current is very strong, this may be impossible, in which case you'll have to use a fast forward ferry combined with a strong downstream lean -- a sophisticated tactic called the "peel-out." Here's the procedure:

The canoe is angled *at least* 45 degrees to the current (a somewhat steeper angle than is used for ferrying) and forward power is applied. As the bow crosses the eddy line, the bow person reaches far out on a high brace and leans the canoe downstream (Figure 8-8). The stern supports the lean and "sweeps" the canoe around. As the boat re-aligns with the current, the pair re-centers their weight and resumes normal paddling.

Here's the alternative method (Figure 8-9) -- bow person paddling on the left, stern person on the right: As the bow crosses the

Figure 8-8   The Peel-Out: Canoe enters the current at about a 45 degree angle. Bow paddler uses a high brace and leans the canoe downstream as the bow crosses the eddy line.

Figure 8-9   The Peel-Out: Using a low brace on the downstream side, the bow paddler stabilizes the canoe with a pry (illustrated) or a crossdraw as the current spins it downstream.

eddy line, both partners lean downstream; the bow person pries or cross-draws while the stern applies a low brace.

Here again, I prefer the former practice (high brace on the *inside* of the turn) as it seems to provide greater stability as the bow crosses the eddy line. But perhaps I'm simply more experienced in the procedure.

When paddling difficult rapids you should proceed from eddy to eddy. At each new stopping place you can survey the conditions ahead and determine the safest course. Eddies can be used to your advantage only if you can perform competent ferries, so the importance of these tactics cannot be overemphasized!

CHUTES

When the river narrows sufficiently for its flow to be severely restricted, a chute of whitewater is formed. When the fast water racing through the chute reaches the calmer water below, its energy dissipates in the form of nearly erect standing waves called *haystacks*. A series of uniform haystacks indicates deep water and safe canoeing -- that is, if they are not so large as to swamp the canoe. To help the bow lift over large haystacks, you can slow the canoe's speed by back paddling or you can quarter into the waves at a slight angle. You can also lighten the front end by putting the bow paddler behind the seat. Running a chute with large standing waves below is one of the few times when you may wish to stop and rearrange the load in your canoe.

FALLS AND DAMS

Low falls can be successfully run if there is sufficient water flowing over them and if they are not so steep as to produce a heavy back roller at their base. If after checking a falls you decide it is safe to run, pick the point of strongest water flow, align the canoe, and proceed at river speed over the falls. Upon reaching the base of the falls, dig your paddles hard and deep to climb out of the trough below.

It is almost always unsafe to run a dam -- any dam, even a low one -- unless, of course, part of it has broken away. The trouble with dams is not the lack of flow over them, or even the steepness of their drops. Rather, the danger lies in the well-formed back roller at their bases. The back roller is actually an extremely powerful eddy, and the upstream current of this eddy can stop you dead in your tracks. Your canoe can be flipped broadside to the current and may spin over and over like a rolling cigar, perhaps to remain trapped until a period of drought lowers the volume of the river. Because some ledges and falls produce the same effects as dams, they should be considered extremely dangerous until proven otherwise.

CHOOSING A SAFE COURSE THROUGH RAPIDS

Negotiating a complex rapid without incident requires skill, cool determination, an accurate appraisal of the dangers and a good partner! Here are the rules for safe passage:

1. An *upstream* vee indicates the location of rocks (Figure 8-10); a *downstream* vee is the safe approach.

Figure 8-10   Choose a safe "downstream vee" when entering a rapid.

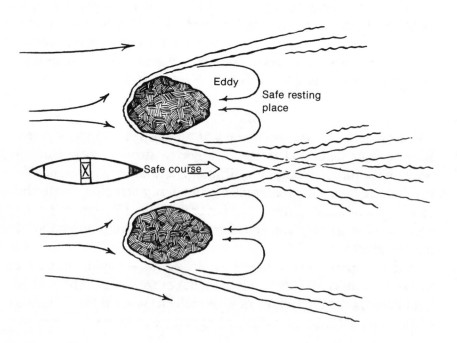

2. You can't steer around obstacles in a fast-moving river: Rely instead on ferry techniques or side-slip maneuvers (the bow person draws while the stern person pries, or vice versa).

3. Scout the rapids from shore before you run them, and view everything from a *downstream* vantage point. Often, a substantial drop (ledge) which is invisible from above, will be immediately evident from below. A binocular (not a monocular!) is useful for checking questionable spots.

4. Proceed downstream *slowly* -- backpaddle to reduce speed. Maintain control with effective draws, prys, cross-draws and ferry techniques.

5. Take advantage of eddies to recover your strength and plan your strategy for the water ahead.

After years of teaching whitewater skills, I remain unconvinced that you can learn to read whitewater -- to choose a safe course through rapids -- from reading books. Certainly, you can learn the important paddle strokes and procedures, but that's not enough. Studying whitewater tactics on a printed page is akin to poring over a map of Great Slave Lake, only to discover its harsh realities from the seat of your canoe. If you want to become proficient at reading and running whitewater, you'll have to paddle in it -- or more accurately, "play" in it. A weekend of on-the-water practice in the company of paddlers who understand the ways of running water will teach you more about "choosing a safe course" through rapids than a winter of fire-side reading.

AND A WORD ABOUT YOUR PARTNER

Some canoeists are lucky enough to paddle with the same partner all the time. Others are less fortunate; they have to adjust to the ways and incompetencies of a new person on every trip they take. Whitewater training sessions? Are you kidding? Learning comes out of necessity in the course of "the canoe trip!" By trip's end the new man or woman is "trained". Too bad we may never see him or her again! All of which brings us to the ultimate bottom line: WHITEWATER TACTICS ARE FOR PRACTICED WHITE-WATER TEAMS. IF IN DOUBT ABOUT YOUR PARTNER'S ABILITY, PORTAGE, PORTAGE, PORTAGE!

Early in my paddling career I discovered that the best way to train a new partner was to make all route decisions (and shout commands!) from my position in the stern -- a practice complicated by the fact that the person up front is closer to the obstacles and can therefore see them much better. So I developed the habit of angling the canoe about forty-five degrees to the current whenever I ran rapids. This improved visibility temendously and enabled me to make more accurate judgments. A quick draw or pry instantly put the canoe back in alignment with the flow. Drifting at an angle to the current had another advantage; the boat was correctly set up for an immediate back ferry. To avoid a rock dead ahead, I'd simply call "BACK!," and the canoe would respond with sideward motion.

Running angled also has the net effect of shortening the waterline of the canoe, which, like "quartering" lake waves, translates into a drier ride. Negotiating rapids out-of-alignment to the current is common practice among experienced northwoods guides, though the value of the technique is seldom expounded in the canoeing literature.

HEAVY WATER

"Heavy water," per se is defined as rapids which generally rate high Class III or better (see the AWA River Rating Scale below). Here, waves rise to impressive heights with deep canoe-engulfing troughs below. Where large volumes of water flow over big subsurface rocks, a "hydraulic jump" or eddy set-on-edge appears. This is the "souse-hole" -- a play-ground for decked whitewater canoes manned by expert paddlers, but no place for open canoes, no matter how skilled their occupants.*

Negotiating huge waves, powerful currents and boiling eddies calls for skill, iron-tough nerves, specialized equipment, a good partner, and a philosophy different from that of the cautious slower-than-the-current (back-ferrying and back-paddling) procedures I've outlined. When waves grow to human size and the trough below threatens to swallow you up, you must shift into high gear -- paddle forward with gusto so as to have sufficient momentum to climb the

---

*Amazingly, souse holes have been negotiated by skilled paddlers in open canoes!

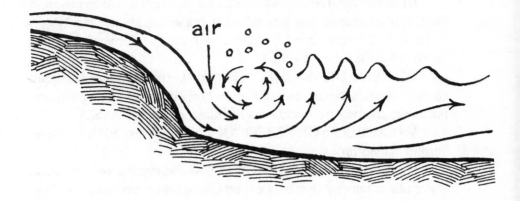

Figure 8-11   Souse Hole: The air-filled back-roller of a souse hole can swamp a canoe and trap it. To escape, you must swim out the side of the hole or shed your life vest and dive below the foam into the bottom current — procedures which require skill and determination. Souse holes are no place for open canoes!

faces of the big waves. Even then, a swamping may be inevitable unless your canoe has plenty of speed and a fabric splash cover.

Heavy water is something you should look at, reverently photograph, then confidently portage around!

Many of the new guide books rate rapids according to the AWA (American White-Water Affiliation) International River Rating Scale. This is most handy, as it allows you to plan a trip with confidence. In guide books where this rating scale has not been followed, you must rely on the individual judgment of the writer, which may be considerably different from your own. The International River Rating Scale is the great equalizer.

AWA INTERNATIONAL RIVER RATING SCALE
Water Class and Characteristics

I. EASY — Bends without difficulty, small rapids with waves regular and low. Obstacles like fallen trees, bridge pilings, and so on. River speed less than hard back-paddling speed.

II. MEDIUM — Fairly frequent but unobstructed rapids with regular waves and low ledges. River speed occasionally exceeding hard back-paddling speed.

III. DIFFICULT — Small falls; large, regular waves covering boat. Expert maneuvering required. Course not always easily recognizable. Current speed usually less than fast forward-paddling speed. (Splash cover useful.)

IV. VERY DIFFICULT — High, powerful waves and difficult eddies. Abrupt bends and difficult broken water. Powerful and precise maneuvering mandatory. (Splash cover essential.)

V. EXCEEDINGLY DIFFICULT — Very fast eddies, violent current, steep drops.

VI. LIMIT OF NAVIGABILITY — Navigable only at select water conditions by teams of experts. Cannot be attempted without risk of life.

Several years ago I drove for many hours to Wisconsin's Flambeau River to run a section of Class III rapids. Despite the fact that water levels were high, the rapid really rated only a class II on the AWA Rating Scale. I learned later that the guide book I had consulted rated all rapids one step above their official AWA difficulty ratings. Of course I enjoyed the run, but I had come for the whitewater excitement, which, on this stretch of the river, just wasn't there.

For all practical purposes a loaded wilderness canoe should not be taken into rapids of a higher classification than II. The risks are just too great. You should realize that a heavy spring rain can turn mild Class I rapids into wild IIs or IIIs, and an early fall drought can tame a III to where you can walk right down the middle of it. Water levels are extremely important in sizing up rapids. Where gauging stations exist, interpretive information can be secured from the administrative unit responsible for the gauge. This is usually the U.S. Army Corps of Engineers, the U.S. Weather Bureau, or your state's department of natural resources or conservation.

Your most accurate information, however, will be available from local canoe clubs which maintain their own gauges. These can be anything from a paint mark on a bridge piling to a rusted pipe. Primitive though they are, club gauges reflect the needs of canoeists and hence are most useful.

LINING AND TRACKING

One morning, after some two hours of leisurely paddling down Ontario's Moose River, my partner suddenly realized that he had left his three-hundred-dollar camera at our last campsite. Somewhat begrudgingly and with unrepeatable expletives, I grabbed a painter and helped him tow the canoe seven miles upstream to our island campsite of the night before. I doubt that we could have paddled that distance very easily.

Upstream tracking is not only useful for retrieving lost cameras, but also for getting around rapids when a portage is difficult or impossible to make. For best results while tracking, the upstream end of the canoe should be kept up. If your towing link or ring is located very far above the water line, you will have to disconnect the bow rope and rig a towing harness. You want the line pulling right from the keel, if possible. The stern line is less important and can remain at its usual place of attachment.

Upstream tracking is just like ferrying. By keeping the canoe at a slight angle to the current (bow out, stern toward shore) while towing, you can walk upstream along the bank and the wash of the current will carry the canoe out to the center of the river. Changing the angle of the canoe while pulling on the ropes will return it to shore. Obviously, tracking is impossible if shorelines are too brushy or rugged to walk along.

The opposite of tracking is lining. This procedure is considerably more common than upstream work and is widely used to get around small falls, ledges, and other obstacles in the river. Some authorities recommend attaching lines to keep the upstream end of the canoe raised. They also advise attaching the bow line to a gunwale near the seat. I have found it best to leave lines attached to their customary rings at the bow and stern (which should be located close to the water line). Often, while lining, you will be working above the canoe or, possibly, hopping from rock to rock, sometimes pulling from different sides of the canoe. If, for example, you let the canoe down a chute and for some reason need to pull it back up to realign it with the main current, you will be at a serious disadvantage if your lines are attached anywhere other than at the ends.

Canoeing texts make lining sound easy. It isn't! Controlling the path of a heavily loaded canoe in the powerful side-wash of a rock-studded passage requires practice. And agility! The recommended procedure is to use lines at both bow and stern. However, coordinating two ropes -- and two people -- requires much more skill than you might believe. Even the smallest miscalculation can send the canoe reeling sideways where it may fill with water and wrap neatly around a rock or be broken nicely in two. For this reason, many experienced canoeists prefer to line their canoe alone, with a single tail rope, even though it results in some loss of control.

Practice lining in easy riffles near your home before you attempt it in difficult waters in the backcountry. Even then, if you're not sure-footed or simply "unsure"...portage! It is considerably safer. On some arctic rivers where impassable rapids continue for many miles, you may have to line. In the continental United States most river banks are too cluttered with debris to permit lining for any great distance.

WHITEWATER SAFETY

Despite some dangers inherent in the sport of canoeing, it is essentially a safe pastime. Whitewater clubs take to the rivers as soon as the ice melts, and although the water temperature is very cold (sometimes just a few degrees above freezing), we seldom hear of a drowning. This is because experienced paddlers respect the rivers and are well prepared for upsets. Herein lies the key to whitewater safety: *Be prepared for an upset!*

LIFE JACKETS

Many beginners assume that being a good swimmer is the most important safety consideration. While swimming ability is important, a life jacket and a cool head are more important. Except in unusually calm conditions, you should wear your life jacket at all times. On a wilderness trip, especially, you are burdened with the extra weight of heavy clothes and boots. An upset in even a moderate rapid or mildly choppy lake can be hazardous. Lack of a life preserver has accompanied almost every canoeing fatality.

In 1974 a canoeist lost his life on the Coppermine River in the Northwest Territories of Canada. The man was a good swimmer and an experienced whitewater paddler. He and his partner put ashore just above a difficult rapid known as Rocky Defile. After considerable scouting the pair decided to run the rapid. As soon as they started downstream, the canoeist realized that he was not wearing his life jacket. He had taken it off while checking the rapids and had neglected to put it back on. But it was too late. The canoe nosed into a heavy roller and began to climb. When it reached the top of the large wave, it teetered and flipped over on its side, throwing both paddlers out of the canoe. Four weeks later the body of the unfortunate canoeist was found. His partner, who wore a life jacket, survived and completed the remaining two hundred miles of the journey alone. It is ironic that in the many miles these experts had paddled together, this was the first time that either had neglected to wear his life jacket. It was not incompetence that cost the life of this canoeist. Rather, it was an oversight -- a simple procedural omission -- like forgetting to buckle up your seat belt before you drive. Wilderness rivers bear no malice toward unprepared paddlers; neither, however, do they grant immunity from error.

Because your life jacket is so important, you should select a model that you can wear comfortably all the time. Eliminate from consideration the bulky orange horse-collar type; they are too confining and chafe the neck badly. Choose instead a vertical ribbed

Figure 8-12 Type III Style Life-Jacket (vertical ribbed): Get a life-jacket that does not interfere with swimming!

Figure 8-13   Type III Style Life-Jacket (panel style)

or panel style vest filled with PVC or polyethylene foam. Every canoe equipment shop carries them. And don't choose a personal flotation device (PFD) on the strength of Coast Guard approval tags alone. The life jacket requirements of whitewater paddlers are not the same as those of powerboaters. For example, the proper procedure for swimming in rapids is as follows: Lie on your back, feet pointing downstream; keep your feet high to prevent somersaulting in the current, and use your feet and canoe paddle to ward off rocks; swim on your back or side, at an angle to the current, to reach shore. This technique is similar to the canoeist's back ferry.

To do this you need as much flotation on your back as on your chest, and the bulky horse collars offer virtually no back flotation. Horse collars are designed to float the wearer head up for extended periods of time, at the expense of maneuverability. You are seldom in the water for more than five minutes in a typical canoe upset. In order to avoid obstacles you need a jacket that does not interfere with swimming. This should be a major consideration. Fortunately, the Coast Guard now realizes that the needs of canoeists are best

Figure 8-14   Safest Way to Swim a Rapid. Keep your feet high to prevent somersaulting in the current and use your feet and paddle to ward off rocks.

met with Type III flotation devices*. Consequently, some of the best life jackets, which a decade ago were outlawed, are now receiving Coast Guard approval. The safest life jacket is the one you're most likely to keep wearing, and this is usually the one that is most comfortable. Buy the *best* life jacket available, even if the cost seems prohibitive. Your life is too precious to skimp here.

It is interesting to note that there is little relationship between your weight out of water and your weight in water. Prospective buyers of life jackets assume that a 250-pound man needs more flotation than a 130-pound teenager. If the man is overweight and the teenager is mostly muscle, quite the opposite may be true. It is not uncommon for children to need as much flotation as their parents. Manufacturers have done an excellent job providing properly sized life jackets. The important thing, however, is to realize that the buoyancy rating of the jacket may or may not meet your requirements. You should test your life jacket in both calm water and rapids to assure that it will adequately support you.

KEEPING WARM

Most canoeists rely on wool or acrylic outer garments and polypropylene long johns for warmth. This combination won't substitute for a wet-suit in near freezing water, but it will keep you cozy in an icy all day rain. Before venturing down difficult rapids in the cold water of early spring, I usually don a waterproof paddling shirt under my life jacket. The shirt fits tightly at the neck, waist and sleeves, provides great warmth for its weight, and considerably reduces the possibility of getting chilled both in and out of the water.

As the table below shows, your body will remain functional in cold water for only a short time. Even this doesn't tell the whole story, because the initial shock of the cold water on your chest saps much of your energy. A paddling shirt can reduce this shock somewhat, but only a wet-suit can eliminate it completely.

*These must keep a *conscious* person in a vertical or slightly backward position. Adult vests must have a minimum of 15.5 pounds of buoyancy; 11 pounds for medium child's sizes, and 7 pounds for small children. Many Type III PFD's feature much more buoyancy than this.

	AMOUNT OF TIME
WATER TEMPERATURE	BODY WILL REMAIN FUNCTIONAL
less than 40 degrees F.	less than 10 minutes
40-50 degrees F.	15-20 minutes
50-60 degrees F.	15-40 minutes
60 degrees F. and above	one or more hours

Although your body may remain functional for several minutes in cold water, you can die from hypothermia after you've been rescued. Hypothermia occurs when body temperature drops below ninety-five degrees Fahrenheit. As blood is rushed to the vital organs, chilling spreads throughout the body. This is accompanied by clumsiness, slurred speech, and loss of judgment. Coma and death may occur within a few hours if body temperature is not raised.

Should a member of your party experience hypothermia, he or she must be treated immediately. If the victim is shivering noticeably (a *possible* symptom of early hypothermia), he may be rewarmed by conventional means -- dry clothing, a fire, lots of loving bear hugs, hot soup, etc. However, if he is shivering *uncontrollably** or is incoherent -- stumbles around and mumbles, you've got to act fast; his core temperature has dropped into the dangerous range and his body may have lost the ability to warm itself. At this point, piling on warm clothes is about as effective as adding insulation to a house when the furnace has gone out. There's a real possibility the victim will die unless you provide a heat source!

Field treatment for advanced hypothermia (and for anyone who has fallen into ice-cold water) consists of stripping off wet clothing

---

Mild shivering does not indicate impending hypothermia. It is merely the body's way of fine tuning its heat conservation and heat production. *Uncontrolled* shivering, however, IS an indicator of hypothermia!

It's important to realize that not everyone has a "shivering reflex." It is quite possible to experience hypothermia (and to die from it!) without ever shivering at all. This is especially true if the victim has become thoroughly exhausted, in which case, there may be insufficient energy to produce the shivering response. The most reliable indicator of hypothermia is the temperature of the body core -- a variable you can monitor with the aid of a special low-reading hypothermia thermometer (available from Indiana Camp Supply, P.O. Box 344, Pittsboro, Indiana 46167).

A practical method of diagnosing hypothermia in the field is to ask the suspected hypothermic to walk a straight line for a distance of thirty feet. If the person wavers from this line you have good cause to suspect a decrease in brain function brought about by a dangerously low body core temperature. (I am borrowing information from Dr. Forgey's excellent book, HYPOTHERMIA, published by ICS Books, Inc.)

and placing the victim into a sleeping bag with one or two people. If the victim is *clearly conscious* and can swallow, you may give him or her hot water or soup as a psychological boost. *Do not* administer stimulants such as alcohol or coffee or place the individual too near a fire. Radiant heat should be applied *gradually* and *gently*! Through it all, handle the victim with a delicate hand. Roughhousing may initiate ventricular fibrillation of the heart...and death could result!

To *summarize*: Mild cases of hypothermia may be treated by simple re-warming procedures -- dry clothes, a fire, and warm hugs. For severe cases -- and all cold water immersion incidents -- use the sleeping bag sandwich treatment, and take care to handle the victim as gently as possible.

A final note: Victims of hypothermia are almost always unaware of the seriousness of their situation. They will continually proclaim, "I'm okay!" It's up to you to diagnose the problem. And to treat it quickly!

In 1980 I led a group of teenagers on a trip into the Boundary Waters Canoe Area. There was an icy drizzle and light wind on Saganaga Lake when we put in that morning -- nothing serious, just fair warning to dress warm and wear rain clothes. Within the hour, the rain picked up. But the kids were all singing and having a grand time, so I saw no reason to put ashore.

As we rounded a point, we overtook another group who was paddling in dead silence. "How's it goin'?" I called encouragingly. Groans of displeasure followed. I paddled alongside the lead canoe and struck up a conversation with the leader.

"Some of these kids don't have good rain gear," he commented. "But they're tough; they can hack it -- besides, we'll be in camp within the hour."

"I dunno," I responded. "Your passenger (a teenage girl) doesn't look so good."

"How ya doin, Linda?" he questioned. "You wanna go ashore and change clothes?"

"I'm okay," she whimpered softly. "I can make it 'til we camp."

The youngster didn't look very well at all. Her lips were blue and she shivered constantly. She had no seat cushion to protect her from the cold wet bottom of the aluminum canoe. It was a perfect set-up for hypothermia.

"I think we better get those clothes changed *now*," I quipped. "C'mon, let's put ashore on that point."

There was another round of "I can make it" from the girl, and "these kids are tough" from the leader, but I was insistent, so he finally routed the crew to shore.

The seriousness of the situation became evident when the leader observed that Linda could not get out of the canoe without help. Her legs simply refused to support her body! While we set up the tent and pulled sleeping bags and dry clothing from packs, the kids crowded around the girl and hugged her to provide as much warmth as possible. Then two girls ushered her into the tent and administered the classic sleeping bag treatment.

Within the hour, Linda was revitalized. But the group decided to remain ashore for the remainder of the day -- a wise decision, as hypothermia is a very draining experience, one which requires plenty of rest to fully recover from.

You don't need to paddle a remote wilderness river to encounter an episode of hypothermia. People have died while canoeing familiar streams near their home! You have a moral responsibility to use your knowledge of hypothermia to help others you meet in the wilderness. It is not bad manners to strongly suggest that a group bivouac because one member is too cold or tired to go on. The most inexcusable act you can commit in the outdoors is to say and do nothing when you know there's a possibility that another human being may become injured or die. A human life is an unfair price to pay for ignorance!

BASIC PRECAUTIONS

When you are canoeing whitewater, avoid long coats, ponchos, or anything dangling around your neck on a string. Should you overturn, these items are likely to be caught on submerged tree limbs or between rocks. Also avoid heavy boots, and *never* wear waders while paddling. Water-filled waders can make swimming in even a moderate current impossible.

If you overturn, your best life preserver is the canoe, and you should stay with it unless doing so will endanger your life.* If you have waterproofed your gear and outfitted your canoe with rubber ropes as recommended, the additional flotation of your packs will keep your canoe floating high. Since whitewater is mostly air, you will have difficulty breathing, even with a good life jacket. A high-riding canoe will keep you above the foamy water.

Upon upsetting, swim immediately to the *upstream* end of the canoe. A water-filled canoe weighs more than a ton, and should you get between it and a rock you will be crushed. Hang onto the grab loop or stern painter and try to swim the canoe to shore. The canoe-over-canoe rescue touted by the Red Cross and Scouts works well on calm lakes with *empty* canoes, but cannot be done with loaded canoes on fast water. Unfortunately, this is where most canoe upsets occur.

---

*If the water is very cold and there is no support crew to come to your rescue, your best bet is to leave the canoe *immediately* and strike out for shore. Hanging hopefully to a canoe in near-freezing water when there is no chance of rescue, only hastens your early demise. Contrary to popular belief, and the writings of some canoe authorities, it is not easy to swim a swamped canoe to shore. And if you rely on the action of wind or currents to bring the craft (and you) to land, you're in for a much longer wait than you can afford!

9.
Canoe Rescue and Repair

Kettle River -- a delightful blend of exquisite scenery and intriguing rapids, a federally protected wild and scenic river that deserves to be. And, a favorite play-ground for midwestern boaters -- kayaks and canoes.

Mike and I had made a deal: I'd help him teach the intermediate whitewater course and he'd provide meals and lodging plus an opportunity to learn some new salvage and rescue techniques developed by the Nantahala Outdoor Center.

My mistake was bringing old Mantoy -- a well used, well patched wood-strip solo canoe which friend Bob Brown and I designed. Mantoy had seen tough service on some of the rockiest rivers in Minnesota and Canada and she had the scars to prove it. Best described as a "nice paddling wreck," Mantoy was just the boat that every whitewater paddler needs to enjoy a river.

Mike watched enviously from shore as I ferried out, eddied-in, and did a host of other playful maneuvers, all designed to solicit envy from the crowd. It worked. Mike was jealous; he asked to paddle Mantoy. "Sure," I beamed. "I can paddle solo anytime!"

DRAW! DRAW!

For the better part of the day we practiced in easy Class I-II rapids. The crew gained skill and by early afternoon they had learned their lessons well enough to begin the "canoe trip."

"Can I take her downriver?" asked Mike, pointing hopefully to the little wood canoe. Before I could answer, he climbed confidently aboard and slipped quietly into the water and out-of-sight around the next bend.

It was then that I remembered that Mike had the pack with all the rescue gear -- the climbing rope, carabiners, pulleys, slings and the like. Suppose we wrapped a canoe around a mid-stream boulder? How on earth would we ever get it free?

Well, that wouldn't happen -- I'd see to that!

It wasn't a big tree but it was enough to command concern. It jutted three-fourths across the river on the inside of a tight hair-pin turn. But there was a clear three foot channel on the outside -- plenty of space for a canoe to scoot through.

My partner and I slipped through the opening then put ashore to wait for the students and signal them to the outside of the turn. They came through like veterans, first one canoe, then two, then...*capsize!* Suddenly, there were two paddlers in the grip of the icy water.

Seconds later I saw the comforting sight of two sunlight-yellow life-vests skimming the surface. I thanked God that the tree had no submerged branches to entrap the swimmers. I quickly belayed the throwing line around a tree and tossed it out. The woman grabbed it and together my partner and I towed her to shore. Downstream, in the shallows, I observed the man struggling ashore.

The water was a cold 47 degrees and the air temperature was only slightly warmer. But the flush of excitement had provided a surge of warmth and the pair had not yet begun to shiver. Nonetheless, an immediate change of clothes, hot tea, and affectionate hugs were in order.

And now, to rescue the canoe. The Grumman had bellied-up against the foot-thick log -- open and exposed to the full force of the current. Reluctantly, I shuffled along the tree trunk to the pinned canoe. No way could I budge it. "Damn!" I said aloud, "If only we had the proper rescue gear!" But no sense whining; we'd have to extract the boat with what we had -- 100 feet of three-eighths inch nylon rope and one carabiner (an aluminum link through which mountain climbers run their ropes).

First step, to get a rope around the hull and attached so that it would pull the submerged gunwale *up and away* from the raging current -- a feat of engineering that required the better part of 20 minutes. That accomplished, we rigged a make-shift block and tackle around an upstream tree with a power-cinch (see Chapter 11, Tying It All Together) and carabiner. Then everyone pulled...and pulled. No luck.

Next, we tried prying the canoe free with a six foot length of log. Again, a blank. "Maybe if we pry and winch at the same time," suggested someone. That did it; the gleaming metal hull groaned and popped free, like a cookie from a mold. All that remained now was to haul it ashore, dump out the water, and stomp it into a shape that could be paddled.

In this instance, salvaging the canoe was no big deal. We could have simply left it and continued downstream in the remaining boats. Later, we could have returned with the rescue equipment. However, had this occurred on a wilderness river, miles from the nearest road, the picture would be much different. Then we could choose between our ingenuity and a long walk home!

EQUIPMENT

If you'll be leading groups down rivers where there's a real possibility you may have to extract a pinned canoe, then you'd better carry some serious climbing gear -- 120 feet of Perlon rope, a half-dozen carabiners, a couple of nylon pulleys, nylon webbing, etc. Otherwise, 100 feet of stout three-eighths inch rope, two carabiners, and a rescue pulley should suffice. With these, you can rig a two to one (or greater) mechanical advantage pulley over a short distance. If the canoe is hung up so badly that a solid harness, a pry bar, and your best efforts won't get it free, at least wait around for a few days before abandoning it. Rivers often fluctuate greatly from week to week, and an inch or two less water may provide just the edge you need.

If your canoe should ground firmly upon a rock in a fast-flowing river and turn broadside to the current, the entire side of the craft will be exposed to the force of the rushing water. This force may equal several thousand pounds and may be enough to bend or break the canoe. However, as long as the craft is kept upright, the rushing water will usually pass harmlessly beneath the rounded hull. But if the upstream gunwale should dip below the water and expose the inside of the canoe to the power of the current, the craft may be broken in half or damaged beyond repair. Therefore it is important that you *never* let the open end of your canoe become exposed to the current. You should make every effort to keep the upstream gunwale up, even if it means leaving your canoe. If necessary, jump into the water on the *upstream* side of the canoe. Hold tightly to the gunwale and try to work the canoe loose. Usually the removal of your weight is all that's necessary to free the hull. Do not, however under *any* circumstances, enter the water *downstream* of the canoe. Should the craft slide off the rock while you are in the water, it could crush you against a downstream obstacle.

REPAIR

Modern canoeists use silver duct (furnace) tape almost exclusively for field repairs of canoes. Duct tape sticks -- to anything! In fact, canoe owners often neglect more permanent hull repairs simply because furnace tape works so well. A small roll of duct tape should be carried on *all* canoe trips -- close to home or otherwise. In thirty-five years of canoeing I have yet to damage a canoe so badly that tape and ingenuity would not repair it.

In the case of aluminum canoes, there is little you can do in the way of field repairs other than apply tape. Where rivets have been pulled they can be retightened by administering several blows with the back side of an axe. Small gaps and holes can be filled with liquid aluminum or epoxy, and these items should be included in your repair kit. Since aluminum canoes usually bend rather than break, physical force will be required to straighten them. An aluminum canoe that has had its gunwales or sides caved in can be placed in shallow water, sand, or mud and stomped back into a semblance of shape. A wood block, the hammer face of an ax, and true grit will produce amazing results. At home a break in the skin should be repaired by affixing a riveted patch. Complete patch kits, available from the Grumman Corporation, include patching material, rivets, and instructions. Although a good-quality welding job appears to hold satisfactorily, the aluminum adjacent to the weld may become brittle and cause problems later on. I have seen some fine repair jobs by master aircraft aluminum welders, and these are probably adequate.

One canoe owned by a very skilled whitewater paddler has been lovingly named *Super Beater.* This ancient Grumman canoe was broken completely in half in a Class III rapid and welded back together. The gunwales have been welded in perhaps a dozen places, and the keel was ripped off and a shoe keel fused in its place. *Super Beater* seems to perform unusually well in heavy rapids, despite its appearance. Its owner remains totally oblivious to the possibility of any future damage.

Fiberglass, Kevlar, and wood-strip canoes are easily repaired by applying epoxy resin and fiberglass cloth directly to the break.* You can substitute polyester resin for epoxy, but it isn't nearly as strong.** Unfortunately, there are dozens of formulations for epoxy and not all are ideal for boat repair. For the past five years, I've been using WEST SYSTEM epoxy (available from the Gougeon Brothers, Inc., P.O. Box X908, Bay City, Michigan 48707) and I highly recommend it. This product is as handy as it is strong -- unique plastic pumps dispense the correct mix so there's no mess or waste. And, WEST SYSTEM EPOXY kicks solid in temperatures as low as forty-five degrees Fahrenheit.

It's unlikely that you'll ever have to repair major damage to a well built fiberglass or Kevlar canoe. However, you may need to mend chipped gel-coat on the ''nose'' of your canoe after every trip down a shallow rocky stream -- easy enough if you *don't* follow the manufacturer's directions. The ''book procedure'' calls for filling the break with color-matched liquid gel-coat, then sanding, buffing, and polishing to blend the repair.

Nothing could be more difficult. Or frustrating! Catalyzed liquid gel-coat is so runny that it's impossible to contain. The solution is to prop the boat at an awkward angle to ''level the flow'' then build a well of masking tape around the resin. You then have to nurse the slowly hardening liquid with a flat stick to keep it from

---

*See my book, CANOEING WILD RIVERS, for detailed methods of repairing structural damage.
**You can patch polyester canoes with epoxy but not vice-versa.

over-flowing the well. If your patience holds out, the completed patch will hardly be noticeable.

There's an easier way. All you need is a small can of *polyester putty* (available at nearly all marinas) and an aerosol can of good acrylic enamel or auto lacquer to match the color of your boat. There's enough variation among automotive paints to match the most faded boat pigments. Add masking tape and sandpaper, and your boat will be ready for the river within an hour.

Mask the area and catalyze the putty. Work it into the break to overflowing. The putty is thick and won't run, so there's no need to prop the canoe or build a tape well.

When the putty is firm (about five minutes) slice off the excess with your pocket knife. Allow the remainder to cure completely (another ten minutes) then sand it level and paint it. Use a light touch on the spray button and repeat to build up a fairly thick coating. When the paint has dried, wet-sand the masking tape lines and buff the area to a high luster with pumice. Apply paste wax to the patch and your repair is complete -- and virtually unnoticeable.

ABS Royalex hulls are so tough that they are nearly puncture-proof. Repairs are usually made with fiberglass cloth and epoxy resin. Kits are available from nearly every company who manufactures these canoes.

If you own a fine wood-canvas canoe, you are probably well aware of how to maintain it. Old Town Canoe company offers everything you need to restore these craft. Wood-canvas canoes never die; they just accumulate new parts. For detailed instructions on how to repair wood-canvas canoes, consult the American Red Cross's canoeing manual; it provides a wealth of information on the subject.

10.
Tripping with Tots and Teens

TRIPPING WITH TOTS

The Indians call it "Chautauqua," which means "traveling show." And it aptly describes a family of canoeists on a pleasant float downstream. Put these together *in the same canoe*: Mom and Dad, a wiggling two year old and inquisitive five year old, waterproof packsacks filled with dry clothes, an ice chest stocked with pop, a thermos of milk; bags of disposable diapers, sunscreen and bug dope, toilet paper, facial tissues and Handi-Wipes, jackets, hats and paddles, a camera and pair of stuffed Teddy Bears, potato chips, pretzels and candy snacks...and the view from dock-side is in every sense, a "Chautauqua!"

At these times you're sure to wonder if all the pre-trip planning and packing, the stern instructions to the kids, and the hopeful prayers for a brilliant rain-free day, are really worth the joys of a family canoe outing. Is canoeing with children all it's cracked up to be? Or is it really more trouble than it's worth?

The first time you see the bright eyes of your child come alive with wonder at the sight of a big blue heron standing knee-deep in sea-green duck weed a dozen feet away, or soothe the frightened cry that results when a foot-long fish jumps brashly across your

163

bow; or thrill to the bubbly laughter of a breezy glide down gentle rapids, you'll "know." Then no amount of pre or post trip drudgery will ever again chain you to the dull confines of house or garden work when on the river there awaits the sun-lit morning of a new day.

Children are magic. And canoes are the perfect vehicle to transport them into the ever-changing, always entertaining world of nature. There's no better way to keep a youthful heart than to paddle with young people. Canoes provide all the entertainment kids need to provide all the laughs you need!

So much for philosophy. Now let's be deadly honest: Canoeing with children can be a trying experience, even when you do everything right. Your role as a parent and leader requires canoe handling knowledge, a perceptive eye, and patience, patience, patience! Even then, don't expect miracles. Kids *will* behave like kids.

THE RIGHT ATTITUDE

Uppermost in your mind should be the realization that you're canoeing for the *sake of the children*, not the adults. Everything should be structured around *their* safety, well-being, and concerns. I've seen parents set toddlers on the cold damp floor of a metal canoe without so much as a square of plastic for insulation. Without a dry place to sit, a comfortable backrest, and a soft pad to sleep on, they'll respond by crying, screaming, and kicking -- exactly what you can't tolerate in the tippy confines of a canoe. The right equipment and a detailed battle plan will eliminate most problems.

Before committing yourself to a canoe trip with preschoolers, prepare yourself for an onslaught of disapproving stares, glares, and verbal assaults at any mention of plans for putting little nonswimming Johnny or Jenny into a "tippy" canoe. Your qualifications as a parent may come under question. Nevertheless, once you're convinced that canoeing with toddlers is safe (and it is if proper precautions are taken), you will be well prepared to deal with the criticism which you are sure to encounter.

FIRST, GET SOME INSTRUCTION!

Although it is seldom mentioned, the greatest safety margin that you can provide for your children is for you to be both a competent swimmer and a reasonably good canoeist. These two factors will keep you out of trouble in almost all situations in which you have non-swimmers aboard. If there is a canoe club nearby, join it. If not, read and reread the good books on canoeing available in your local library. Then, get out and practice -- without the kids. At any rate, do join your state canoe association. If you don't know its address, your state's department of natural resources has probably worked with the canoe association from time to time and should be able to tell you how to contact it. As a member of a canoe club, you will become acquainted with other canoeing families, and your mind will be more at ease knowing there are others to share your experiences and help with problems.

THE PROPER EQUIPMENT

First and foremost is the life jacket. Toddlers absolutely must wear their life jackets at all times. A bit of psychology helps -- and generally this means that both mom and dad set an example. Since the rocking motion of a canoe is conducive to extra-long naps, it is important that the life jackets your children wear be extremely comfortable ones that they can sleep in. The $8.98 kapok models are excellent in case of an upset, as they float the child's head well out of the water, but they are very uncomfortable and should be avoided if at all possible.

Several companies now make specialized life jackets for pre-schoolers, all of which have been thoroughly tested and Coast Guard-approved. Although expensive, they are an excellent investment for the safety of your child, since children will wear them contentedly even through their naps. Swim-aids, while more attractive and less expensive than Coast Guard-approved life jackets, should be avoided, for they will not keep the head of a nonswimmer afloat.

The bottom of a canoe (aluminum models, at least) may run only a few degrees warmer than the temperature of the water. Consequently it is important to cover the bottom with adequate cushioning for both insulation and comfort. The best solution is to place an air mattress, nylon-covered foam pad, or piece of Ensolite foam on the bottom of the canoe for the children to sit on and later to curl up on for a nap. Children will want to sit up and view the countryside, so a backrest of some kind should be provided. A foam cushion makes a suitable backrest when propped up against a canoe thwart, and when nap time rolls around it makes a good pillow as well.

Each child should have his or her favorite blanket and toy. By all means provide a canoe paddle of miniature dimensions, for children love to paddle (it is wise to tie a string to the paddle and to secure this string to a canoe thwart). Don't become disenchanted by your passenger's inability to paddle properly. Let kids play with their paddles as they wish (just so they don't hit each other, or you), for this is part of their good time.

A complete change of clothes from nose to toes must be provided, and rain gear is very important. The best rain covering for toddlers is a poncho. The hood and extra-long body of the poncho will cover a child completely. A less expensive solution is to provide each child with a plastic leaf-and-lawn-size garbage bag. Merely cut a slit for the head in the top of the bag and furnish a "souwester" style hat to go with it.

It is also advisable to bring along a spare blanket. When children fall alseep in the canoe, they may need additional insulation not provided by their security blankets. Lastly, a lightweight nylon or plastic fly of about eight by ten feet is desirable for shelter in case you want to get off the water during a heavy rain, or as a cover for the kids when they are sleeping, should a light rain begin.

Proper footgear is always a concern. After years of canoeing with children I'm completely won over to sneakers *and* galoshes (or slip-on rubber boots). This combination keeps feet dry in rain and when wading ashore or exploring the river's edge. Once aboard the canoe -- or in camp -- the boots are quickly removable.

In addition to food and drink for the day, bring a thermos of milk for the kids and some penny candy. Plan to stop for a few minutes each hour, and allow time for fun and games during the lunch break. Generally, river trips of about ten miles are ideal; longer trips tend to get somewhat trying for both children and adults, and three or four hours on the water is plenty with young children. For toddlers in diapers, the disposable kind are indispensable. Take several, packed in a waterproof plastic bag, and place used diapers in a plastic bag to be brought home for proper disposal.

All clothing, food, and equipment must be adequately waterproofed. An easy and inexpensive way to do this is to place everything into an ice chest (pop cooler). Seal the lid of the ice chest with a band of duct tape. The tape seal can be removed and resealed often without losing its effectiveness and the rigid plastic container will protect crushables.

Insects: Nothing can spoil a trip faster than determined mosquitoes and black flies. Repellents are essential but mustn't be too strong. Super-effective products which contain more than 40 percent DEET (diethylmeta-toluamide) may be too caustic for sensitive young skin. Citronella or cream base formulas are best. If bugs are really a problem, provide a headnet and gloves for everyone.

It should go without saying that river sections with rapids should be avoided -- even by highly skilled canoeists. Very mild, bouncing water can, of course, be paddled and adds to the fun. Such "rapids" are generally shallow enough to walk through. A final word of safety: If you have two nonswimmers aboard, decide before the trip how you will handle an upset should it occur. Generally one parent goes after each child. *Do not* take three nonswimmers on a canoe trip when there are only two swimmers to watch them. Should you overturn, your first responsibility is to your children. With everyone wearing life jackets in a slow-moving river or placid lake, rescue should present no problems, especially if another canoe is nearby.

I must admit that my wife and I have never overturned our canoe with young children aboard, but we have helped rescue other families who have. When the initial displeasure is followed by warm clothes, a roaring fire, and hot chocolate, even the crankiest child is ready for more. A family canoe trip brings the kind of warmth and well-being which too many of us have forgotten in this age of electronic gratification.

CANOEING WITH TEENAGERS

It's a familiar story: A group of teens from a local community ask their youth director to take them on a canoe trip. "Marvelous idea," thinks the director, "but I don't know much about canoeing." A phone call to the local expert -- you! -- and a plea for help gets you the job of putting together a four day outing. "I'll handle the kids," reasures the voice on the phone. "You just find us a river and get us safely down it. We'll have an orientation meeting a few weeks before the trip. It would be nice if you could attend."

The phone rings off, but the nonchalance and casual assured-ness of your contact lingers. You know that making an "event-free" canoe trip with young people is much more demanding than your new acquaintance realizes. It's already mid-April and the event is just two months away. To insure success, you'll have to begin work immediately!

PICKING THE ROUTE

By and large, teenagers are out for a good time. For them, a canoe trip is more a "social experience" than a wilderness en-counter. So choose a route that is commensurate with their physical and mental capabilities. Days should be challenging but not exhaust-ing. A 15 mile day, or five hours on the water is about right. Kids need time to swim, explore and socialize.

It goes without saying that all but the easiest rapids should be portaged. Even the best trained teenagers often freeze up when water conditions get hairy.

THE PRE-TRIP MEETINGS

Unless kids are taught correct procedures *before* the trip, they will make life miserable for themselves and you. Young people are unbelievably careless, even with their own equipment. I have seen teenagers who should know better throw expensive down sleeping bags into the wet bottom of a canoe, or lay them out in muddy grass or too near a fire. Unthinking teenagers leave food lying around which attracts animals, and they procrastinate dishwashing well into the night. They almost never remember to remove drying clothing from clotheslines before they retire, and in spite of stern warnings to the contrary they burn up at least one boot or pair of socks in the campfire while attempting to dry them. Their sanitary habits are usually completely undeveloped. If no latrine is available, they just go in the woods. They wash their hair, bodies, and dishes in the river or lake with little concern for possible water contam-ination, and less than ten minutes later they draw water for drinking from the same spot.

These pitfalls are common to the age group and can be pre-vented with proper planning and training. Planning begins with the first "pre-trip meeting," which should be scheduled at least a month in advance of the trip.

FIRST MEETING

Distribute these forms at the first meeting:

Swim form: Summer camps usually require would-be canoeists to pass a minimum 100 yard freestyle swim test. Frankly, I think that's overdoing it. Canoeing fatalities are more often the result of entrapment (getting a foot caught between rocks in a whitewater capsize), hypothermia, or failure to wear a life jacket, than to "poor swimming ability." If a kid can swim 50 feet, is comfortable in the water with a life vest on, and is not exposed to the dangers of cold or rough water, he'll get along fine. If you don't have time to test swimming ability yourself, get a signed statement from a parent or school coach to verify what you need to know.

Medical history form: Your doctor can help you design a medical history form. You'll want to know about allergies, back problems, special medications and phobias.

Allergies and physical disabilities are seldom reason enough to eliminate a youngster from going along. You can provide for a bee sting allergy by carrying the appropriate kit; a girl with scoliosis can participate (even wear a brace!) as long as she doesn't carry heavy packs or canoes. To be forewarned is to be prepared!

Medical release form: Situation: A canoe overturns in a current. One kid panics and gets caught between the canoe and a large rock. The result is a mangled leg which requires immediate surgery. Fortunately, you're able to quickly evacuate the youngster to a nearby hospital. The hospital calls the parents for permission to operate but they can't be reached. So surgery is postponed until permission can be secured.

The "medical release form" is a statement, signed by the parent(s) which allows a doctor to perform essential medical treatment without first contacting the parent. In a life-threatening emergency, a conscientious physician will probably do whatever is necessary anyway, but the signed form eliminates frustration and delay.

Equipment list: Provide each teenager with a list of personal equipment which he or she must supply. Rain gear and a change of clothes is generally enough for day trips, but overnight's require specialized items (see the suggested "Equipment List" in Chapter 12). A *written* list of essentials is essential when communicating with teenagers!

Go over each item on the equipment list and explain its value. Parents are apt to minimize the importance of certain things, especially when the trip is a short one. But be emphatic -- indeed, demanding -- that items which are critical to comfort and safety be provided even if it means parents must buy them.

For example, to many parents, a sleeping bag is a sleeping bag, and girls, especially, will show up with twenty dollar slumber bags unless told otherwise. And rain gear is always a problem. To save money parents will usually buy their children cheap plastic ponchos or rain suits which won't hold up for more than a day or two in rough weather. This type of rain gear may be adequate for an especially dry time of year, but it won't make the grade in a two day storm. Remember, the kids are *your* responsibility, and so is a case of hypothermia!

SECOND MEETING

Now is the time to develop a sense of responsibility and environmental awareness. I begin by explaining a typical day on the river (a good slide show helps). Kids are shown how to pack their sleeping bag and personal gear; how to treat canoes and equipment; how to manage camp chores, etc. Throughout the discussion I continually stress environmental etiquette.* For example, I tell young people that hair washing is not permitted within fifty feet of a waterway. This, I explain, is to prevent water pollution. The kids enjoy doing their part for the environment and soon develop a cooperative method of shampooing, complete with hot water and a bucket brigade.

Teenagers will forget much of what you say at this meeting but they will leave with an understanding that there are important expectations, and that a canoe trip is not a "do-as-you-please" experience.

THIRD MEETING

This should be an on-the-water practice session. Rent or borrow canoes, paddles and PFD's and get out and teach *safe* canoeing. Eight hours of intensive instruction is minimal to insure an event-free canoe trip. The leader who allows a teen group to first set foot into

---

*See Appendix "C" for a test on backcountry ethics which you can share with your group.

a canoe on the morning of the scheduled trip is certain to encounter a number of "upsetting experiences".

FOURTH MEETING

Sometime or other you'll have to pack food and equipment. The job will be easier if each youngster supplies two nylon stuff sacks -- one for clothing, the other for toiletries and personal items. Have a "full field" inspection of all but the most personal items before you start packing. Don't trust teenagers to follow the equipment list!

When the packing is complete, go over these rules:

RULES

1. *Everyone*, regardless of swimming ability, must wear a life jacket when canoeing. To this end, it's essential to supply each youngster with a comfortable PFD which can be worn long hours without complaint. This eliminates bulky horse-collar styles which will be removed as soon as you're not looking!

2. Life jackets are *life-saving* equipment. Don't sit on them or throw them around!

3. Take life jackets *inside* your tent when you retire. Do not leave them outside! This rule promotes respect for the PFD and keeps it clean and dry. No one wants to wear a vest that's been left in the rain.

4. Before retiring, canoes are turned over and tied to a tree so a high wind won't turn them into a kite. The first time you chase a paddlerless canoe down a bleak river in the black of night you'll understand the importance of this rule.

5. No whittling! *Every* cut I've bandaged on teen canoe trips has been the result of lackadaisical whittling!

COMFORTS

Most teen groups travel with three to a canoe which means one person rides "dead weight" in the cold wet bottom of the hull. A sitting pad -- boat cushion or square of waterproof foam -- is essential to the warmth and well-being of your passenger.

Fitted wood yoke: If your route includes portages, you'll have to provide a yoke for each canoe. The commercial variety with shoulder pads set eight inches apart (inside dimensions) is too wide to fit the narrow shoulders of most teenagers. The result is an impossibly painful carry. I suggest you make your own down-sized yokes according to my plans in Chapter 3. Even slightly built teenagers can carry heavy canoes with this rig.

Don't bolt the yoke to the gunwales. Use the clamp device illustrated, instead. That way you can remove the yoke to provide more room for your passenger.

SAFETY

First aid kit: It goes without saying that a good first-aid kit -- and the knowledge how to use it -- is essential. Figure on using lots of bandaids, aspirin, and Ace bandages. Most common injuries are sprains, burns and small cuts (which are easily infected if you don't attend to them). Be sure to include some surgical scrub (anti-septic soap), cotton swabs, and insect sting medication in your kit.

If a canoe capsizes in cold water or chilly weather, you'd better be prepared to treat hypothermia. I always carry a fire-making kit which consists of a flattened milk carton, some cedar shavings, fine kindling, and a chemical fire-starter. With this outfit I can make a roaring fire in a matter of seconds in any weather. A one quart Thermos filled with hot soup or tea rounds out my arsenal against hypothermia.

Continually stress safety, safety, safety! Admonish kids to slow down and look where they're going when carrying a canoe or pack. Nearly all accidents are the result of hurrying a task. Kids require a steady flow of energy to keep their motors running at peak efficiency. And they need frequent rest stops too. Teens can paddle long and hard if they're well (and continually) fed. For this reason, a smart trip leader always includes a bag of cookies or snacks on all his or her canoe trips.

RESPONSIBILITY

Unless a group of teenagers has had considerable canoe-camping experience, they are apt to forget items of equipment on the portage trail or when they break camp. The only effective way I've found to deal with this problem is to make each youngster respon-sible for something. For example, one boy might be responsible for a food pack and the gas can (for the stove). He should be able to recite the contents of that pack and verify that it and the gas jug are present at the end of each portage. Another group member might be responsible for an equipment pack and fishing rod case, etc. Youngsters quickly learn the importance of each item and accept their responsibility without complaint. On the few occasions where an article is left behind, the person responsible for it will usually volunteer to go back after it.

In June 1975 I took seven teenagers on a one-week trip into Minnesota's Boundary Waters Canoe Area. It happened that another teen group had selected the same route as ours, and for three days we trailed about an hour behind them. At the end of the three days we had accumulated two canoe paddles, one rain jacket, one sweatshirt, a pair of sunglasses, a bottle of insect repellent, and one gallon of gasoline. When we finally caught up we were able to effect a trade of needed items. We swapped their lost equipment for two pounds of popcorn and some margarine. We were all well satisfied with the exchange.

DELICATE CONCERNS

Seemingly insignificant things, like "how and where to go to the bathroom" really frustrate teenagers. So write the rules in technicolor so everyone understands. For riverside rest stops, I simply point and say, "Girls upriver, boys go thataway." Co-ed overnights, however, require more finesse. If there are screened out-houses for men and women, your problem is solved. Otherwise you'll have to dig a "uni-sex" latrine. Here's my procedure:

I dig a 12 inch deep rectangular hole well away from the main camp and screen it with a nylon tarp if the vegetation permits seeing the tent area. A foot long piece of aluminum tube with one end flattened serves as a shovel. Toilet paper is bagged in plastic and kept inside a bright colored nylon bag which is hung in a conspicuous place at the edge of camp. When someone needs to use the facility, he or she simply takes the "TP" bag and goes. No one is to go to the latrine until the TP bag returns.

The procedure works wonderfully and is one time kids listen to the rules!

FOR YOUR SANITY

Every teen group must have a strong leader, capable of making rational decisions. A lot of private camps team eight kids with one instructor on all their canoe trips and have few problems. I commonly trip this way but don't think it's the best procedure. *Two* adults per group of ten makes more sense: If someone becomes hurt, one leader can go for help while the other maintains control. When it comes to kids, one grownup can't possibly be everywhere at once!

On the other hand, too many cooks can spoil the stew. The last thing you need is an argument when there are important decisions to be made.

Generally, teenagers don't like to canoe with adults, even their own parents. Kids are most comfortable in the company of other kids; adults should pilot their own canoes!

Kids are pretty honest with adults. If they don't like something, they'll tell you right off. It may be the food, the rain, the ruggedness of the trip, or the way you are running things that they find fault with. And youngsters are often right -- from their point of view. This is an important consideration, for if you are tripping with teenagers you are doing so for *their* benefit, not yours. In planning a trip, remember that youngsters lack your experience and maturity. Their kind of trip may not necessarily be your kind of trip. You'll discover exactly what this means the first time you want to fish and the kids want to swim; when you want to absorb the majesty of a sunset in silence and they want to sing. Discipline is essential on teen canoe trips, but so is understanding.

Rainy days: Suppose you encounter a heavy rain on a week-long trip? Should you lay-over until the sun shines? No way! The worst thing imaginable on a rainy day is a bunch of grumbling kids who "can't find anything to do." Feed 'em well, dress 'em warm, and work 'em hard, and they'll respond with smiles no matter how bad the weather. When ol' Sol smiles again, *then* stop and spend the day. Teenagers will find plenty of ways to entertain themselves when the weather is cooperative.

ESSENTIAL EQUIPMENT FOR OVERNIGHT TRIPS*

1. Bring along an extra wool shirt or two, and a few large leaf and lawn size plastic bags which can be fashioned into emergency waterproof garments. Kids do occasionally lose their raingear!

2. One ten by ten foot (or larger) waterproof tarp for every five people. If you encounter heavy rains and have to prepare meals and do camp chores under cover, only a generously sized tarp will do.

3. Stove: When rains come, put up your tarp, fire up the stove, and prepare gourmet meals in comfort. I would never forego my campfire, but I always cook on a stove in any weather.

4. Folding saw and hand-axe. Making fire when the woods are soaked from a week-long rain is not easy without the right tools. So I always carry a wood-frame folding camp saw** and a quality-built all steel hand axe, which I *do not* allow the kids to use for chopping. All wood is cut with the folding saw; the axe is used only as a splitting wedge. I permit only one method of splitting (Figure 10-2): The hand-axe is driven into the upright log with just enough force to hold it in place; the splitter then uses *both* hands to grasp the handle firmly; a second person uses a length of log to hammer the axe head through the log to be split. This method necessarily requires two people -- one to hold the axe, and the other to hammer. Because the axe is all steel, no damage to the handle can result. But most important, there is no danger of cut toes, knees, or thighs.***

Making kindling from the splittings requires extreme care so I *always* tackle this project myself. Kindling splits easier from the end grain -- a process that is made easier (and safer!) if you use a stick of wood to hold the upright piece in place (Figure 10-3).

Over the past twenty years I have organized and guided more than sixty canoe trips (more than 500 kids) and I have always had an axe in camp. I have never had an accident or come close to having one. When used properly -- and with an ever-watchful eye -- the hand axe is a safe and valuable tool. It has been bad-mouthed

---

*See Appendix "B" for a checklist of essential gear and river rules.
**Best camp saw I've ever used is the "Fast Bucksaw", available from Indiana Camp Supply, P.O. Box 344, Pittsboro, IN 46167. Write for their free catalog.
***A thin-ground aluminum splitting wedge makes a moderately effective substitute for a hand axe.

Figure 10-1   Splitting wood is easy if you use the axe as a splitting wedge rather than a "chopping" tool. Thick logs can be easily split by this method.

Figure 10-2   Kindling splits easier from the end grain — a process that is made easier (and safer!) if you use a stick of wood to hold the upright piece in place.

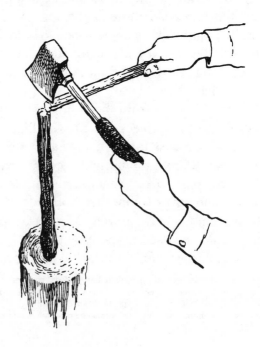

for too long by people who don't understand how to use it. Contrary to popular belief, not everyone who carries an axe plans to chop down the forest with it!

5. One hundred feet of quarter-inch nylon rope is essential for rigging tarps and clotheslines.

PACING THE TRIP

I have found it best to go slow and easy the first day of a canoe trip, and to pick up the speed on the second day. Stop early enough each day to allow plenty of time for play and fishing. Include at least one day that is a real challenge, begin at dawn that day and camp at sunset. Paddle hard and, where they are available, select rugged portages. Such a day is necessary to mold the group into oneness. Plan to spend a full day in camp after your rugged day.

A teen group which I tripped with in August 1975 was extremely slow, both in paddling and on the portages. Where other groups of similar age would complete a portage in forty-five minutes, they would take ninety. I jokingly nicknamed them "my sweet pokeys." Then one night while we were sitting around the campfire, I asked to read their diaries (I require that each individual keep a diary). I found that most had written beautiful, poetic things about the trees, the lakes, and the beauty of nature. With this came a realization. Unlike faster groups, my sweet pokeys had gained a respect and appreciation for the wilderness. They had developed the exact attitudes that I was trying to instill. Instead of rushing through the wilderness, they were looking at it. I was ashamed that I had mocked them, and I apologized for my thoughtlessness.

As you can see, canoeing with teens is much more than a "casual experience." At times you'll be mother, father, doctor, lawyer, teacher, and disciplinarian. You'll have to find ways to include unpopular kids in group activities, and to get the rest of the group to accept them. On occasion, you may even have to give up the shirt on your own back to warm that of a child.

Rewards? You bet! I've paddled dangerous whitewater and remote rivers north of the arctic circle. I've stood amidst thousands of caribou, even been "charged" by grizzlies. But nothing warms my heart more than the tearful hugs and "Thanks, Cliff," I often receive at the end of a teen canoe trip.

Canoeing with teens is the best way I know to be honestly appreciated, and to rediscover the forgotten innocence of being young.

11.
Tying It All Together

Every canoeist should have a fundamental knowledge of knot-tying and rope-handling techniques. You will use ropes for lining and tracking your canoe through rapids, erecting a rain tarp, making a clothesline, lifting a bucket of cold water from the depths of a lake, securing your canoe to a car-top carrier, salvage and rescue operations, and many other purposes.

Many outdoors handbooks define a dozen or more knots. In reality, unless you are a mountain climber or intend to chop down the forest to build rope-lashed furniture (which isn't even remotely humorous in this age of environmental awareness), you can get along very nicely with just two hitches and two knots. These are the *double half-hitch* (two *half-hitches*), *sheet bend, bowline*, and *power-cinch*. Those familiar with rope-handling techniques will note the conspicuous absence of the square knot and the tautline hitch. Except for limited first-aid applications the square knot is generally useless, and the much touted tautline hitch has gone the way of the passenger pigeon. The tautline was useful in the days of cotton tents and manila rope; it has been replaced with the much handier, more versatile, power-cinch.

Admittedly, I find that most canoeists can usually get by with just one knot and one hitch -- the power-cinch and the sheet bend. These are a must, however, and they should be mastered before you undertake a voyage of significance.

THE DOUBLE HALF-HITCH
(two half-hitches)

The double half-hitch is useful for tying a rope to a tree or to the towing link of a canoe. The knot is very secure and tends to tighten itself when a load is applied to the rope.

Figure 11-1   Double Half-Hitch:

THE SHEET BEND

Use the sheet bend for tying two ropes together. The knot works well even if the rope sizes differ greatly. The sheet bend is about the only knot that can be effectively used to join the ends of slippery polypropylene rope.

A friend of mine won five dollars when he fixed a broken waterskiing tow-rope with this knot. When the tow-line snapped, the owner of the ski boat bet my friend that he couldn't tie the two

Figure 11-2   Sheet Bend:

ends of the polypropylene rope back together tightly enough to hold. My friend won the bet and skied the remainder of the day on the repaired line.

It is important that the free ends of the sheet bend be on the *same side*, as shown in Figure 11-2. The knot will work if the ends are on opposite sides, but will be less reliable.

THE BOWLINE

The bowline is a very secure knot which won't slip, regardless of the load applied. It is commonly used by mountain climbers to tie their climbing ropes around their waists. Use this knot whenever you want to put a nonslip loop on the end of a line.

Beginners are often told to make the bowline by forming a loop, or "rabbit hole." The rabbit (free end of the rope) comes up through the hole, around the tree (opposite or long end of the rope shown in Figure 11-3) and back down the hole. The bowline will slip a few inches before it tightens, so allow an extra-long free end.

Figure 11-3   Bowline:

THE POWER-CINCH

Perhaps the most ingenious hitch to come along in recent years is the power-cinch (there seems to be no widely accepted name for this hitch; hence, I took the liberty of naming it the "power-cinch"), which effectively replaces the tautline hitch and functions as a powerful pulley when used properly. Skilled canoeists use this pulley knot almost exclusively for tying canoes on cars. It is also widely used by truckers who tie heavy loads in place. The power-cinch may be the canoeist's most useful hitch.

Begin the power-cinch by forming the loop shown in Figure 11-4 step 1. Pull the loop through as in step 2. It is important that the loop be formed *exactly* as shown. The loop will look okay if you make it backwards, but it won't work.

If the loop is formed as in step 2, a simple tug on the rope will eliminate it. This is preferable to the common practice of tying a knot in the loop, which, after being exposed to a load, is almost impossible to get out.

If you are tying a canoe into place on top of a car, tie one end of the rope to the canoe's bow or stern and snap the steel hook on the other end of the rope to the car's bumper. Run the free end of the rope (a) through the loop in step 2. Now apply power to the free end. You have, in effect, created a pulley with a two-to-one mechanical advantage. The power you can get out of this system has to be seen to be believed; if it is used to secure the bow or stern of a car-topped canoe to a car bumper, you can, if you are careless, actually pull the rope hard enough to break the back of a wood canoe or seriously bend an aluminum model. You can pull a clothesline tight enough to cause it to sing like a taut guitar string when plucked with the fingers.

Complete the hitch by securing a double half-hitch around the body of the rope, or use a "quick-release" loop as illustrated.

For additional power, which is needed, for example, in canoe salvage operations, you can form additional loops in the rope body like the ones shown in step 2. The more loops, the greater the mechanical advantage and the more power you can exert (after about two loops, the system gain is lost in friction). When you form additional loops, however, it is important that each pulley be completed separately. For example, to form an additional pulley

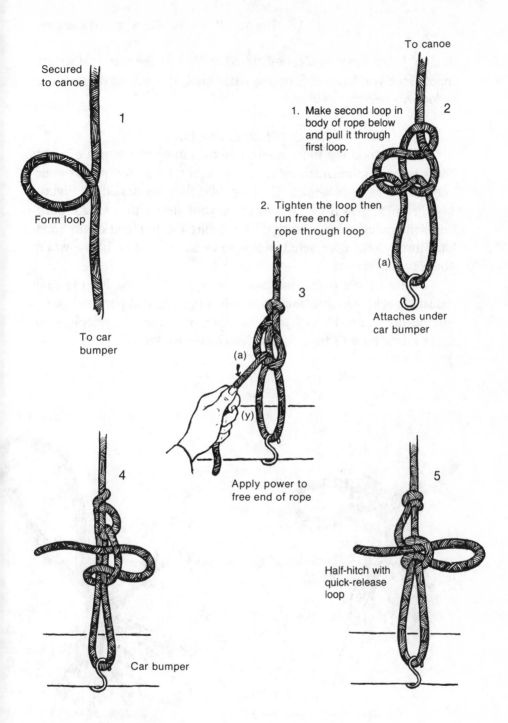

Secured
to canoe

1

Form loop

To car
bumper

1. Make second loop in
   body of rope below
   and pull it through
   first loop.

To canoe

2

2. Tighten the loop then
   run free end of
   rope through loop

(a)

Attaches under
car bumper

3

(a)

(y)

Apply power to
free end of rope

4

Car bumper

5

Half-hitch with
quick-release
loop

Figure 11-4   Power Cinch:

in step 3, the loop would be formed at "y" -- the free end of the rope. Once you learn to form the basic knot, the principal of adding loops will become evident.

THE QUICK-RELEASE LOOP

There's nothing more frustrating than untying a bunch of tight knots when you're breaking camp in the morning. If you end your knots with a "quick-release" loop like that illustrated in Figure 11-4, step 5, you'll be able to untie your ties with a single pull. Form the quick-release feature by running the free end of the rope back through the completed knot -- same as making a "bow" when you tie your shoes.

Use a simple overhand knot with a quick-release loop to seal the stuff sacks which contain your sleeping bag and personal gear. The plastic "cord-locks" sold for this purpose are for people who don't know how to tie effective quick-release knots.

Figure 11-5   Secure your stuff sacks with a quick-release loop.

SECURING A LINE

On a wilderness trip several years ago one canoe of our party swamped in a heavy rapid. There was a bouldery falls about two hundred yards downstream, and it was imperative that we get a rope to the wet canoeists immediately in order to avoid disaster. Luckily, a fifty-foot line was at hand and was properly coiled for throwing. The line was heaved to the two men who were hanging onto the gunwales of the water-filled canoe. Fortunately the men caught the rope, and both they and the canoe were pulled safely to shore, avoiding what might have been a serious mishap.

You should always keep your ropes coiled and ready for use. The best system I have found is an old Navy method:

1. Coil the rope (taking care to lay each coil *carefully* into place), grasp the main body of it with one hand, and place your thumb through the eye of the coils to hold them in place, as shown in Figure 11-6, step 1.

2. Remove the last two coils of rope, take this long free end, and wind it around the main body of the rope several times (Figure 11-6, step 2). Wind the free end *downward*, toward the hand

Figure 11-6a   Securing a Line: Steps 1-2

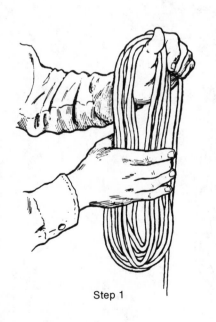

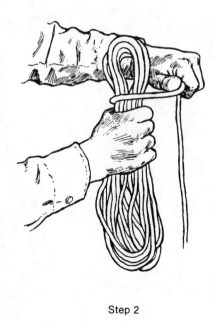

Step 1

Step 2

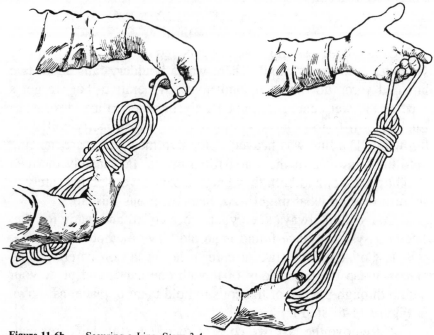

Figure 11-6b   Securing a Line: Steps 3-4

Figure 11-7   Bind your fifty foot line by the old navy method outlined in figure 11-6, then tie it to a thwart as illustrated here. A quick pull of the "free end" releases the rope instantly.

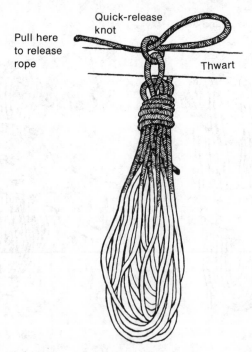

Quick-release
knot

Pull here
to release
rope

Thwart

holding the rope body. Wind evenly and snugly. Don't make the coils too tight.

3. Form a loop with the free end of the rope, as shown in step 3, and push it through the eye of the rope body.

4. Grasp the wound coils with one hand and the rope body with the other hand and slide the coils upward tightly against the loop. The rope is now coiled and secured (step 4). Pulling the free end of the rope will release the line, which can quickly be made ready for throwing.

I bind all my fifty foot utility ropes in this manner and store them under a pack-flap so they'll be quickly available when I need them. When running whitewater, I often keep a throwing line tied around a thwart as illustrated in Figure 11-7. A single pull releases the line from the thwart; a second tug makes it ready for use. Fast and convenient...and possibly a life-saver!

12.
The Necessities

Some years ago, the staff of a high quality equipment store invited me to join them on an overnight canoe trip. It was to be a high-tech affair, administered by the pros of the shop. The idea was to use store equipment for the event to give employees a chance to try first-hand what they'd been selling on a daily basis. Later, what they learned in the field would be shared with customers on the retail floor.

The plan was to run the shuttle after work on Friday and camp that night at the put-in. This would permit an early start (kick-off time down river was scheduled for nine a.m.) on Saturday.

I arrived Friday evening to a plethora of brilliant color and sophisticated geometry. Every imaginable type of tent was represented, from A-frames and tunnels to domes and pyramids. And amidst the flamboyant display there mingled a weathered crew of around a dozen young men and women, each nattily clad in state-of-the-art woods attire.

I looked down at my bland castoffs -- military surplus chinos and Marine Corps wool shirt. Suddenly I felt quite inadequate, like a peasant in Camelot.

But my uneasiness was instantly dispelled when the young store manager thrust out his hand and with a broad grin said, "Welcome aboard, Cliff. Glad you could come." Then he waved nonchalantly about and in a low tone commented, "Don't be intimidated -- all this is store gear -- we can't afford it either!"

With that I settled for a cold beer and arrogantly pitched my ancient Gerry Fireside tent within whispering distance of a geodesic dome that cost hundreds of dollars more.

Equipment talk raged far into the night. Gore-Tex was hot new stuff then as were Jan Sport domes and MSR stoves. Wilderness camping was in revolution. It would require diligent study to keep abreast of "what was best."

It began innocently. A few drops at first, then substantial patter. Suddenly, it erupted into a full blown thunderstorm. We bid hasty good nights, and filled with enthusiasm, hurried reluctantly off to our tents. The spell was broken.

Like the others, I'd pitched my tent in a slight depression; the lay of the land was plainly uncooperative. But I'd installed a new four-mil thick plastic ground cloth *inside* my tent. The plastic was cut over-size to wrap well up the side-walls. Previous foul weather experience with this set-up proved it alone was enough to deter all but a veritable flood.

The full force of the storm passed quickly but heavy rain continued most of the night. At around five a.m. I awoke to a dead calm and mumbled conversation. I dozed off again but by six the camp clatter had reached full crescendo. It was evident that everyone was up but me.

As I struggled into the pre-dawn of the day, I was greeted by another round of equipment talk. Finally, one woman asked me how I'd slept in my "little" tent.

"Great, 'til you guys started yapping," I replied.

"Didn't ya get water in?"

"Nope...not a drop!"

"Oh..."

Frankly, I'd expected more than just "Oh."

Right then I decided it would take more than casual prodding before I'd divulge the genie who protected me from last night's rain.

Within minutes a golden sun that predicted a perfect day streamed boldly through the rising fog and suddenly everyone began scurrying around in an effort to dry gear and prepare breakfast. Two stoves sputtered threateningly but wouldn't flame. In desperation, their users finally abandoned the endeavor and just hung around another group in hopes of using their ancient two-burner Coleman the moment it was free. No one even tried to build a fire. After all, there were "the stoves."

By ten a.m. breakfast was finished and attention was turned to the gear drying on the clotheslines. It was a comical sight; just about everything imaginable from down bags to unmentionables were strung hither and yon on an intricate web of parachute cord.

It sort of reminded me of a World War II D.P. camp!

The first canoe touched water at five minutes after eleven. Within the hour there was an upset in the first rapid. Too bad, I thought, that these "experts" -- amiable as they were -- lacked the skills to use effectively all the fancy gear they'd brought along. In the words of the late Cal Rutstrum: "Too bad they never learned how to camp and canoe!"

The notion that state-of-the art equipment will take the "wild" out of wilderness is valid only if you're already expert at wringing out the best from your traditional gear. Sort of like the casual fisherman who spends a fortune for a sonar equipped bass boat and dynamite assortment of lures only to discover that he's still no match for the local Indian guide who has "none of the above."

It's nice of course to have the very best. But all you really need to be comfortable in the backcountry is a modicum of sensible, sturdy gear and the knowledge how to use it. So please keep things in perspective as you read this chapter, and be aware that many substantial canoe trips have been completed with much less (and much worse) gear than I've suggested. Also be aware that equipment which is suitable for backpacking is not always well adapted to canoeing. Wading in knee-deep water for hours at a time or sloshing through a mucky mosquito-infested swamp is very unlike walking down a wind-swept mountain trail. When selecting equipment, consider how it will perform when soaked with water or covered with sand and mud. These are some of the realities that determine its suitability for backcountry canoe tripping.

Lastly, question the long term durability of any product you buy. If a zipper looks weak, it probably is; if there are loose parts which may get lost, they probably will; if high wear areas are not reinforced and failure seems imminent, bet on it. Some products which work well in the short run fail miserably when the years turn to decades.

PACKS AND SUBSTITUTES
FRAMELESS PACKS

For short, close-to-home trips you don't need expensive pack sacks. You can make do very nicely with inexpensive duffel bags. Line duffel bags with one or two heavy plastic sacks before inserting your belongings; this will make them completely waterproof. Two duffel bags can easily be stuffed under the center thwart of most canoes and still allow plenty of room for two children or an adult passenger.

For short portages you can carry duffel bags "army style" over your shoulder, but for long carries it will be best to rig a tumpline. Make the tumpline by attaching two stout ropes or strips of cotton webbing to a 2-foot length of 3-inch-wide canvas. Tie the ropes or buckle the webbing tightly around the bag. Place the tump strap just above your forehead, lean forward, and take off. Once you get used to it, you can carry moderate loads up to a mile with little difficulty using this system.

If you're planning a trip of a more serious nature, you will want to invest in one or more authentic pack sacks. The most popular, and the best for wilderness canoeing, is the Duluth pack, or "grunt sack," as it is often called. The Duluth pack is a large envelope-style sack made of 15- to 20-ounce per square yard canvas. Straps are usually made of heavy leather and are well secured to the pack with brass rivets and waxed thread. A stout tumpline is sometimes provided. Needless to say, Duluth packs are extremely rugged. They are commonly sized as follows:

Number 2: 24 inches wide by 28 inches deep; weight about 2½ pounds

Number 3: 24 inches wide by 30 inches deep; weight about 3½ pounds

Number 4: 28 inches wide by 30 inches deep, with a 6-inch side wall (set out); weight about 4 pounds

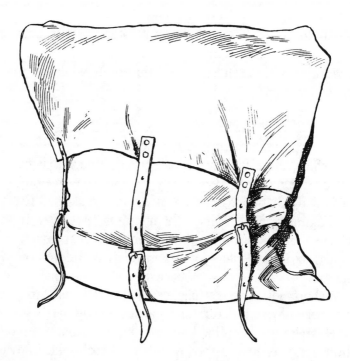

Figure 12-1 The Duluth Pack — still the best choice for canoe tripping.

The number 3 size is the most popular, although some canoeists prefer the larger number 4 for lightweight, bulky items like sleeping bags and clothing.

Even with the tumpline in place, a heavy Duluth pack weighing from sixty-five to eighty-five pounds is not a pleasure to carry. Nevertheless, Duluth packs have been the standard canoe-tripping packs for well over a century, and frankly, nothing better has come along. First of all, grunt sacks are commodious. There are few frame packs which can carry the load of a number 3 or 4 Duluth. Second, it's easy to waterproof the contents of these packs by inserting a nested pair of six mil plastic bags into them (see ''Waterproofing Your Outfit'' at the end of this chapter for the specific procedures). And last, Duluth packs are designed to sit upright in a canoe instead of on their backs or bellies, like packs of more conventional design.

This stand-up feature is of especial value when you take water in rapids or heavy waves. You can literally fill the canoe with water, and as long as you remain right side up no water can enter the plastic liner of the pack. This is because the weakest part of any waterproof bag is its closure, and this closure is just beneath the flap of the erect Duluth pack -- out of contact with accumulated water. This seemingly unimportant design feature became evident to me on a Canadian river trip during which my partner and I repeatedly filled our canoe with water in the heavy rapids we encountered. At no time did we get a single drop of water into any of our food or equipment, although our companions in another canoe had some problems with a specially built, extra-long pack they were carrying. To keep the canoe's center of gravity low, our friends laid the long pack on its back. In spite of reasonable waterproofing precautions, a small leak developed at the closure of the single pack liner. That night we resmoked two pounds of damp, homemade deer jerky -- though I must admit the smoke was more useful in controlling the black flies than in drying the jerky.

A virtue of Duluth packs that should not be overlooked is the ease with which they fit into the unique contours of a canoe without wasting space, enabling you to pack your gear closely around the yoke to keep the ends of the canoe light for better response in rough water. And because a fully loaded number 2 or 3 Duluth pack only comes a few inches above the gunwales of most canoes (number 4 packs come somewhat higher), the center of gravity of the canoe can be kept low for greater stability. All of which means Duluth packs, especially in the number 2 and 3 sizes, are just about perfect for wilderness canoe tripping.*

PACKS WITH FRAMES

Packs with exterior aluminum frames have three major failings when used in canoes: The frames catch on seats, gunwales, and thwarts during loading and unloading operations; the rigid design prevents efficient utilization of space, which can result in a poorly balanced load; and it is difficult to waterproof the contents of the many zippered compartments. Frame outfits, however, are easier to carry, and if you do as much backpacking as canoeing, they may be a better investment that the less versatile Duluth packs.

*Your most complete source of Duluth packs is: Duluth Tent and Awning Co., Inc., 1610 West Superior St., Box 6024, Duluth, MN 55806.

I know of no good way to waterproof frame packs, short of stuffing each compartment with a multitude of plastic bags. Bring plenty of extra bags; failure is frequent!

The best way to use a pack frame (if you must use one) is to pack everything in duffle bags and lash them to the frame (you'll have to remove the packsack, of course). If you don't have duffle bags, try this: Lay out your tent or nylon tarp and place sleeping bags, foam pads or air mattresses and clothing in the center. Fold over the edges of the tarp and roll the whole thing up. Tie the roll to your pack frame and the outfit is complete.

Some canoeists prefer packs with internal frames (stays) for canoeing because they fit well in canoes yet carry more comfortably than Duluth packs. True enough, but the problem of length still remains -- these packs are simply too long to be set upright; they must be laid on their backs in direct contact with bilge water. The first time you strike out across a portage trail with a wet, muddy packsack riding firmly against your new Pendleton shirt, you'll understand how important the "stand-up" feature is.

WATERPROOF PACKSACKS

There are a variety of tough waterproof packs and bags which are designed especially for whitewater rafting and canoeing. The most reliable models are constructed of heavy nylon coated with neoprene or poly-vinyl-chloride (PVC) and feature rapids-proof closures and sturdy carrying straps. Many models are in use by commercial rafting companies who will vouch for their effectiveness.

Whether or not these sophisticated (and very expensive!) packs are ideal for wilderness canoeing depends entirely on your perspective...and your pocketbook. Frankly, I think there are less costly solutions which work as well. After you've read "Waterproofing Your Outfit" at the end of this chapter, you may agree.

RIGID PACKS

A lot of canoeists scorn rigid packs, correctly suggesting that they don't fit well into the rounded hull of a canoe. That's true enough, but there are times when you'd give your eye teeth for a pack that won't munch its contents everytime you set it down. For years, the standard solution to crushed crackers has been to line food packs with shellacked cardboard cartons. This set-up is still considered state-of-the-art by some commercial outfitters in Minnesota's Boundary Waters and the Allagash of Maine. Unfortunately, the maximum lifetime of a well-shellacked cardboard box is one summer. For this reason, you may want to consider a more permanent form of protection for your breakables.

The traditional hard pack is the Maine pack basket -- an artistic affair that's woven from splints of black ash by Indians in the east and north central states. Pack baskets have become very popular among New England canoeists while remaining virtually unknown in other canoe areas. Consequently, they are not readily available in most parts of the country. Until recently, the most complete source of pack baskets was L.L. Bean, Inc., Freeport, Maine 04032. However, Bean no longer lists them in their catalog, and I am unaware of any other mail order outlet which carries them.

Fortunately, there are alternatives. Here's the least expensive one: The next time you go discount-store shopping, take your Duluth

Figure 12-2   The Maine Pack Basket. Items which are breakable or which might be uncomfortable in a conventional "soft" pack are placed in the pack basket. To make a watertight unit, the basket is first placed in a waterproof army clothes bag.

Figure 12-3   The E.M. Wanigan: A tough polystyrine box that's portable and watertight. The Wangan has padded shoulder straps and a 5,200 cubic inch capacity (about the same as a number 3 Duluth pack).

pack with you (so what if you look a little crazy; most canoeists are anyhow). Now, when you pass the housewares section, try to find a plastic trash can that fits inside your pack. The cheaper the trash can, the better. The cheaper cans tend to be more flimsy, and hence conform better to your bony contours than the more expensive rigid models. When you find a plastic can that fits -- buy it!

Then, insert the can into a waterproof bag (the tough army waterproof clothes bag is ideal). It's best to insert the trash can *in* the bag, not vice versa. This way sharp objects within the pack won't puncture the waterproof liner. Finally, insert the whole combo into your Duluth pack. You can pack camera, stove, cook-kit, thermos, or anything else which might be uncomfortable against your back in this unit.

Another alternative is to purchase one of the new plastic hard packs which are available at many camping shops. For the past year I've been using the E-M Wanigan* -- a tough polystyrene box that's portable and watertight...and sized to fit crossways in the belly of even the skinniest canoes. The box has padded shoulder straps, suitcase-style lifting handles, and fast, effective latches. It holds 5,200 cubic inches of gear -- about the same as a number 3 Duluth pack. The E-M Wanigan is a fairly expensive unit, but worth it if you want reliable protection for your breakables.

*E-M Wanigan, 10411 Kelman Court N., Stillwater, Minnesota 55082

WATERPROOF CAMERA BAGS

Canoeists are great storytellers. It's too bad most of them (myself included) don't have pictures to back up their whopping good tales. Usually canoeists dismiss photo requests with a simple comment like, "No way am I gonna take my four-hundred-dollar camera on a canoe trip and dump it in the river." And there is much wisdom in that statement. Although many paddlers carry expensive cameras on canoe trips, most keep them well hidden in the bottom of watertight packs and bring them out around suppertime when all the gear is unpacked (this explains all the pictures of happy campers sitting around the fire eating).

Whitewater paddlers commonly stow their cameras in 50-caliber ammunition boxes (army surplus). This is a fine solution, but ammo boxes are heavy and cumbersome on portages, and the loud snapping noise of the lid-latch frightens away wildlife.

An ideal camera bag can be found on the shelves of your military surplus store. It's called an *amphibious-assault* gas-mask bag. This canvas-covered rubber bag is just the right size to accept a 35mm camera and telephoto lens; it's *absolutely* watertight, lightweight, and extremely rugged. Moreover, it opens and closes by simply releasing three solid brass fasteners. You can strap the bag to your hip on portages and have your camera available when you need it. Phoenix Products, Inc., U.S. Route 421, Tyner, KY 40486 makes a less sturdy version of the military gas mask bag that is quite popular with whitewater canoeists. If you can't find the original army version, buy the Phoenix bag. It's plenty strong!

Figure 12-4　　The Amphibious-Assault Gas-Mask Bag — the best protection for your camera. It's absolutely waterproof!

TENTS

You can be a bit lavish when selecting a canoe tent. After all, the longest portage in most canoe country is seldom more than a mile -- hardly a backbreaking distance to transport a tent of "reasonable" weight. What's "reasonable" depends, of course on your perspective, though most canoeists would agree that *twelve* pounds is about maximum for a tent that will be used by two people.

Size: It works out that each camper needs a space of around seven feet by two-and-one-half feet just to stretch out and store gear. Increase the area to eight by three and you enter the realm of "comfort." Widen it another six inches and ahhh...pure luxury. A *seven by eight foot* floor plan and enough room to sit fully upright is ideal for two! Evidently most canoeists agree, for nearly all the tents you see on canoe trails are technically classified as "four person" models, even though they're commonly (and wisely) occupied by just two.

Sleeping two in a tent built for four may seem like needless pampering, until...

1. You encounter a storm. Now, extra space is essential, not just for sanity, but to keep your bedding dry. Even the best tents will deform some in high winds, and if you're snuggled against a sidewall, water is sure to condense on your sleeping bag. And if your tent has a "cap" fly (a three-quarter length fly that doesn't extend to the ground), wind-driven mist may blow in through the breathable nylon canopy. Now if you can just put some distance between the tent sidewall and your sleeping gear...

2. You become wind or bug-bound and have to eat, relax, and make repairs to equipment inside your tent.

3. Your neighbor's tent destructs in a high wind or is inadvertently left sitting on a rock at your last campsite. Thank God you've got a four person tent and can handle the overload!

Fabrics: The only suitable tent material is nylon. Cotton tents are too heavy; they gain weight when wet, and they mildew. When you buy a nylon tent, make sure you specify two-ply construction. This means that the tent consists of two layers of fabric. The main tent body is built of a porous nylon or mosquito net, to let body-produced water vapor out. To keep the rain from getting in, a chemically coated waterproof *fly* is suspended a few inches over the inner tent.

The result is a shelter that is completely watertight, breathable, and lightweight. You can pitch the tent without the fly on clear nights, or you can remove the rain-fly and use it separately as your only shelter for camping in the fall when bugs are no problem.*

Bulk: Bulk is more important than weight. You can live with a few extra pounds, even on a go-light canoe journey, but not with a tent that won't fit in your pack. The culprit is usually the length of the poles. Sections longer than 23 inches simply won't fit cross-ways in most packs without protruding from under the closing flap. And anything that's secured by friction alone can work free and be lost.

A good canoe tent should pack small enough to fit *completely* inside the waterproof confines of your packsack. Unfortunately, some otherwise outstanding canoe tents do not.

Here's how to pack a tent with obnoxiously long poles:

1. Stuff or roll the tent without the poles or pegs. Pack the tent inside your pack.

2. Place poles and pegs in a sturdy nylon bag with drawstring closure. Sew a loop of nylon webbing to each end of the bag and attach lengths of parachute cord to the loops.

3. Pack the pole set under the pack flap and snake the closing

---

*Some of the best canoe tents have *integral* flies which cannot be removed.

Figure 12-5 The Cannondale Aroostook — the author's favorite canoe tent. Location: along the Hood River, Northwest Territories.

straps through loops in the cord ends. Now your pole bag can't possibly fall out of your pack.

Geometry: You'll pay much more for sophisticated geometrics (domes, tunnels and such) than for simple-to-sew but reliable A-frame designs. Canoe camps are commonly pitched on solid rock, sand, or the pebbles of a passing gravel bar, so choose a model which is free-standing or nearly so. And be aware that price does not necessarily indicate foul weather performance or how easy (or difficult) the tent is to pitch. Surprisingly, some of the best canoe tents cost less than some of the worst!

In case you're wondering, my favorite canoe tents are the Cannondale Aroostook and Wabash, and the venerable Eureka Timberline, with heavyduty outfitter poles and optional vestibule.*

THE TARPAULIN (RAIN-FLY)

How do you cope with camp chores in an unrelenting rain? Why rig a rain-fly of course! Then move your gear beneath it, fire up the stove, and assume mastery of the situation. For greatest versatility, select a tarp about ten feet square, or larger if you prefer. Look for polyurethane-coated nylon fabric in 2-to 3-ounce weight per square yard. Then customize your tarp according to the directions given in the next chapter.

GROUND CLOTH

A plastic ground cloth is essential for storm-proofing your tent. Read the next chapter and you'll see why!

SLEEPING BAG

This is one of your most important purchases, so don't buy the first good deal that comes along. A well-made sleeping bag may last a life-time so it pays to shop around and buy the best you can afford.

DOWN-FILLED SLEEPING BAGS

A good-quality sleeping bag, filled with sufficient duck or goose down to keep you comfortably warm in temperatures to 25 degrees Fahrenheit, will weigh around three and one-half pounds and stuff into a waterproof carrying sack scarcely larger than a

---

*Eureka Tent, A Division of Johnson Camping, Inc., P.O. Box 966, Binghamton, NY 13902
Cannondale Corp., 9 Brookside Place, Georgetown, CT 06829

two-pound coffee can. These characteristics -- warmth, light weight, and compactness -- have made down-insulated sleeping bags a popular choice among outdoors people everywhere.

However, down-filled bags are expensive, drying wet down is difficult, and down has a tendency to absorb moisture in humid weather. As down bags absorb water, their loft (thickness) decreases and their weight increases. On a humid or hot, sweaty night, a down bag can absorb several ounces of water from the air or your body. Ultimately, the interior atmosphere of the bag will become muggy. Camping along river bottoms is, by nature, a muggy experience, and down bags compound the problem. For this reason, many canoeists prefer the efficient new synthetics.

SYNTHETIC-FILLED SLEEPING BAGS

At this writing, the only suitable substitutes for down are Dupont's Quallofil and Celanese's Polarguard. From the standpoint of thermal efficiency, it takes about 1.3 pounds of these polyesters to equal a pound of good down. Average canoe-country temperatures seldom go below freezing, and in this climate a bag filled with 1½ pounds of high quality down or 2 pounds of Quallofil or Polarguard, is very adequate. In fact, I would rule out as *too warm* any closely fitting bag with more filler than this.

A bag filled with 2 pounds of either of these synthetics will weigh about 4 pounds and will stuff into a sack of 9-by-18 inches -- ideal for canoeing. And, the cost of such a bag will be considerably less than a comparable down-filled model. It will not, however, have as broad a comfort range as an equivalent down bag. For example, a down bag that's comfort-rated to 25 degrees Farhenheit will be usable from about 25 to 60 degrees. An identically rated synthetic bag will become *too warm* when the temperature reaches 50 degrees.

A real advantage of Quallofil and Polarguard is that these synthetic materials, unlike down, stubbornly refuse to absorb water. If a Quallofil or Polarguard bag gets wet it can be wrung out and will retain a good share of its warmth. Down, on the other hand, possesses almost no insulating value when water-soaked.*

---

*As I've already pointed out, there's no excuse to get your sleeping bag, or anything else, wet on a canoe trip. If you don't know how to waterproof your gear or storm-proof your tent you need to learn basic skills, not buy bomb-proof equipment!

Despite the advantages of these man-made materials, you may like down-filled sleeping bags because of their excellent draping qualities (if you've ever slept under a feather-and-down comforter you know what I mean) and longevity -- a good down bag will outlast a synthetic one by many years, if it is well cared for. Buy what you can afford; but whatever you buy, make sure it has a hood to keep your head warm, and a full-length two-way zipper to keep your feet cool. In addition, the smaller the bag, the lighter it will be, and the less area you will have to heat to keep warm. For these reasons you should select a fairly close-fitting bag with a tapered mummy shape.

Obviously, if you commonly share your bag with someone, a pair of zip-together semi-rectangular sleepers will be the best choice. The inefficiency of these larger, harder-to-heat bags will be more than compensated for by the warmth of togetherness.

CUSTOMIZING AN INEFFICIENT SLEEPING BAG

Here's how to make a bulky overweight sleeping bag warmer and lighter: Climb inside the bag and snuggle against the zipper. Have a friend push in the material on the side opposite the zipper until it barely touches your body. Then, back off the fabric until you're comfortable and mark the location with chalk or pins. Climb out of the bag and set heavy diaper pins through the material along the marked line. Voilá! Project complete.

By decreasing the amount of space your body has to heat, you increase thermal efficiency. This is the easiest way to make an adult-sized sleeping bag suitable for use by a child. As the youngster grows, simply re-fit and re-pin the bag.

Pinning increases warmth but does absolutely nothing for the bulk or weight of the bag. The solution is to cut off the excess fabric, bind the raw edges with seam tape, and sew along the marked line -- a ten minute job for a tent-and-awning maker or shoe repair man.

Next, install a 12-inch wide draft flap around the neck area of the bag to keep warmth in and cold out. Make the draft flap out of cotton flannel and sew it directly to the top of the bag as shown in Figure 12-6.

These simple alterations will reduce the weight of an average

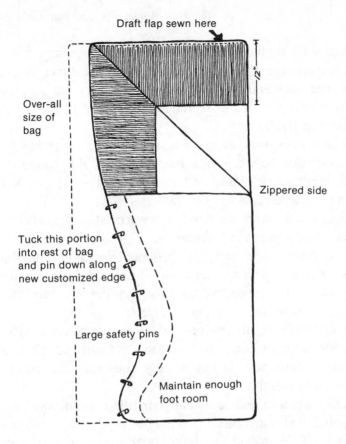

Figure 12-6   Customizing an Oversize, Overweight Sleeping Bag

"station wagon" bag by one-third or more, and will extend its temperature range by at least ten degrees.

TRAIL MATTRESSES

A good trail mattress should smooth out the lumps and insulate your body from the cold damp ground. It should also be lightweight, compact, and reliable.

When temperatures are much below fifty degrees, an air mattress is unsuitable. The air in an air mattress is continually moving from one tube to another, ever so slightly; if the ground is cold, this cold will be transmitted right to your bones. You will, in effect, be sleeping on a recirculating refrigerator. Down, especially, compresses to almost nothing, and to a lesser extent, so do Quallofil and Polarguard. This is less of a problem with old-style kapok or wool-filled sleeping bags, because the filler in these bags is so thick and uncompressible that an effective insulative layer is created between your back and the air mattress. The price you pay for this thermal barrier is weight and overall rolled size; hence the popularity of smaller and lighter bags.

For adequate warmth in early spring, you must have some kind of insulation between your back and the cold ground. Either open-cell urethane or closed-cell Ensolite, polyethylene, or EVA (ethyl-vinyl-acetate) foam is satisfactory.

One of the most comfortable, and warmest trail pads currently being manufactured is the "ThermaRest" -- a self-inflating foam-filled air mattress. Essentially, the product is nothing more than an open cell foam pad with a waterproof (and airtight) cover and brass inflation valve. I've used two models very heavily over the past ten years and have had only one failure.

For the ultimate in comfort and insulation, team a nylon air mattress with a quarter-inch thick closed cell foam pad. This combo weighs about four pounds but is very compact. The comfort is worth the extra weight.

It's important to realize that any air-filled product will eventually fail, so if cost *is* an object, you may want to consider something more foolproof. Whatever you buy, cover it with breathable cotton or cotton-polyester. Nylon covers are hot and sticky against the skin -- use one in warm weather and you'll wake up in the morning with a drenched back. And, nylon-covered pads slide out from under your sleeping bag and wander all over the tent floor!

If you're on a budget buy a piece of carpet padding about 62 inches long and 20 inches wide. Carpet padding works great as a mattress and is much less expensive than store-bought pads. Additionally, carpet pads are ideal if you are canoeing with toddlers who wet their sleeping gear every night. In the morning you need only rinse the wet pad in clean water and hang it in the sun to dry. Although nylon-covered pads seem attractive for toddlers, in practice they don't work well. The younsters roll, slide, and squirm right off them. An uncovered pad produces more friction and keeps children moderately immobile.

STUFF SACKS

The best way to organize items is to place them in color-coded waterproof, nylon stuff sacks. Make a variety of different size stuff sacks and install drawstrings to tie them shut.

Traditionally, I place all my personal clothing for a canoe trip into a lobster-red nylon sack about 10 inches wide by 20 inches long. I make waterproof sacks for the repair kit, cook set, first-aid kit, rain gear, and foodstuffs like Bisquick and pancake mix (food sacks are first lined with plastic Zip-Lock bags).

When placed inside paired waterproof liners in a Duluth pack, nylon stuff sacks provide additional waterproofing insurance. They are also convenient for keeping your things dry while packing or unpacking in a rain. In early spring, waterproof stuff sacks are indispensable.

COOKING GEAR

See Chapter 15, "The Menu" for a discussion of essential cooking gear.

STOVES

For most kinds of canoe-camping a stove is a necessity. Scrounging for wood on a denuded, over-used campsite is not conducive to having a good time, and neither is the inconvenience of cooking in the rain. Fire bans, too, can be a problem. You never know when the forest service will disallow fires for reasons of low humidity and inadequate rainfall. Although the traditional campfire has not yet been abolished in most wilderness areas, it is disappearing. There simply isn't enough wood available to support the number of campers who want to build fires. Then, too, in many locales all land adjacent to rivers is privately owned, and fire building is strictly prohibited.

If you are on a limited budget and must choose between a camp stove and an axe and saw, choose the stove. The cost will be about the same -- not to mention the labor you will save by not chopping down the forest.

Gasoline Stoves

When selecting a stove, remember that canoeing is not backpacking. You can afford to carry a bigger, more powerful, and more reliable stove than a packpacker. For the past 15 years I have been using an Optimus 111B gasoline stove. This one-burner, pump-equipped "blow torch" weighs 3½ pounds, is extremely rugged, and absolutely reliable under virtually any conditions. The stove is also quite economical to operate. I used the 111B exclusively on a twenty-one-day trip to James Bay in 1974 (I built a fire only twice). I prepared food for six people, made popcorn, and heated dishwater -- and used only two gallons of gas on the entire trip.

I am also very fond of the tiny Svea-Optimus (Primus) stoves, which are commonly sold in backpacking shops. These stoves are quite adequate for canoeing and they put out good heat. But they lack a really stable pot support, are temperamental, and not very wind-proof. Nevertheless, any one of these stoves is a good invest-ment and will give you years of good service.

Starting a small Svea or Optimus stove can be a problem because no pump is provided to generate pressure (an optional minipump is available at extra cost). The lighting instructions fur-nished with this type of stove tell you to cup the tank in your hands, warming it slightly, to provide sufficient pressure for starting. An easier way is to prime the stove with an eye dropper. Just suck some gas out of the tank with the dropper and squirt it below the burner plate. Cap the stove tightly, light the gas, and stand back. When the flame is almost burned out, turn up the heat.

For serious wilderness trips I always carry a small Svea stove in addition to my 111B. Although I seldom use the Svea, it's good to have a second burner -- just in case the infallible Optimus 111B proves fallible!

The best way to carry gas is in liter-size (1 liter equals 1.06 quarts) SIGG aluminum bottles. These bottles, which tend to be rather expensive, are available at almost every camping shop. A cheaper solution is to use the heavyduty plastic gallon jugs designed especially for gasoline. These jugs are absolutely leak-proof, almost indestructible, and cost only a few dollars. I have used these con-tainers on dozens of trips with teenagers and they are still in fine shape. Any product which hangs together in the hands of fourteen-year-olds is to be highly recommended.

I generally allow two liters of gas per week for a party of four to six people (not including the original stove-tank filling). This is plenty of gas if you don't waste it by running your stove indiscrimi-nately.

Butane Stoves

In recent years a number of simple-to-operate butane gas stoves have appeared on the market. These stoves require no pumping, no priming, and no pouring of gas. Just turn the adjuster knob and light. Unfortunately, butane stoves don't put out much heat, and most work poorly unless they are well shielded from the wind. The heating efficiency of bottled butane is directly related to the outside temperature -- the warmer the temperature, the greater the gas pressure, and the better the stove performs. If the temperature drops much below freezing, the butane will liquify and the stove won't start. Then there is the problem of what to do with the spent gas containers. Obviously you can't leave them lying all over the woods, and you can't bury them, so the only solution is to pack them out. On a long trip you may have to carry up to a dozen fuel cylinders, which is certainly less convenient than a single gallon can of gasoline.

You won't find experienced wilderness canoeists using butane stoves. They're okay for two- or 3-day local trips, but stick with gasoline or kerosine for serious ventures.

Kerosine Stoves

Kerosine stoves are very efficient and economical to operate. They are also safe to use, mainly because kerosine is less volatile than gas. Unfortunately, kerosine stoves cannot be started unless they are first primed with alcohol or gasoline, and they don't burn as hot as comparable gas models.

Sterno and Alcohol Stoves

These are good for keeping food warm. Avoid them for serious cooking -- three or four candles work about as well.

A final thought regarding stoves. Keep one-burner models in a light cotton or nylon stuff sack when not in use. This will keep lint and dust out of the burner parts and will protect the stove from dents and scratches. If your stove has a pump, be sure to include some oil in your repair kit to lubricate the leather pump washer.

CUTLERY

KNIVES

For daytripping, any jack-knife will do, but for more adventure-some canoeing you'll want a blade that's long enough to produce kindling, slice lunch meat, and reach to the bottom of the peanut-butter bottle for the last scrapings.

Basically, I dislike sheath knives on canoe trips. Granted, they look woodsy, but they are uncomfortable to wear in a canoe; the knife handle gets caught in your life jacket and the tip of the sheath catches on the seat. If you upset in rapids and the leather sheath gets wet, you'll feel like you're carrying a slab of bacon on your hip. Besides, sheathing a knife in wet leather is just asking for trouble.

Most of the time, I carry my favorite folding knife -- a hefty Puma Plainsman (4-inch blade) in a special snap pocket sewn into my field pants. But sometimes I disregard my own advice and wear my old fixed-blade Gerber shorty (4½-inch blade) in a heavyduty sheath on my hip. The Gerber is handy when I'm guiding groups and need to slice large amounts of meat and cheese. I also prefer the sheath knife when I'm paddling my solo canoe with its fabric cover attached. The Gerber is ''there'' when I need it if ever I upset in a rapid, become trapped in the cover, and have to cut my way free -- an unlikely possibility, but one that's real enough to cause concern.

If you plan to catch fish, include a fillet knife with your equipment. Don't wear the knife on your hip; rather store it in your pack for the ultimate in safety.

AXE AND SAW

Axes are still necessary on canoe trips, even though the tree-felling, cabin-building days are over. You need an axe for splitting kindling, driving stubborn tent stakes, setting rivets in torn pack straps, and repairing bent aluminum canoes. But you *don't* need a big axe. Many of our nation's most able woodsmen -- Daniel Boone, Davy Crockett and Jim Bridger -- depended entirely on a not-very-efficient tomahawk for all their camping chores. If you saw your wood into 10-inch lengths, you will have no trouble splitting them with a good hand axe.*

Perhaps more useful than a hand axe in the lowlands of the far north is a Swedish Brush Axe (Woodsman's Pal). This interesting tool combines the power of a hatchet with the blade of a machete. There is even a brush hook at one end. Where a good deal of overgrown vegetation must be cleared along portage trails, this or a machete will be useful.

Whatever edged tool you select, keep it well sheathed when not in use. Most sheaths that come with cutlery are much too thin. To make a knife or axe sheath, obtain some heavy sole leather and soak it in water for ten minutes or until it is flexible. While the leather is wet, mold and cut it to the shape of the tool (you should make a paper pattern first). When the leather is moderately dry, glue the sheath together with contact cement. Seal the protective edges of the sheath with hammer or pop rivets; or, if you prefer, your shoemaker can sew the sheath for you for a dollar or two.

WHETSTONE

You can't put a good edge on a knife with the stones commonly sold in hardware stores. For an adequate job only an Arkansas or genuine "diamond" stone will do. I like my knives razor-sharp, so I carry both types, plus a bottle of special honing oil. You don't need all this, but a good whetstone of some sort is a necessity.

Incidently, the small butcher's steels commonly available are fine for touching up a knife's edge. They cannot, however, be used for sharpening, as they don't really remove steel; they just realign the microscopic teeth on a knife's edge. Only a stone possesses the abrasive properties necessary to remove metal, and for this reason should not be omitted in favor of a steel.

SHOVEL

An ultra-light shovel of some sort is handy on canoe trips. The most compact type consists of a foot long piece of aluminum tube with one end smashed flat.

---

*See Chapter 10, "Tripping with Tots and Teens" for the recommended procedures for using the hand-axe.

WATER JUG

On most canoe trips, you'll need some sort of container to carry water. For trips without portages, rigid gallon jugs work best, but for touring the backcountry, you'll want something more compact.

For years, I carried a folding plastic water jug with mixed results. Granted, it was light and handy, but it developed pin holes after a single trip. Each season I bought a new one. Then one day, I bought a five liter box of Italian Swiss Colony wine and discovered the tough mylar-coated plastic liner inside. Now, I simply sew a ring of one inch wide nylon webbing around the empty wine jug liner (there's plenty of seam allowance) and leave a loop for a handle. My wine-jug water bag is incredibly strong; it lays flat on a rock or hangs securely from a tree branch; it fills and dispenses easily, and it doubles as an air pillow. I've used the same wine bag for two years now and it's just beginning to show wear. Perhaps this spring it will again be "necessary" to imbibe some fine wine in order to update my camping gear.

FOOTWEAR

Canoeists are not in complete agreement as to the most suitable footwear for canoe trips. There is, however, universal agreement among seasoned trippers that leather boots should be avoided. For casual outings and most whitewater canoeing, canvas sneakers are almost universally used. These inexpensive shoes provide good protection, are very light and easy to swim in, and dry quickly. But for serious tripping you should choose from the following:

1. Rubber boots with steel shanks and ten- to twelve-inch-high tops -- preferred mostly by arctic travelers, who often wade icy rivers.

2. Rubber-bottom-leather-top shoe-pacs of the L.L. Bean type -- popular with canoeists who want more support and comfort than that provided by all-rubber boots.

3. Vietnam (Jungle) boots -- liked by guides in the rocky Quetico-Superior country of Minnesota and Canada. These canvas-top-leather-bottom boots have heavy-lugged soles, steel shanks, and breathable mesh liner. Since jungle boots were designed for stomping through rice paddies in Vietnam, they are well adapted

to the wet, swampy conditions often encountered on a canoe trip. Once they are wet, Vietnam boots dry quickly -- generally within an hour, in warm weather. Because their ten-inch-high tops offer good protection from leeches and other pests, these boots are a good choice for Georgia and Florida swamp trips. Vietnam boots are very inexpensive and extremely rugged. Virtually every military surplus store carries a good supply of them.

After years of experimenting, I am won over completely to the L.L. Bean shoe-pac. These boots can be had with tops up to sixteen inches high (I prefer 8-inch tops) and with light, medium, or heavyweight bottoms. I have found that pacs with mediumweight bottoms are very adequate, even though they look and feel as if they won't take much abuse. I carry 2 pairs of leather insoles for my pacs. If one pair of insoles gets wet, I merely remove them from the rubber boot bottoms and install a dry pair.

For wilderness canoeing you need an extra pair of boots or shoes. A pair of sneakers for wading or in-camp use is fine, and so is a pair of comfortable leather moccasins. I prefer two pairs of shoe-pacs; a mediumweight pair for general use, and a very supple, lightweight pair for relaxing.

PERSONAL CLOTHING

For one- or 2-day trips, bring a complete change of clothes. For outings longer than two days, add two changes of underwear and three or four pairs of socks. Be sure to take a mediumweight wool jac-shirt or knitted wool sweater and a cotton or nylon windbreaker. There is no need to take additional clothing. Canoe-country temperatures seldom go much below freezing and you can always put on your extra clothes if you get cold.

Regardless of the clothing you select, it should be unrestrictive to allow freedom for paddling. Shirts and jackets should be comfortable to wear under a life jacket. For this reason, bulky down and fiberfill jackets are not recommended. Jacket hoods too, can be a nuisance; in a wind they may blow about your face and obscure your vision. Your canoeing wardrobe should consist almost exclusively of wool or acrylics for warmth and quick-drying nylon for wind and water protection. Cotton is acceptable only for wind parkas or for use in very warm weather. You can find good buys on wool garments, cotton ski parkas, army field jackets (the forerunner of modern mountain parkas), fatigues, and field pants at military surplus stores.

LONG JOHNS

Long johns are unnecessary for canoe trips in most of the lower states, but are essential for trips into Canada or Alaska or for any April, May, or early June trips in the far northern states. For years, the premium fabric was wool, and even today, many canoeists (including myself) still prefer it. Now, there's polypropylene, the rage in cross-country ski wear. This unique *plastic* fabric is non-scratchy, non-allergenic, inexpensive, and it doesn't absorb water. Not a drop! Capsize in an icy rapid and it'll be dry within minutes after you. Perspiration? No sweat! Body moisture passes through the fabric to your outer clothing leaving you warm, dry, and in command.

Miracle fabric? Perhaps. But there are problems: First, polypropylene holds body odors and so must be washed frequently -- not always easy on a long trip. And, its effectiveness diminishes as it accrues dirt -- another reason to keep it clean. It is also instantly dissolved by certain solvents, such as those contained in insect repellents. You'll definitely want to check out your longjohns if your bottle of bug dope ruptures in your pocket! A friend of mine experienced this problem on an arctic trip. The repellent ate away a six-inch swatch of underwear in a most embarrassing place.

As to longevity, there's no contest. Good wool -- or nylon-reinforced wool will outlive polypropylene by a wide margin -- a factor to consider if you're very budget conscious and use your gear a lot.

Nonetheless, polypropylene has rightfully earned its place on the canoe tripping scene. It is versatile and reliable, and compact enough to carry along for "emergencies" on all your trips.

A seldom-mentioned virtue of long johns is their ability to almost completely eliminate black fly bites (nothing *completely* eliminates them). These pesky insects, so common in the far north, have an uncanny ability to find the smallest patch of unprotected skin. The solution is to cover up completely, and long johns help considerably. Many old-time woodsmen carry rubber bands and secure their pants legs at the ankles to prevent the tiny flies from crawling up their legs and biting. Rubber-banded trousers do reduce black fly bites, but tight-fitting long johns help even more.

The best rain gear is a two-piece coated nylon suit. Ponchos and below-the-knee rain shirts are easy to put on and take off, and are well ventilated, but they are dangerous in a canoe, for in the event of an upset, they make swimming difficult. While a rain suit is more bother than over-the-head rain clothes, it is much safer.

Fabrics: There are those that work and those that don't. And the difference between the two is not necessarily a function of price. In fact, some of the best rain gear costs much less than some of the worst!

If you want a reliable, inexpensive rain suit, check out the ones at industrial supply stores -- the same places where construction workers shop. The new industrial rain suits are much lighter than those manufactured a decade ago and are constructed of fabrics similar, and often identical to, those used on the best foul weather suits. But because there are no pockets, form-fitted hoods, Velcro wrist tabs, and other niceties, they cost much less.

Most camping stores carry a wide selection of rainwear, but the "el cheapo" polyurethane-coated outfits are usually the best buy -- that is, if you're willing to seal the seams yourself with the special glue provided.

At the far end of the cost spectrum are PVC and neoprene-coated foul weather sailing suits that absolutely, positively won't let you down no matter how bad it rains. And these are worth every penny if you need them and can afford them.

Gore-Tex: Gore-Tex has achieved enormous popularity in the decade or so that it has been available. The secret is in the micro-thin Teflon coating which, purportedly, makes the fabric to which it is applied both waterproof *and* breathable. Everything from running suits to mitten shells have been constructed of Gore-Tex, and new ideas for use of this product emerge almost daily. In fact, Gore-Tex gear is so popular that it is almost impossible to find a camping shop that doesn't carry it!

Unfortunately, my own experience with Gore-Tex has not been very satisfactory. I own and use three expensive jackets of varying vintage made by two different manufacturers. They are wonderful wind garments -- excellent for cross-country skiing, and they perform superbly as spray jackets for paddling whitewater. But they all leak in heavy rains. And so do the majority owned by friends and acquaintances. For this reason, I cannot recommend Gore-Tex for canoeing in areas where long hard rains are common.

Buy what you can afford, but don't waste your money on frills you don't need. And get your outfit big enough to fit over baggy trousers and a foam-filled life vest. Rains are frequently sporadic in the canoe country; stripping off a life jacket every time you want to put on or take off your rain gear is a hassle.

Incidentally, some rain trousers are equipped with snaps or Velcro at the ankle. Avoid these closures, as they severely restrict ventilation.

EQUIPMENT LIST FOR TWO PERSONS

FOR A TRIP OF ONE WEEK OR MORE

GROUP EQUIPMENT

Tent (preferably with self-supporting framework)
Plastic ground cloth
10 x 10 foot (or larger) coated nylon rain-fly
3 Duluth packs (#3 size) or 2 Duluth packs and 1 pack basket or "Wanigan" box.
Waterproof liners for Duluth packs
100 feet of ¼ inch nylon rope (two 50-foot coils)
100 feet of nylon parachute cord
1 all-steel hand axe
1 compact folding saw
Repair and miscellaneous kit:
> 1 small pliers wth wire cutter, 1 roll fine copper wire, 1 roll silver duct tape, needles, thread, instant epoxy, 12-inch square of fiber-glass cloth for canoe or paddle patching, 6 hammer-driven rivets, 2 aluminum carabiners, 1 nylon pulley, small file for sharpening axe, soft Arkansas stone, oil, 3-inch square of scrap canvas for repair, 2-inch square of heavy leather for repair, sharp sewing awl, safety pins, sandpaper

6 heavy-duty rubber ropes with steel hooks attached
Large sponge for bailing

Thermos
Fillet knife
Cook kit and oven
Graduated plastic shaker (2 quart)
Folding plastic water jug or nylon water bag
Biodegradable soap and abrasive pad for dishwashing
Stove and gasoline
Matches: carry 3 separate supplies of wooden stick matches, each in a screw-cap plastic jar. Place each supply in a different pack.
4 or more candles
Folding candle lantern (nice, but not essential).
First-aid kit* in waterproof box (minimal, unsuitable for expeditions):
> Band-Aids, butterfly strips, Telfa pads, 2-inch wide roller gauze, adhesive tape, antiseptic soap swabs, Bacitracin ointment, tweezers, scissors, antacid tablets, aspirin, toothache medicine, Chapstick, Moleskin for blisters, Compazine (5 mg. tablets) for nausea or vomiting, thermometer, water purification tablets, poison ivy cream, ammonia inhalant, needle for removing splinters, first-aid manual

INDIVIDUAL EQUIPMENT

Life jacket (vest type)
Two paddles
Sleeping bag and foam pad
2 pairs of military fatigues or field pants (choose wool pants in spring and fall)
Cotton webbed belt (dries faster than leather when wet)
2 lightweight, long-sleeved wool shirts
1 medium-weight wool jac-shirt, or medium-weight knitted wool sweater
1 cotton T-shirt
1 pair wool or polypropylene long johns (spring and fall trips)
4 pairs wool socks (at least 75% wool content)
1 light nylon wind parka (not waterproof)

*If you want an easy-to-follow description of first-aid equipment and its use, see Dr. William Forgey's excellent book, WILDERNESS MEDICINE, published by ICS Books, Inc.

1 waterproof 2-piece rain suit
1 brimmed hat or cap for sun; 1 wool stocking cap for chilly days
Souwester hat for rain (optional)
Extra glasses if you wear them
Sunglasses
Security strap for glasses
3 changes of underwear
1 towel (old baby diaper is ideal)
2 red bandannas
1 pair rubber-bottom boots
1 pair sneakers, moccasins, or other soft footwear for camp use
1 pair lightweight leather gloves (for arctic trips use leather-faced
     wool or plastic-coated cotton gloves)
1 flashlight, extra bulb and batteries
Heavy-duty pocket knife
Toiletries (include hand lotion for chapped hands)
Compass (orienteering style)
Map set in waterproof case
Butane lighter (handy for relighting stoves, candles, etc; saves
     matches)
Insect repellent -- at least 2 bottles. (Hint: repackaging repellent in
     empty roll-on deodorant containers enables you to apply just
     the right amount of repellent in just the right places, with only
     one hand.)
Wristwatch
Insect head net; essential for trips into northern Canada, otherwise
     unnecessary.

OPTIONAL AND INTERESTING ITEMS

Fire ribbon -- a chemical for emergency fire-starting. At most camp
     shops.
Red smoke bombs, mirror, for emergency signaling.
Air splints for broken limbs (for isolated trips).
Ultralight mountaineering hammock (rolls to fist size, weighs about
     three ounces -- for general relaxing and can be used to make
     a stretcher.
Small pocket thermometer (to settle temperature arguments).

Small barometer (for amateur weather forecasters).

Hypothermia thermometer (low-reading thermometer to monitor hypothermia).

If money is no object, you can simply buy state-of-the-art neoprene or PVC-coated packsacks that are guaranteed not to leak -- at least when new. And you can patch, glue, and ultimately replace them after a few dozen mean portages. That's because no matter how substantial a pack fabric is, it will ultimately succumb to the effects of abrasion. For example, how long will the best PVC-coated pack last when it's loaded with 60 pounds of gear and drug solidly across sharp granite? Or slammed hard onto a pebble beach? These are the harsh realities of wilderness canoe travel.

The inner fabric of a packsack is also subject to considerable abrasion. Every time you stuff a pair of sneakers, hand-axe, or sleeping bag deep inside the pack, you rub off a micro-thin layer of its waterproof coating. Eventually, the bag will leak and you'll need to repair it. Far better to devise a waterproof system that can be maintained at low cost -- one which will keep out water *and* provide the abrasion protection you need.

Key to the system is to sandwich inexpensive plastic bags between layers of abrasion-resistant material.

For example, to waterproof your sleeping bag: First, stuff the bag into its nylon sack (which need not be watertight), then set the sack *inside* a four-mil thick plastic bag. Pleat and twist the end of the bag, fold it over, and secure it with a loop of shock-cord. Then, place this unit into an oversize nylon sack (again, which need not be waterproof). Note that the delicate plastic liner -- which is the only real water barrier -- is protected from abrasion on *both* sides!

If you line your nylon stuff sack with a plastic bag *then* stuff your sleeping bag into it as advised by some authorities, you'll abrade and eventually tear the plastic liner. The method I've suggested creates a waterproof seal *and* eliminates the damage caused by the most careful stuffing.

To make a Duluth pack (or other "soft" pack) completely watertight, you'll need two *36 inch by 48 inch, six-mil thick*, plastic bags.* Don't use "leaf and lawn" size plastic bags -- indeed anything you can buy at the supermarket. Even the largest and strongest (three-mil) grocery bags are too small and weak.

Nest *two* of these six-mil thick bags inside each Duluth pack. The inner bag may be well worn -- even have some pin holes -- as it functions merely as an *interior* abrasion liner for the *absolutely watertight* plastic bag outside.

PACKING OUT

For a trip of one week, you and your partner will need three #3 Duluth packs, or two Duluth packs and a 3-peck (18-inch high) pack basket. Canoe partners should pack together as follows:
Duluth Pack #1

Place the two "water-proofed" sleeping bags in the bottom of the Duluth pack. Set your foam pads or air mattresses on top and complete the package with one or two clothes bags (each canoeist should have his or her own clothes bag. This is a 10 x 20 inch waterproof stuff sack into which all your clothes and personal gear is placed).

When the pack is completely filled with gear, exhaust the air (give it a big hug!) then pleat and roll the inner abrasion liner down tight. Atop this place your tent or rain tarp. This isolates items which may be damp or wet from the dry contents of the pack below. It also "barricades" the mouth of the reasonably watertight abrasion liner.

Next, twist, fold over, and secure the *waterproof* plastic outer bag with a loop of shock-cord or a band cut from an innertube.

You now have a completely watertight pack -- one which will withstand the abrasion of stuffing and dragging. Note that the sleeping bag -- your most important item -- has been placed at the *bottom* of the pack. Here's why:

To reach the sleeping bag, water must first penetrate the mouth of the outer waterproof sack (unlikely, if you've sealed it properly). That which does get in must bypass the tent or tarp below, then trickle through the folds of the abrasion liner and work down through nearly two feet of gear to the "sandwiched" sleeping bag.

*Order these tough plastic bags from Indiana Camp Supply, Inc., P.O. Box 344, Pittsboro, Indiana 46167. At this writing they cost three dollars apiece.

As you can see, there's no reason why you should *ever* get your sleeping bag wet on a canoe trip!

The advantage of Duluth packs and twin six-mil liners over more sophisticated set-ups is long term reliability, low cost, and easy maintenance. With judicious use of duct tape, the plastic bags will last for years.

Duluth Pack #2

Place the nylon bags containing your food in this pack. Organize soft items so they won't gouge your back. If you select dehydrated and freeze-dried foods, a two-week supply for two people will take up about half the pack. The remaining space can be filled with sundries. Everything should be placed in nylon stuff sacks -- more for utility than protection from the rapids. Items which *must* be kept dry are "sandwich-bagged" in the same manner as the sleeping bag.

Seal the waterproof liners as explained, place your rain gear on top, and cinch down the closing flap.

The Pack Basket

Place your cook kit, in its protective stuff sack, in the bottom of the pack basket. Atop this set your stove and gasoline, thermos, repair and first-aid kits, fishing reel and lures, hand-axe, and other items which are breakable or might be uncomfortable in a "soft" pack. Seal the waterproof liner and cinch down the pack flap.

PACKING THE CANOE

Place the food pack directly behind the yoke, centered in the canoe. This is your heaviest load and you want it perfectly balanced. Set your pack basket on the other side of the yoke and put your light clothes pack next to the pack on the side of the lightest paddler. This should provide sufficient weight to level the canoe. If a fourth pack is carried, as on extended trips, packs can be placed sideways (parallel to the gunwales) in the canoe. The important thing is to have a low, well-balanced load, with the major portion of the weight as close to the middle of the canoe as possible.

Finish loading by installing your shock-corded security system as explained in Chapter 3. If you capsize, your gear will be locked tightly in place and the canoe will float high. Figure 3-2 shows the procedure.

You can pay a great deal of money for sophisticated waterproof bags and fancy packs of all types. However, for reliability and versatility I heartily recommend this packing system.

OVER THE PORTAGE AND THROUGH THE WOODS

The standard procedure for portaging is as follows: Each person takes a pack and a paddle and strikes out across the portage. While walking, both canoeists look for shortcuts back to the river or lake ahead as well as for obstacles that will have to be circuited when the canoe is brought over the trail. Packs are dropped at the end of the portage, and the pair returns. On the second trip one person carries the canoe and the other person takes the last pack and any remaining items. Usually the person with the pack leads, so that when the canoe-carrier becomes tired he or she can call to the person ahead to look for a suitable stopping place -- like an out-jutting tree limb where the bow of the canoe can be set. When such a limb is found, the canoe-carrier sets the bow in place and steps from beneath the yoke to rest. This procedure requires much less energy than setting a canoe on the ground and later lifting it to the shoulders.

In heavily traveled wilderness areas wooden rests are often provided to prevent people from jamming canoe ends into tree branches. Although such rests spoil the primitive nature of the portage, they are essential to minimize environmental damage to foliage. In parklike areas where portages are known to be clear and in good condition, the canoe is sometimes carried over the trail first -- primarily because it is the heaviest load and requires the greatest expenditure of energy.

13.
Weathering the Storm

I pitched the old Eureka Timberline tent on a gentle knoll amidst a clump of birch trees. There was a much better spot about twenty feet away -- a well worn site where hundreds of tents had stood before. But the barren place was in a slight depression that was devoid of ground cover -- a good rain could mean a flooded tent. Besides, a long dead spruce tree, its limbs poised menacingly overhead, stood nearby waiting patiently for the first big wind to send it crashing down.

At about seven p.m. it began. Slowly at first, with a gentle rain that lasted an hour. Then the storm intensified; soon rain fell in thick sheets, driven by hurricane force winds of sixty miles an hour!

For awhile, I just stood complacently in the pre-storm drizzle and watched the chilling blackness expand across the sky. Then methodically, I began to make the necessary adjustments.

First, I pulled a coil of parachute cord from my pack and strung two taut guylines from each tent peak to trees nearby (The Eureka Timberline is self-supporting and theoretically does not need to be guyed). Then I weighted each stake with heavy rocks which I drug from the stream bed below.

Within minutes, it struck. The big Eureka shook and groaned as the initial swish of the wind tore at her. But she stood fast.

The heaviest part of the storm passed quickly, but a steady forty to fifty mile per hour wind continued unrelentlessly throughout the night.

We awoke the next morning to the scene of disaster. Trees were down everywhere. The dead spruce lay about where I predicted. And every depression was overflowing with water. Smugly, my wife and I exchanged glances. We'd weathered the storm!

Admittedly, storm-proofing a camp requires luck as well as skill. Really, what would I have done if that clump of birch hadn't been there? Or if rocks or brush prohibited placing the tent on high ground?

It's unrealistic to expect any woodland tent to withstand sustained winds of over forty miles per hour, regardless of how you pitch it. But rain is another matter. A sophisticated expedition tent that's pitched badly or set in the wrong spot is sure to admit water, while a simple forest tent that's rigged right won't. In the end, your skills at coping with the weather are much more important than your gear.

KNOW THE SHORTCOMINGS OF YOUR TENT AND CORRECT THEM

Blowing rain or ground water is most likely to enter a tent through ground level or exposed perimeter seams. Obviously, all tent seams should be waterproofed -- either with a special seam glue or liquid compound. (I prefer "Thomspon's Water Seal," a brush-on chemical formulated for waterproofing concrete floors. "TWS" is flexible and stable in all temperatures and is available at most hardware stores. The product is also useful for waterproofing maps and clothing.) And of course, no tent floor will remain impervious to water forever. The solution is to *always* use a plastic ground sheet *inside* the tent. Water which wicks through the floor seams or fabric will then be trapped beneath the ground cloth and you'll sleep dry.

Some "experts" suggest that you place the groundcloth under the floor to save the floor material from abrasion and punctures. You'll really have a sponge party if you follow this advice, for ground water will become trapped between the plastic sheet and

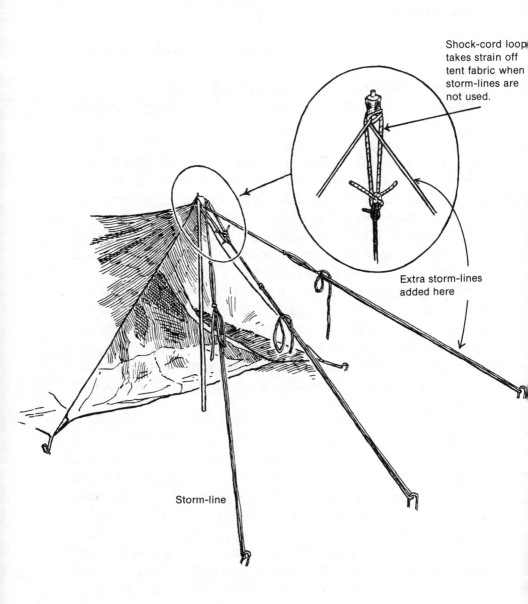

Shock-cord loop takes strain off tent fabric when storm-lines are not used.

Extra storm-lines added here

Storm-line

Figure 13-1   Storm-proofing the tent.

floor and be pumped (the weight of your body creates a pressure differential) into the tent!

The use of an *interior* ground cloth is the best wet weather tip I can give you. And, it will also reduce the number of holes and abrasions in your tent floor.*

The best way to improve the wind-stability of any tent is to run *twin* guylines from *each* peak. Extend the lines outward at forty-five degree angles to the poles. Don't mess with the original tent guy. What you want is *three* lines emanating from each end of the tent. Whenever possible, attach guy and stake lines to an immovable object -- tree or boulder. Or, weight stakes with rocks or logs so they won't pull out when the ground softens from a rain.

Next, attach loops of three-eighths inch shock-cord to every stake and pole loop (the extra guys are added only during a storm, but the shock-cord loops should be a permanent part of your tent's anatomy). The elastic loops will take the wind stress normally reserved for the tent's fabric and stitching.

At home, take a hard look at your tent's design. Pitch it tightly on level ground and check out the lay of the fabric. If you have an inexpensive tent there'll probably be some sag along the roof line. You can string out the ridge so it doesn't luff, but only at the expense of the base. If the fly sags along its border -- looks as if it needs more stake loops to support it, it probably does. Get out your sewing machine and add them -- as many as necessary to make the fabric drum tight and wrinkle-free. Use the storm loops like you'd use reef lines on a sailboat -- only in rough weather emergencies.

While you're handy with the needle and thread, reinforce questionable stitching, especially at the corners and peak of the tent. Afterwards, carefully waterproof all the seams you've sewn!

THE RAIN-FLY

Waterproofing and windproofing your tent is only half the solution to weathering a storm. The other part is providing a dry place to cook and relax. Customize your nylon rain tarp by sewing five equally spaced nylon loops to one side (Figure 13-2). These loops provide anchor points for rigging cords and allow you to

---

*If you don't believe this, begin a trip with a new plastic groundsheet in your tent. At trip's end, count the number of holes in it -- holes which would otherwise have been in your tent floor!

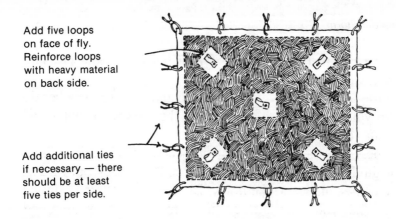

Add five loops
on face of fly.
Reinforce loops
with heavy material
on back side.

Add additional ties
if necessary — there
should be at least
five ties per side.

Figure 13-2   Customizing the Rain Tarp: Add ties to all the grommets and sew five equally spaced loops to the face. This will allow you to pitch the tarp in a variety of geometric configurations.

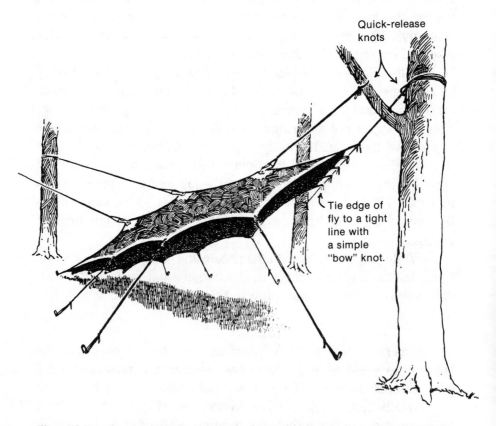

Quick-release
knots

Tie edge of
fly to a tight
line with
a simple
"bow" knot.

Figure 13-3   A customized rain tarp can be rigged in less than three minutes and will withstand 30 mile per hour winds.

pitch the tarp in a variety of geometric configurations. It's almost impossible to rig a tarp tightly if it doesn't have cord loops on its face. Be sure to reinforce all the loops with a backing of strong fabric. And remember to seal all the seams you sew.

Rigging procedure:

You can pitch a rain-fly in an unlimited number of geometric configurations. There are so many possible patterns that most people don't know how to rig a single wind-stable design quickly. When you see storm clouds moving in, feel the temperature drop, and suddenly everything becomes still, you generally have only a few minutes to get some rain-cover over your gear. The majority of campers are pretty haphazard about fly pitching, and as a result the first good wind that comes along rips the corner grommets right out of the fly. Consequently, some canoeists believe that tarps should never be set up in a wind-driven rain. Unfortunately, this is when you need their protection most.

After years of experimenting, I've come to prefer this simple, strong, and efficient method of rigging (Figure 13-3).

MATERIALS

A fly customized like the one shown in Figure 13-2
50 feet of nylon rope
6 lightweight aluminum tent stakes
2 trees, not over 30 feet apart

PROCEDURE

1. Locate 2 trees about 15-20 feet apart. String a drum-tight line between the trees about 5 feet off the ground. Use 2 half-hitches at one end of the rope and a power-cinch with a quick release knot at the other end (see Chapter 11 for a review of knots).

2. Take the pair of ties at one corner of your fly and wind one tie of the set around the rope in a clockwise direction and the other tie in a counterclockwise direction. Take at least 4 turns around the rope. Secure the ties with a simple overhand bow.

3. Pull the other corner of the open end of the fly tight along the rope and secure it with the ties, as in number 2 above. The tie

wrappings will provide sufficient tension to keep the corners of the tarp from slipping inward along the rope when the fly is buffeted by wind.

4. Secure all remaining ties to the rope with a simple overhand bow. (By securing the fly at several points along the length of its open end, rather than just at the corners, as is commonly done, you distribute the strain across a wide area, thus increasing the strength of the fly.)

5. Go to the back of the fly, pull it out tight, and stake.

6. Run the center cord over a tree limb or a rope strung just above and behind the fly. Snug up the center cord (use a power-cinch with a quick-release knot) to pull the center of the fly out. Add additional lines if necessary.

7. Secure the sides of the fly with extra cord. Complete all knots with a quick-release loop. You now have a sturdy, rain-free shelter that won't flap in the wind. Total rigging time? Under three minutes!

Don't feel intimidated because you don't own the latest eye-popping super-shelter or state-of-the-art foul weather gear. If you're always warm, dry, and comfortable on the canoe trails, there's no reason to change your gear or your methods, despite the pressure of advertisers or my recommendations.

On the other hand, if bad weather prevents you from enjoying the day, then you'd best learn how to rig a snug camp!

14.
Wilderness
Navigation

The Fond du Lac River begins in the northwest corner of Saskatchewan at the far end of Wollaston Lake. It is described by Eric Morse (author of CANOE CANADA) as a "remote challenging river for expert whitewater canoeists." The Fond du Lac is all of that and more, though getting to the river is the harde t part of all.

First, there's the bone-jangling ride over the Missinnippi Tote Road -- 200 miles of fist-sized gravel that is guaranteed to fully depreciate the toughest vehicle. Then there's the 30 mile crossing of Wollaston Lake -- a sprawling piece of water with hundreds of islands and bays to confuse you. The Fond du Lac begins innocently in an obscure bay at the northwest corner of the lake. All you have to do is find it!

The trip sprang from an assignment for CANOE magazine -- one whose article deadline came just five days after our scheduled return. No way could I knock out a story that fast. I'd have to do some writing enroute and find a way to shorten our time on the river.

The solution was to hire a tow from Wollaston Lake lodge to the mouth of the Fond du Lac. That alone would save two days of paddling. The tow would cost us seventy Canadian dollars; but no matter, we'd come to run the river, not fight wind and waves.

We unloaded our gear at the Wollaston dock, packed the canoes, and tied them to the waiting motor boat. The sandy-haired man who was to guide us to the river seemed amiable enough: He was a college student from Toronto -- a cracker-jack fishing guide who purportedly "knew the lake blindfolded."

Within minutes we were waterborne, skimming northward at full throttle.

Casually, I looked at my map then nudged my friend beside me. "Look here, Darrell...this guy's going the wrong way, too far east. Whatcha think?"

"Aw c'mon, Cliff; he's the guide! Keep the faith, friend!"

"Yeah...okay."

With that I folded my map contentedly and simply watched the scenery pass. Ultimately, I heard a coughing sound that suggested we were out of gas. No problem; our guide shut down the twin Mercs and plugged in the auxiliary tank. Then he quietly drew forth a tiny Xeroxed copy of a 1:500,000 scale map of the area and squinted boldly at it.

"Hey, this guy's really a pro," I muttered to my friend. "Look at that map. Man, I'd need bifocals just to tell the water from the land!"

There was a long silence. Then came a sheepish grin and the words, "Any of you guys know where we are?"

I looked at Darrell and together we burst out laughing. Our guide was *lost*!

Reluctantly, I pulled out my detailed 1:50,000 scale map and stared intently at it. "I dunno," I replied, "but one thing's certain; we're too far east!"

After that, it was merely a matter of intensive map study and fancy compass work to determine our location. Within the hour we chugged confidently to the hidden bay which marked the Fond du Lac -- no thanks to our "expert" guide.

As this case illustrates, anyone can get confused on a complex waterway, even when it is "familiar turf." The wilderness has a delightful way of humbling the most confident of egos. The remedy is to carry a good map and compass and to become expert in their use.

"But I'm not a lake canoeist -- I only paddle rivers," you might say. All well and good. You still must be able to read and interpret a river map, and because of variability in water conditions, channel erosion, and the influence of man, interpretation of river guides and maps calls for a much higher degree of resourcefulness than you might imagine. Whether you canoe local rivers or wilderness waterways, you will feel more confident and secure if you understand the basic principles of direction finding.

EQUIPMENT

MAPS

Of foremost importance is the map. Except for going in a straight line, a compass is totally worthless without a map. Get the best topographic maps available; these can be purchased from a variety of sources (see Appendix A -- Map Sources). Cost, including postage, seldom runs over $3.00 a sheet. For advance trip planning it is best to write to the U.S. Geological Survey's map distribution office in your area (regional addresses are given in Appendix A). Request a free "Index to Topographic Maps." This index will tell you what maps are currently in print, in what scale, and the cost. If much of your travel will be on large, complex lakes, request the largest scale available. 1:24,000 scale maps are best for picking your way across mazelike lakes, although at this large scale you will need several of them. Smaller 1:50,000 scale maps are ideal for most wilderness canoe travel (the larger the denominator of the scale, the smaller the actual map scale). Usually, however, you can't afford to be so choosy. Large-scale maps are readily available for heavily traveled or civilized areas, while more remote sections of the continent may be available only in small scale. Avoid maps with scales smaller than 1:250,000 (1 inch = 4 miles). Such small-scale maps are useful to experts, but they don't inspire confidence in beginners.

When you have secured your maps, cut and glue (use rubber cement) the sections together so as to completely cover the area you wish to canoe. Although a large, single map is somewhat cumbersome, it is certainly less bother than several independent map sheets -- especially when you find yourself working on the edges of two adjacent sheets. Discard the map portions you don't need and you'll eliminate carrying a lot of unnecessary paper.

I prefer to coat non-waterproof maps with Thompson's Water Seal. A single light coat, applied with a foam varnish brush makes maps reasonably waterproof and allows you to write on them. Or if you prefer, you may want to cover them with clear contact paper to insure an absolutely waterproof seal. If you like more stiffness to your map, purchase some Chartex dry-mounting cloth for the backing from Forestry Suppliers, Inc., 205 West Rankin St., Jackson, Mississippi 39204. Forestry Suppliers has a number of navigational aids you might find useful. Write for their catalog.

MAP CASE

A map case is a must, whether maps are waterproof or not. Plastic map cases take a lot of abuse on canoe trips so get something sturdier than a Zip-Loc bag. If your canoe was properly outfitted with shock-cords as explained in Chapter 3, your map case can be secured by sliding it under a shock-corded thwart. When you encounter rapids, simply stuff the map into your nylon thwart bag for the ultimate in security.

THE COMPASS

Buy a decent compass. In fact, buy two, since one can be lost or broken. You don't have to spend a lot of money for a serviceable instrument unless you want sophisticated features like optical sights and a mechanical adjustment for declination (discussed in the sections which follow).

Floating Dial Compasses

These are the easiest to use. They have no dials to turn and you read the compass in the same plane as your objective. You merely point the instrument toward your destination and read the dial directly. There is nothing to set, and usually not even a cover to raise. If it is filled with liquid to slow the swing of the needle (damped), this model may be the fastest of all styles to use.

Cruiser Compasses

Cruiser compasses are almost identical to compasses used on surveyors' transits. Their basic design dates back many decades. Designed for use by professionals, cruisers come in solidly constructed aluminum cases and have long, free-swinging (undamped) needles. To use a cruiser, open the cover, hold the compass waist-high, and point the instrument at your objective. You read the dial where it is intersected by the north end of the magnetic needle (number graduations are reversed to permit reading the compass in this fashion). All cruisers have an internal means for offsetting local magnetic declination. Most compasses of this style are very heavy (8 ounces or so), cumbersome, and slow to use. Few are really waterproof, and none are usable at night. They are very expensive. Although quite accurate, there are better styles for the canoeist.

Fixed Dial Compasses

The stationary or fixed dial compass has for years been the traditional route-finding instrument of the wilderness traveler. The design of these instruments dates back hundreds of years. Best typified by the gumball machine variety, they are still manufactured because most people just don't know how to use any other kind. These models are fine for playing at navigation but should be avoided for any kind of serious route finding.

Lensatic and Prismatic Compasses

These are floating dial compasses with sophisticated sighting devices. Unfortunately, most are not very good. Expensive models work well and are by far the most accurate hand compasses in production. The cheapies (under twenty dollars) generally have poorly aligned sights, rickety mounting systems, or sufficient parallax to prevent accurate sightings. Moreover, the lack of versatility of these compasses is a drawback (see ''Orienteering Compasses'').

Orienteering Compasses

The most versatile and suitable compass style for the canoeist is the orienteering model. Orienteering compasses have built-in protractors which allow you to quickly and accurately compute direction and scale distance from a map without first orienting the map to north. This means you can define a *precise* direction (to the nearest degree) while sitting in your bobbing canoe. Additionally, the direction is physically set on the compass by turning a dial. There is nothing to remember and nothing to write down.

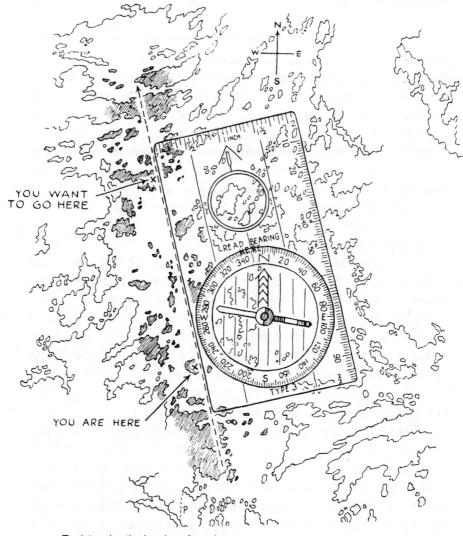

YOU WANT
TO GO HERE

READ BEARING
HERE

YOU ARE HERE

To determine the bearing of a point on your map:

1. Place the left or right edge of the compass over your position in line with your destination, shown in figure 14-1.

2. Hold the compass base steady and turn the needle housing until north on the *dial* points to north on the map (top of the map).

3. Read your bearing at the index (350 degrees in the illustration). Note that the magnetic needle *is not* used for this computation!

4. Now, remove the compass from the map and turn it (turn your body with the instrument) until the north end of the *magnetic needle* points to the north on the *dial*. You are now facing in a direction of 350 degrees. Simple, isn't it?

Figure 14-1   Orienteering Compasses have built-in protractors which allow you to quickly and accurately compute directions from a map without first orienting the map to north.

Since all orienteering models are liquid-damped, finding the direction of travel once it has been determined from the map can be done quickly -- generally within seven seconds. Orienteering compasses are very waterproof, light, compact, and unusually rugged. I once saw a jeep run over a Silva Ranger model. Although the cover was ruined, the compass was still usable for rough work. (When the instrument was returned to Silva for repairs a note of inquiry sent to the manufacturer was returned with the comment, "No charge -- Silva compasses are indestructible!") To determine the bearing of an object with an orienteering compass, point the compass at the object, and while holding the base steady, rotate the graduated housing until the north end of the magnetic needle points to *N* (North) on the dial. The direction you are facing, in degrees, is locked onto the compass dial and can be read at an index inscribed on the base. The compass can then be slipped back into your pocket for reference later. And you don't have to remember the direction that was set on the compass, either, since it will remain positioned on the dial until you turn the housing. To verify your direction with this style of compass, merely point the instrument away from your body and rotate your body and the compass until the north end of the magnetic needle points to *N* on the dial.

Since you don't have to read the numbers set on the dial, orienteering compasses are ideal for use at night or under conditions of rain or poor visibility.

(Hint: Strap a small wrist compass around a thwart or seat frame and you'll be able to check directions without fumbling for your pocket compass.)

Although all high-quality compasses come with adequate instructions for average use, you should have an in-depth understanding of basic navigational principles if you intend to use your compass for serious route finding. There are many excellent books available dealing solely with navigation that should be consulted before undertaking a wilderness trip of much significance. At the end of this chapter there is a practice map you can use to test your route-finding ability. If you can successfully complete the map exercise, you are ready to set out on a wilderness trip on a reasonably complex waterway.

FIRST, THE BASICS

The compass is graduated in degrees. There are 360 degrees in the compass rose. The cardinal directions (north, south, east, and west) are each 90 degrees apart. The northeast (NE) quadrant encompasses the direction from 0 to 90 degrees, the southeast (SE) quadrant from 90 to 180 degrees, and so on. Learn to think in quadrants. Before determining the precise direction you wish to travel, ask yourself, "In which quadrant am I traveling?" This will help eliminate the most common of compass errors -- the 180-degree error. For example, if your map tells you to go southwest and your compass points to 45 degrees (NE quadrant), you know something is wrong; you are facing 180 degrees in the wrong direction. It is not uncommon to transfer data from map to compass and make serious directional mistakes. A knowledge of your approximate direction of travel should be known *before* you get down to the specifics.

Using the map of Lost Lake on page 245 (Figure 14-6), assume you are at point A. You want to go just north of point H and take the portage trail to the South Arm of Maze Lake. A glance at the map tells you to begin by heading northwest until you hit the shoreline, then to follow it around until you pass Bays 1 and 2; then on into Bay 3 and straight to the portage. Very simple, right? Wrong! Look at the map scale. You won't be able to decipher islands from mainland or one bay from another. When you look out across a lake of this size and complexity you will see green as far as the eye can see. Physical features will blend with one another until the entire landscape is one of sameness. Because of wind and waves you will lose all sense of distance traveled. You can rely on your watch for a rough estimate, but it will be difficult for you to judge whether you have completed two miles or three. You can easily bypass Bay 3, or you can get turned around completely and become convinced that a channel between islands is a large bay, or vice versa. One of the greatest tragedies of twentieth-century canoeing occurred because of a map misinterpretation. In 1904 Leonidas Hubbard, Dillon Wallace, and George Elson attempted to penetrate the interior of an unexplored part of Labrador. "How vividly I saw it all again," said Wallace later on, "-- Hubbard resting on his paddle and then rising up for a better view, as he

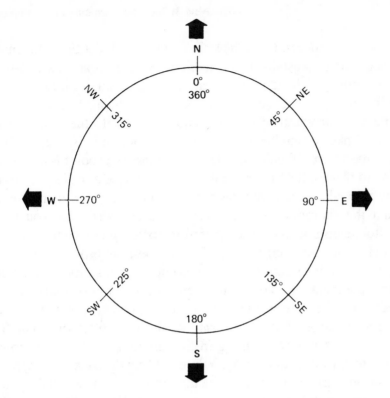

Figure 14-2   The Compass Rose:

said, 'Oh, that's just a bay and it isn't worthwhile to take the time to explore it. The river comes in here at the end of the lake. They all said it was at the end of the lake.' And we said, 'Yes, it is at the end of the lake; they all said so,' and went on.'' The Susan River they wrongly ascended was a dead end. With provisions gone and winter setting in, the expedition ended at Lake Michikamau, many miles from their destination. Hubbard, weakened by hunger and exhaustion, could not continue. He died on Sunday, October 18, 1904. His two companions, Elson and Wallace, retraced their fateful steps down the Susan Valley to civilization. We will never know why Hubbard, a man of experience, did not take the time to check his map and compass at such a critical point in his journey.

USING COMPASS AND MAP FOR
PRECISION DIRECTION FINDING

In order to keep track of where you are on a body of water of any size, you must know, within reason, your position at all times.

This means you can't just head in a general direction, you must proceed along an established direction, or bearing as it is called.

Assume you have begun a canoe trip at point *A* on Lost Lake (see the map of Lost Lake at the end of this chapter). You plan to paddle the full width of the lake and portage into the South Arm of Maze Lake, which lies just to the west. Horseshoe Island, you've heard, has an excellent campsite on its south end (point *B*), so you decide to make your first camp there. You choose to paddle straight to the campsite rather than take the longer, more confusing route around the shoreline to your west. To accomplish this you will need to determine the *exact* direction (bearing) in degrees from point *A* (your location) to point *B* (your destination).

You can use your orienteering compass or a simple protractor for this computation. To use an orienteering compass, place either the left or right edge of the compass base plate on point *A*. Place the forward edge of the *same side* of the base plate on point *B*. Your compass is now pointing in the direction you want to go -- from *A* to *B* (not from *B* to *A*). While holding the base plate tightly in position, turn the compass housing until north on the dial points to the top (north) of the map. Caution: Don't use the magnetic needle! Your direction of travel -- 292 degrees -- is now locked onto the dial and can be read at the index inscribed on the compass base. Now, while holding the compass in front of you with the direction-of-travel arrow inscribed on the base pointing *away* from your body, rotate your body and compass (you may have to turn the canoe to do this) until the magnetic needle points to north on the dial. You are now facing in the proper direction. Locate a notch or visible incongruity on the horizon that you can identify as being on this course of travel. Put your compass away and paddle toward your objective. Do *not* attempt to watch the compass needle and paddle at the same time! In time your objective (point *B*) will pop into view and you will have found your campsite.

Since precise directions are needed in canoe travel, the orienteering style compass has an obvious advantage over all other types. With a dial or cruiser model precise bearing determination is possible only if you have a good protractor and sharp pencil at hand. And if that protractor should become lost or broken, accurate direction finding will be slow and time consuming at best.

Once you have reestablished your position at point *B*, you can continue your voyage to *C*, then to *D*, and so on. In this manner you can cross a large, complex waterway without fear of becoming lost, for you will know where you are all the time.

AIMING OFF

Assume you are at point *G* and you want to locate the portage to South Arm just north of *H*. There are three portages leading out Bay 3, but only one goes to South Arm. Since one degree of compass error equals 92.2 feet per mile (tan. 1° × 5280 feet), even a slight error can be disastrous.

From *G* to the South Arm portage is about three miles. A 4-degree error over this distance would cause you to miss the portage by at least 1100 feet, or nearly one-fourth of a mile. You would in effect be lost, since you'd have no idea which direction to go to find the portage. Instead, "aim off." Determine the bearing from *G* to a point just south of the portage -- in this case, point *H*. Locate a notch on the horizon which corresponds to the bearing you have computed, and start paddling. When you reach the shoreline, you will be somewhere near *H*, although you may be a few hundred feet north or south. But one thing is certain -- you are *south* of the portage to South Arm. You merely have to paddle up the shoreline (north) until you come to the portage. This principle of aiming off is equally useful on land or for locating the mouth of a river. By aiming off you minimize the possibility of error.

DECLINATON

A compass points (actually, it doesn't point -- it lines up with the earth's magnetic field) to *magnetic* north, not *true* north. This angular difference, called *declination*, must be considered whenever you use your compass (see Figures 14-3 and 14-4). In the eastern United States the declination is westerly and in the western United States the declination is easterly. If you live right on the imaginary line which goes directly through both the true and magnetic north poles (called the *agonic* line), your declination will be zero.

If you live east or west of the agonic line, your compass will be in error, since the true north pole is not in the same place as the magnetic north pole. As you can see from the declination chart, the farther away you are from the agonic line, the greater the declination. Moreover, the magnetic north pole is constantly moving; because of this declination will vary from year to year as well as from place to place. Consequently, it is not possible for compass manufacturers to factory-adjust a compass to account for this variation. To find the exact declination for your area, consult a topographic map or call a surveyor. In the continental United States declination can range from 0 degrees at the agonic line to more than 20 degrees in New England and the far west. Unless your canoeing will be limited to those states very close to the agonic line, you will have to consider declination.

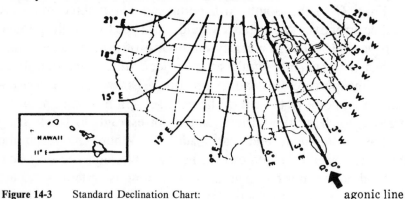

Figure 14-3   Standard Declination Chart: agonic line

The easiest solution to the declination problem is to purchase a compass which has the mechanical means for offsetting this difference. Silva and Suunto both make orienteering models with this optional feature, and all cruisers can be mechanically adjusted for declination. Prices for such compasses are generally in the twenty dollar-plus category; nevertheless, if you are a serious wilderness canoeist, the extra cost is worthwhile. If you are on a limited budget or live close to the agonic line, it is probably not necessary to purchase a compass with declination features. You may instead compute the variation mathematically, according to the following rhyme:

Declination east -- compass least (subtract east declination from
      your map direction)

Declination west -- compass best (add west declination to your map
      direction)

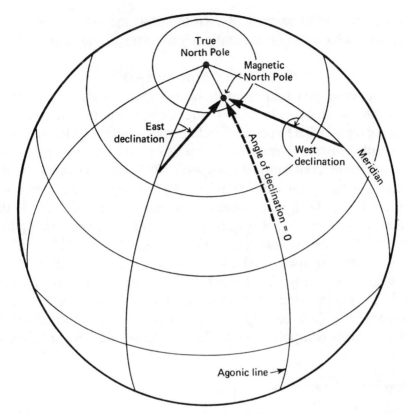

Figure 14-4   Compass Declination — The Angular Difference between *True* North and *Magnetic* North (the direction the compass points).

Maps are almost always drawn in their *true* perspective (any variation is so small that it can be ignored). So when you determine a direction of travel or bearing from a map, it is a *true bearing*. The true bearing taken from your map will have to be converted to a *magnetic bearing* to be set on your compass.

Assume a declination of 10 degrees east. Applying the rhyme "Declination east, compass least," *subtract* 10 degrees from the true bearing computed from your map. In the Lost Lake map exercise a true bearing of 292 degrees from *A* to *B* would equal 292 minus 10, or 282 degrees, using the declination given above. Conversely, if declination were 10 degrees west, it would be added 292° + 10° = 302°), and this value would be set on your compass. If this is confusing and you plan to travel in areas where the declination is large, you would be well advised to spend the extra money for a compass which can be manually adjusted for declination.

POSITION BY TRIANGULATION

Suppose you find yourself on a large, mazelike lake where you can identify two or more topographical features but you don't know exactly where you are. Finding your position by triangulation is simple with an orienteering compass (or you can use a protractor with a more conventional compass). Pick out one point on the horizon which you can identify -- Old Baldy, in this case (see Figure 14-5). With your compass, shoot a magnetic bearing to the point (bearing = 312 degrees). Change this magnetic bearing to a true bearing by reverse application of the rhyme: 312° + 6° = 318°. Draw the *back* (reciprocal) bearing (318° − 180° = 138°) through Old Baldy, using your compass base plate and a sharp pencil. (When using an orienteering compass you don't have to compute the back bearing at all.) Set 318° on the compass dial, place your pencil point on Old Baldy, and put the forward edge of

Figure 14-5   Position of Triangulation:

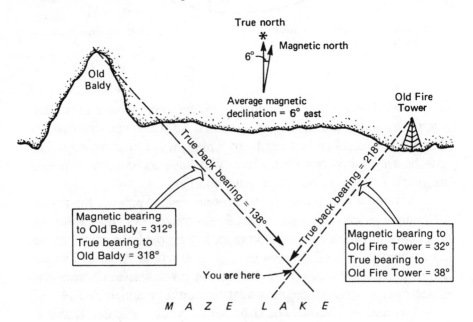

one side of your compass base plate against the pencil point. Rotate the entire compass in an arc about the pencil until north on the *dial* (not the needle) points to the top (north) of the map. Caution: Do not turn the compass housing during this operation, since the true bearing which you just computed to Old Baldy (318°) is set on the dial. This procedure will *not* work if you change the dial setting! Using the base plate as a straight edge, draw your line. Repeat the exercise using another point on the horizon which you can identify (the old fire tower). You are located where the two lines cross. For greatest precision you may wish to take three sightings.

NAVIGATION AT NIGHT

Canoeing by moonlight on a slow-moving river or calm lake is an enjoyable experience. However, no canoeist's repertoire is complete until he or she has done some black-night travel by compass. Some years ago while canoeing in Minnesota's Boundary Waters Canoe Area, I was awakened to find three bears in camp -- Mama and two babies. In spite of previous stern warnings, the youth group which I was guiding had left food scattered about the camp. The dehydrated fruit which was on the lunch menu evidently had a superabundance of prunes, and the youngsters had elected to have a prune fight. Even after a thorough policing of the grounds, enough prunes remained to attract the bears. We blew whistles, banged on canoes, clanked pots and pans, and made a variety of other noises in the hope of frightening away the hungry bruins; to no avail. Our bears were used to people. After they knocked down one tent we became convinced it was time to leave, and within a few minutes we put to sea. The night was black as pitch, but locating a new campsite without a moon to guide us was not difficult. We set course by compass and located a new site within an hour. My compass, a Silva Ranger, had a good luminous night sighting device.

If you travel at night it is important to obtain a compass with luminous points. A flashlight won't do, since the filament coil in a flashlight bulb functions as an electromagnet (and flashlights are made of steel, of course). Besides, navigating by flashlight requires continuous readjustment of your eyes to the light.

As to navigation by the stars, I know of no modern canoeist

who has ever had to resort to such folly. If you are lost or without a compass, you have no business traveling at night, and if you do have a compass you certainly don't need the stars. Moreover, trees and topographical features sometimes prevent you from keeping the North Star in view. Such star navigation makes interesting reading for the armchair canoeist, but it is impractical and, on complex waterways, dangerous. If you are interested in this sort of thing, however, see a Boy Scout handbook or, for more detail, any text on surveying or astronomy.

YOUR WATCH AS A COMPASS

Although of questionable accuracy, direction finding using a watch is at times convenient when you want a rough, quick direction but you don't want to get your compass out. If your watch is correctly set for the time zone in which you are canoeing, you have merely to point the hour hand at the sun (keeping the watch horizontal). Halfway between the hour hand and twelve o'clock is roughly south. Such showmanship will impress your friends when things get dull on a long wilderness voyage (though Robert Owendorff pointed out the unreliability of this method in "How to Get Lost in One Simple Lesson," in the January 1973 issue of the *Isaak Walton League* magazine).

LOST LAKE EXERCISES

On page 245 is a map of Lost Lake (Figure 14-6). Assume you are at point A. Using your compass or a protractor, determine the bearing and approximate time of travel from point to point. Proceed alphabetically, ending your trip at the portage into South Arm. Assume a travel speed of two miles per hour. When you have finished and your answers check, work the triangulation problem below.

TRIANGULATION PROBLEM

You can identify Dunker Hill at a magnetic bearing of 256 degrees and Kaby Lookout at a magnetic bearing of 4 degrees. Where are you located? Clue: Don't forget to apply the declination.

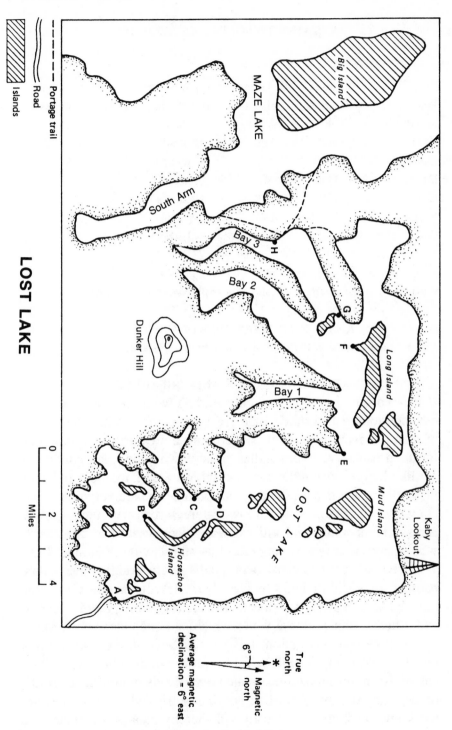

Figure 14-6   Average Magnetic Declination Equals 6 East.

ANSWERS TO LOST LAKE EXERCISE

Point	True Bearing	Distance (miles)	Approximate Travel Time	Magnetic Bearing (to be set on your compass)
A to B	290°	2¾	1½ hours	284°
B to C	341°	1½	¾ hour	335°
C to D	15°	4/5	20 minutes	9°
D to E	338°	4	2 hours	332°
E to F	274°	3¼	1½ hours	268°
F to G	244°	1⅛	½ hour	238°
G to H	227°	2½	1¼ - 1½ hours	221°

H to portage (paddle north up the shoreline to portage): Time -- about 15 minutes.

ANSWER TO TRIANGULATION PROBLEM
You are located at the north end of Horseshoe Island.

RIVER NAVIGATION AND TRIP GUIDES
No discussion of canoe route-finding would be complete without mentioning trip guides and river navigation. With the impact of man on river systems, it is becoming more and more important for the prospective river paddler to know what the water conditions are like before setting the canoe in the water. Many local and even far northern rivers are now dam controlled, and are very dangerous at high water or impossible at low water. Barbed wire fences strung across rivers maim and kill canoeists each year, and the people who string these fences generally have the law on their side. Each year we read about canoeists who inadvertently paddled over a dam because they didn't know it was there. If you paddle rivers you must be able to accurately locate and identify dams, rapids, fences, and other obstacles in the water which can endanger your trip.

Unlike lake navigation, it is very difficult to fix your position on a river. A compass will be useful for rough directions only. You can reaffirm your location at major river bends, identifiable rapids, or incoming streams. On wilderness canoe trips where it is necessary to ascend an incoming stream and thereby change watersheds, a high degree of resourcefulness and competency in map reading may be required, especially if there are many streams to confuse you. For trips on complex waterways near the magnetic north pole (where compass pointings are generally unreliable), a sextant or compact theodolite might be a wise investment to insure navigational safety.

Lastly, some of the best maps of river conditions are the local people who live in the area. Always check with them before embarking on a river, even if you have run it many times. Many things may have changed since your map was drawn. Although you should heed the advice of local persons, bear in mind that most don't understand canoes. Locals have a tendency to exaggerate the dangers of their rivers. Nevertheless, they will provide you with much good information. Especially seek out foresters or professional people who work in the area. Outdoors people will generally tell it like it is, or at least they will exaggerate less.

15.
The Menu

The days of bean-hole and stew-pot cookery are gone. No longer must we sweat and choke over a hot, smoky fire to prepare something palatable. We can, instead, devote our energies to experiencing the joys of nature.

Anyone can prepare gourmet meals on wilderness trips these days. Everything from freeze-dried shrimp cocktail to Neapolitan ice cream can be purchased in packaged form from camping equipment shops. And you don't have to be an accomplished chef to prepare these foods, either; generally you need only boil water, add the product, and simmer for five minutes or so.

Fortunately for our pocketbooks, many of these lightweight, easy-to-prepare foods are commercially available in local supermarkets at substantial savings over the packaged stuff available from outfitters. And, interestingly enough, some of the food items, like soups, puddings, fruit drinks, and cake mixes, are equal to or better than similar products from equipment shops.

Although you can build considerable variety into a wilderness menu by combining the offerings of both supermarkets and equipment shops, sameness in food does not seem to bother most experienced outdoors people. In fact, some hearty wilderness travelers carry only beef jerky, dehydrated fruit, soup, oatmeal, and tea, and get along quite nicely for weeks at a time.

Anything goes on canoe trips of less than a week, and this includes coolers filled with fresh meat, cheese, and fruit. But for extended or whitewater trips where weight must be carefully con-sidered, only freeze-dried or dehydrated foods will do. If money is no object, you can merely pick 'em off the shelf of your local camping store. But if you're on a limited budget you can save tremendously by choosing grocery shelf products and repackaging them. Freeze-dried foods, although excellent for most canoe trips, don't supply enough calories for rugged, physically demanding voyages of several weeks. On rugged trips your body needs at least four thousand calories a day. These calories can be supplied by ample amounts of oatmeal, jam, cornbread, rice, peanut butter, margarine, and nuts.

MEAL MANAGEMENT
PACKAGING

Remove all excess packaging on foodstuffs (like cardboard boxes) and repack each meal separately in a large, heavy-duty plastic bag (Zip-Loc bags are ideal). Place plastic bags in color-coded nylon stuff sacks. If you pack all your breakfasts in a green nylon bag, your lunches in yellow, and your suppers in red, you will avoid much pack groping at mealtime.

Each packaged meal should be a complete unit. It should not be necessary to search for the sugar, instant milk, cocoa, or what-ever. All items should be premeasured in the correct amounts neces-sary to serve the group. Instant puddings, for example, call for the addition of milk. The correct amount of nonfat dry milk should be premeasured and added to the dry pudding mix in a plastic bag. Preparation of the pudding should require the addition of the correct volume of water only. If you premix all your foods in this fashion, you will shorten meal preparation time considerably.

A word of advice: When you repackage meals be sure to include the directions for cooking. I still have several bags of what-is-it-and-how-much-do-I use? left over from previous canoe trips.

The best way to pack breakables and crushables like crackers, candy bars and cheese, is to place them inside a rigid cardboard milk carton. When mealtime rolls around, use the carton for mixing powdered drinks and messy puddings, or save them for use as emergency fire starters.

Make an accessory bag (a large nylon stuff sack). Into this place toilet paper (plastic-bag each roll separately and crush thoroughly before placing in the bag), sugar, salt, pepper, and any special delight such as a package of mixed nuts. Bag items like cooking oil and pancake syrup separately in plastic even though these liquids come sturdily packed in nonleaking plastic bottles. A wilderness canoe trip is surprisingly rough on food and equipment.

COOKING GEAR

For a party of four you will need the following cooking equipment:

Group Equipment	Personal Equipment
3½-quart aluminum pot with cover	insulated or stainless steel cup
3-quart aluminum pot with cover	plastic cereal bowl
6-cup coffee pot	spoon
9½-inch cast aluminum or	fork
stainless steel frying pan	pocket knife
oven (see discussion below)	
2-quart graduated plastic shaker	
with cover	
waterproof salt and pepper shakers	
spatula with 4-6 inch long handle	
aluminum pot lifter (or small	
pliers)	
stainless steel Sierra Club cup	
for use as a soup ladle,	
extra cup, or bowl	
waterproof stuff sack to store	
the cook kit	

If you snap your Sierra Cup to a brass hook attached to the outside of your Duluth pack, you won't have to unpack the cook kit when you need a cup for lunch or a drink of water. A good idea is to keep the graduated plastic shaker tied to a canoe thwart,

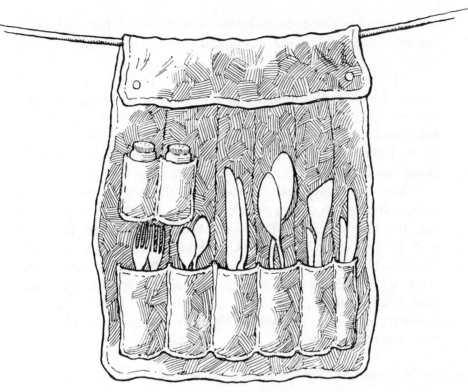

Figure 15-1   When rains come, hang your fabric utensil roll from a tight line strung beneath your cooking fly. Now, everything you need to prepare meals will be clean, dry, and instantly at hand.

where it will become a handy bailer if your canoe takes too much water in heavy waves or rapids. Use the shaker for mixing Kool-Aid, measuring water for soup, or whipping instant pudding. The inscribed graduations enable you to determine the precise amounts of water needed to reconstitute freeze-dried and dehydrated foods.

Tip: Store your silverware and spices in a fabric untensil roll that has a top which folds over and snaps down (Figure 15-1). When rains come, run a tight line just beneath your cooking fly (rain tarp) and hang your utensil organizer from it. Now, everything you need to prepare meals will be clean, dry, and instantly at hand.

OVENS

In the days of large campfires, I used a folding reflector oven for all my baking. Now, however, I cook on a stove or small fire, so the polished reflector is out-of-place. When I wish to bake on a fire, I use a Bendonn aluminum dutch oven.* For trail stove baking, I use a large ring Jello-mold (about three dollars at most discount stores) or a triple-pan Dutch oven (described below).

The Bendonn oven consists of two modified frying pans and a pair of spring steel handles. One pan is inverted over the other and hot coals are placed in a special ring on top. Pastries within the oven cook from the heat above. This versatile cooker can also be used to pop corn, fry potatoes and boil soup. It weighs only 25 ounces and will nest compactly with most cook kits.

You can easily make an acceptable Dutch oven by inverting a large frying pan over a smaller one, or by placing a skillet or cake pan on top of a pot. Put your bake stuff in the oven and build a small, hot fire on the cover. Use almost no heat on the bottom. Best results will be obtained if you set this homemade unit in the warm ashes. Because Dutch ovens receive heat from above rather than below, burning is seldom a problem. Bisquick bread or blueberry muffins will cook in about thirty minutes if plenty of heat is used.

*Bendonn Company, 4920 Thomas Ave. South, Minneapolis, MN 55410.

Figure 15-2   The Bendonn Oven: This versatile cooker can also be used to pop corn, fry potatoes and boil soup.

Figure 15-3 The "Jello Mold" Oven: It works on any trail stove.

To use the Jello mold for baking on your stove...

1. Grease the mold and pour your bake stuff into the outside ring. (Decrease the suggested amount of water by up to one-fourth for faster baking).

2. Bring the stove to its normal operating temperature then reduce the heat to the lowest possible *blue-flame* setting. Center the Jello mold over the burner head, top it with a high cover (necessary to provide sufficient room for the bake goods to rise) and relax. Cooking times are nearly identical to those suggested in the baking directions.

3. Cool the mold by setting it in a shallow pan of water for a few moments.

The triple-pan method of baking on your stove...

You'll need two nesting skillets, a high cover, and a half dozen small nails or stones.

1. Evenly scatter the nails or stones onto the surface of the large (bottom) frying pan.

2. Place your bake stuff into the small frying pan and set it on top of the nails (the two pans *must* be separated by nails or stones to prevent burning).

3. Cover the unit and place it on your stove. Use the *lowest possible* blue-flame setting.

Warning: Don't use this method with a thin aluminum skillet on the bottom; you'll burn a hole right through it!

Though the procedure sounds hokey, it works quite well and is, in fact, the only way to bake if you're canoeing above the timberline and have no Jello-mold oven.

HINTS
TO MIX MESSY PASTRY BATTERS

Pour batter and water into a plastic Zip-Loc bag. Seal the bag and knead the contents with your hands until they are well mixed. When the consistency is correct, punch a hole in the bag bottom and squeeze the mix (use the bag like a cake decorator) into your waiting oven. There is no mess, no fuss, and no washing of utensils. This is the best way to make Bisquick dumplings, which are dropped into boiling soup.

DRYING COOKWARE AND CLEANING EQUIPMENT

Package a half-dozen sheets of paper towels with breakfast and supper meals. The towels are handy for drying cookware, cleaning the stove, and similar chores.

CLEANING POTS AND PANS

If you have hangups about fire-blackened pots, soap each pot bottom with liquid soap or shaving cream before placing the pot on the fire. The bottoms will clean easily with a limited amount of elbow grease. Many experienced campers, however, consider black beautiful and dispense with this foolishness.

TO ASSURE SUFFICIENT SERVINGS OF FREEZE-DRIED FOOD

Virtually all manufacturers of freeze-dried foods are optimistic about the number of servings per package. For nonstrenuous recreational canoe trips increase each serving by one-fourth; for rugged wilderness ventures increase by one-third to one-half. Teenagers, especially, consume much more food on a wilderness trip than you might imagine. Unlike adults, who tend to foresee the consequences of their acts, youngsters often dip into the next day's till to satisfy their voracious appetites.

FOR FISH LOVERS

Excellent main meals can be prepared by dropping chunks of raw fish into boiling soup. Watch the clock carefully because cooking time is less than three minutes. The taste? Indescribably delicious! Once you've tried it you may never again want to return to the mess of frying fish.

FOR POPCORN LOVERS

If you're tired of seasoning popcorn in a pot that's too small, try this: As you complete each batch of corn, pour it into a paper shopping bag (don't use a plastic bag; hot popcorn will melt through it). Season the corn to taste and shake the bag to mix it. After you've eaten the popcorn, fold the bag and store it inside a Zip-Loc bag for future use. The Zip-Loc will protect your pack contents from grease and eliminate odors. In damp weather, use the oil-soaked bag for a fire starter.

FOR THAT GOURMET TOUCH

To give added zest to virtually all dehydrated and freeze-dried entrees, include a small container of thyme and a fresh onion with your cooking gear. A sliver of onion and a dash of thyme will turn mediocre mush into gourmet cuisine.

FOOD PROTECTION AND SANITATION

It has become increasingly difficult to find campsites along heavily traveled canoe routes which are devoid of litter, garbage, and human waste. Filthy campsites are more than just eyesores; they are health hazards. I have observed people deliberately scattering leftover food about the woods under the guise of feeding the animals, and I have watched people who should know better throwing the entrails of fish directly into the lake that provided their drinking water.

Misuse of natural areas is more often due to ignorance of basic ecological relationships than wanton abuse. For example, people don't always understand that it may take many months, or even years, for a small lake to completely flush itself clean of pollutants. Some over-crowded lakes may experience the paddles of more than ten thousand canoeists annually. If each dumps a single cup of leftover camp coffee or washes even a single pot in the water, the environmental impact upon the watershed will be severe. Nature has provided fish and wildlife with sufficient food of the proper kind to insure their health and well-being. The diet of wild creatures need not include man's garbage.

A few people are under the misguided impression that wild animals in isolated areas are dangerous. Such persons, for fear of bodily injury, steer clear of the deep woods. They feel that the presence of a fellow camper a few hundred feet down the lake will keep away the wolves, bears, mountain lions, and other potentially dangerous animals. In practice, quite the opposite is true. A whole new breed of wildlife seems to be evolving -- a breed that has become fond of, if not dependent upon, people's waste. The camp bear and garbage-can raccoon are distinguished members of this new group. A camp bear, for example, who has been unwittingly fed by environmentally unaware campers, may become downright nasty when you attempt to shoo it away from your food pack with conventional means like whistles, yells, and the clank of pots and pans. Camp bears have destroyed entire campsites in their frenzied searches for food. Like humans, animals know a good thing when they see it, and once they find a free meal they're sure to return for another. The number of rampaging bears killed by forest and park personnel has increased substantially from that of a generation ago. The fault is ours. A clean camp area and a well-protected food supply are the main ingredients in a pleasant and event-free canoe trip.

FOOD PROTECTION

Before you retire for the night, your food supply should be carefully sealed in plastic and secured in your Duluth pack. If there is any evidence that a bear or raccoon has recently frequented the area, the pack should be *taken out of the immediate camp area* and treed, or set in the woods or along the shore line. Under no circumstances should you keep food in your tent! An experienced camp bear will casually destroy anything in his way -- even you --

to get at food. Almost without exception, bear maulings can be traced to careless food habits.

The common advice given to beginners is to "tree" food packs -- hoist them up at least fifteen feet off the ground. Unfortunately, this procedure usually *attracts* bears rather than repels them! That's because there are seldom more than one or two trees in a typical campsite with limbs high enough to discourage a hungry bruin. Bears aren't stupid; they quickly learn the location of these trees and they develop ingenius procedures for getting food down. An experienced camp bear will check every one of these trees for the presence of packs on his nightly rounds.

Once, I observed a sow and two cubs dislodge a treed pack by a very ingenius method. When the bear saw (or smelled) the pack, she attempted to climb the tree. But her efforts were fruitless; she kept sliding down the trunk. After a few attempts she gave up in disgust. Then, one of the cubs began to climb. The cub got part way up the tree, stopped and looked down (perhaps for further instructions). Now, mama had a plan: She climbed a few feet up the trunk then nudged the youngster's rump until he continued upward. When junior got within striking distance of the pack, he brought it crashing down with a few persistent swipes of his paw. As I've said, bears are not stupid!

My philosophy is that if a bear can't smell your food, or see packs which contain food, he won't get it! Bears are creatures of habit; they quickly associate camps (and packs and tin cans) with food. On several occasions hungry bruins have come into my camp and nosed around in search of food. Finding nothing, they left empty-handed, not realizing that just 50 feet away, along the shore line, there was a pack filled with gourmet delights.

I've made hundreds of canoe trips through black bear country and I've always grounded my packs *out of the main camp area*. Never once have I lost food to animals or suffered the slightest damage to my equipment. The system works!

Some canoeists rig a night alarm system by placing pots and pans atop their grounded food packs. The idea is that a hungry bear or raccoon will knock the cookware down, creating sufficient racket to awaken the sleeping campers, who will arise and "scare off" the intruder. Don't you believe it. I can assure you that the clang of a few pots and pans *will not* discourage a determined bear from eating his prize!

Occasionally, canoeists place their food packs beneath their canoes in the hope that this will deter a hungry bear. This I consider downright dangerous -- to the canoe, that is. Bears are extremely powerful animals, and they can easily smash a canoe with a friendly swipe of a paw.

What about masking food smells with insect repellent or moth balls, as advised by some authorities? Again, you're wasting your time. A handful of mothballs *will not* stop a hungry bear from eating your food. But an absolutely clean, odor-free camp will!

SANITARY DISPOSAL

For short trips where there are few portages, all garbage should be bagged in plastic and packed out of the wilderness. When this is impractical, as on lengthy outings, the best and most widely accepted method of disposal is burning. Before burning uneaten food, build a good, hot fire so that the remains of soupy foodstuffs won't extinguish the blaze. Burn all garbage *completely*, being sure to pick aluminum foil out of the flames before it melts all over everything. Partially melted and fire-flaked aluminum foil is rapidly becoming the scourge of the wilderness. Cans and bottles have been outlawed in many areas because people refused to pack them out. Soon aluminum foil may follow suit.

Disposing of fish entrails can be a problem. If you throw them in the lake, you pollute the water, and if you toss them back in the woods, they attract wild animals. What then is the best solution?

If you are in a *remote* area where sea gulls are prevalent, place fish innards on a large boulder well away from human habitation. Within the hour the remains will be devoured by gulls, and since fish is the natural food of these great birds, you will have done little to upset their ecology.

In well-traveled areas -- or where no sea gulls can be found, the most satisfactory means of getting rid of viscera is by burying them. Bury fish remains as far away from the camp area as is practical, and cover them with four to eight inches of soil. This depth is best for decomposition and also minimizes the possibility of their being dug up by animals. Where there is only an inch or two of soil cover, as on the Precambrian geologic shield of Canada, place a heavy rock or log atop the buried entrails to hold them in place.

If possible, human waste, too, should be buried four to eight inches deep. Toilet paper and sanitary napkins should be burned. Just light the paper where it is, and when the flames are extinguished, cover with soil. Human refuse decomposes quickly, but paper products, unless burned, will remain an eyesore for at least a complete season, maybe more.

And *please*, don't throw food (or anything else!) into Forest Service box latrines or chemical toilets. Bears commonly upset latrines to get at the food they want. The mess that results is indescribable!

Dishes (or anything else) should be washed on the land, well away from the water's edge. Greasy dishwater is best poured into a small hole in the ground and covered with a few inches of soil. And it should go without saying that detergents should be biodegradable. Better yet, avoid detergents entirely and boil your dishes clean. A little grease on your bowl won't hurt you -- as long as the grease is yours. For this reason you should never use the eating gear of another member of your group. This simple precaution will eliminate minor illnesses.

WATER PURIFICATION

Unless you are canoeing in the most remote regions of the far north where water is still relatively pure, you'll need to give some thought to water quality. If you value your health, you'll "treat" your drinking water or carry it with you.

Most authorities conscientiously recommend that you boil, filter, or chemically treat all water taken from a questionable source. That's sound advice, providing you have the necessary chemicals and/or equipment plus the self-discipline to use them. Though I occasionally boil my drinking water on backcountry trips (I always boil it on local waterways!), I confess to laziness in this respect. As often as not, I drink untreated water, *but* I am very careful where I get it. Here are the guidelines I religiously follow:

1. Go well away from shore to get your drinking water. If you are camping at a spot that is frequented by man or animals, go

upstream of the source to get your water. On lakes, a minimum of 150 feet from shore is recommended -- and the farther out you go, the better.

2. Decay organisms (bacteria, protozoans, etc.) generally prefer the shallows, so the deeper your water source, the better. On large lakes, I often attach a rope to my large cooking pot and drop it down thirty feet or more.

3. Avoid any water which has a green or greenish-brown color. Water with a green tinge contains algae and is usually loaded with microorganisms.

4. Don't take water from backwaters and stagnant areas. These are breeding places for microbes.

5. Never drink any water which has been contaminated by wastes from a paper mill. Secure your water from incoming streams or springs instead. If there is a paper mill located along your route, *you'll have to* boil your water or treat it with chemicals!

6. Do not take water near beaver dams or lodges. Beaver are the favored host of "Giardia lamblia" -- a small protozoan that will make you plenty sick if you ingest it. Giardia enters a water supply through the feces of the host and is extremely long lived. In fact, the cyst of this protozoan can survive up to two months in 46 degree Fahrenheit water, and up to one month in 70 degree water! As you can see, these are incredibly hardy organisms.

The infection caused by Giardia ('Giardiasis'') is characterized by severe diarrhea, cramps, nausea, gas, vomiting, and general fatigue. The incubation time is generally one to two weeks, though some people have gone as long as two months before getting sick.

Giardia is usually diagnosed by stool examination, but this method is not always reliable. And most physicians simply aren't familiar enough with the disease to identify it. As a result, victims of Giardiasis frequently suffer for months before they get the help they need.

Two summers ago, a teenage girl on one of my BWCA canoe trips developed Giardiasis. For two months she suffered while taking one ineffective medication after another. One day, her father chanced to meet me at a community event. When he described the symptoms of the disease, I immediately suspected Giardia and suggested that his daughter be treated for it. The man replied that she had already been tested for Giardia and that the results were negative. Nonetheless, I persisted in my diagnosis and suggested he ask his family physician to administer the appropriate medication anyway. After some persuasion, the doctor wrote the necessary prescription, and within a week the girl was on her way to recovery.

FIELD METHODS OF WATER TREATMENT

1. *Boiling*: Most organisms are killed instantly when water reaches the boiling point. Some obscure pathogens may require 20 minutes or more of boiling time -- impractical on most camping trips. A one minute boil will destroy nearly everything. More time than this is only justified in problem areas or at high altitudes.

2. *Filter* the water with one of the mechanical devices sold at camping shops. Make sure the filter pore size is small enough to remove all harmful organisms. Not all filters will trap Giardia!

3. Chlorinate your water with Halazone tablets or chlorine bleach. If you use Halazone, take an unopened bottle on each trip. Halazone must also be protected from heat and exposure to air.

4. Liquid chlorine bleach with four to six percent available chlorine may also be used to purify water. Use two drops of bleach per quart of clear water and four drops per quart of cold or cloudy water. Let the treated water stand for 30 minutes. You should be able to smell the chlorine gas. If not, repeat the dosage and let it stand another fifteen minutes before using. If the water is very cloudy or cold, let it stand overnight before using it.

5. Water may also be sterilized with iodine by either of the methods below:

Method 1: Buy some iodine crystals at your local pharmacy. Weigh out six grams of iodine (your pharmacist will do this for you) and place the crystals in a one-ounce amber bottle (or a clear bottle covered with tape). Fill the bottle with water.

Sterilize a quart canteen of water by pouring about half the iodine solution into the canteen. Let the canteen set at least thirty minutes before drinking. Allow additional time for cloudy or very cold water.

Recharge the iodine bottle with fresh water after each use. The iodine crystals will dissolve until a saturated solution results.

You may continue to re-use the "iodine decant bottle" dozens of times -- until no more crystals are visible.

Method 2: Treat your water with a commercial tablet like "Potable Aqua" or "Globaline," which contains iodine. Again, use a fresh unopened bottle for each trip.

Note: Chlorine bleach and Halazone tablets *will not* destroy Giardia cysts under all conditions. Your best bet is to boil the water or use one of the iodine preparations suggested. Also, chlorine is carcinogenic, while iodine is not. For this reason, I prefer the iodine decant method or tablets which release iodine.

AND A FINAL THOUGHT...

As you paddle the rivers of North America, you will surely come upon thoughtless people and their refuse. Tin cans, bottles, mattress springs, car bodies, and worn-out appliances are but a sampling of the debris I've observed in my travels. Once, in the Boundary Waters of Minnesota, I was awakened at midnight by an enterprising trumpeteer. On another occasion, a teen group sang ribald songs the whole night through. Four times over the last decade I've put out other people's campfires, and I've cleaned more trashed fire-places and campsites than I can recall. But my efforts are not unique: Everyone who cares about the future of our wild places follows suit throughout each and every camping trip. Doing battle with environmental idiots is a never-ending, non-rewarding process.

Nearly everyone who paddles America's rivers ultimately develops a profound respect for them and an abiding disdain for those who abuse them. Nonetheless, it's important to realize that those who violate the backcountry usually do so out of ignorance not willful disrespect. Unlike you and I, they have no feeling for the land, no knowledge of the proper way to treat it.

To that end, I offer the suggested "Ethics Quiz" in Appendix C. Use it as you wish. Reproduce it in any number you like, and share it with as many people as you can. Education may not be the total answer to eliminating environmental abuses, but it is a start, and we can do no more than that.

16.
The Wet-
Weather Fire

Wilderness guidebooks suggest that making fire in wet weather is easy. Don't you believe it! If it has rained steadily for several days or weeks, even an experienced woods-wise person will have difficulty turning the flicker of a match into a roaring blaze. I remember a canoe trip that I took into the Boundary Waters Canoe Area of Minnesota early one spring. The ground, drenched with the rain of many weeks, yielded only the wettest of wood for fuel. To start a fire under those conditions required at least thirty minutes, a candle stub, some balsam pitch, a few dead cedar boughs, and a goodly supply of kindling cut from sticks robbed from a beaver house.

Unfortunately there is no "right way" to build a fire. What works under one set of circumstances may fail miserably under another. Nevertheless, some fire-building methods always seem to produce more positive results than others. For me, at least, the procedure described below has proved nearly faultless under the most difficult climatic conditions.

BUILDING THE FIRE
Tinder First

A fire begins when a match ignites some very flammable material, called "tinder". In the north country, the tendency is to search for birch bark -- much to the detriment of the trees and displeasure of those who will later occupy the site. Besides, any birch bark you find during or immediately after a good rain is likely too wet to burn anyway. And on a dry day, there are better alternatives!

Instead, seek out the dead, pencil-thin branches which grow near the base of evergreen trees. These shade-killed twigs are protected from rain by the tree canopy and are usually bone dry. They'll break with a crisp snap even after days of prolonged rain. If the branches are wet to the touch but the "snap" is heard, the wood is dry enough to burn. A handful of this tinder is all you need.

If evergreen twigs are rain-soaked or unavailable, locate a log with a dry center. Search the shore line of your campsite for a length of jutting birch, pine, cedar, or other softwood. When you find one of these "blowdowns" poking out from shore, saw off the section that doesn't touch the land or water. Some basic biology here: You'll find deadfalls in the woods as well as along the shore but they're often rotten from the dampness of the forest -- and rotten wood, as everyone knows, burns poorly. However, snags which protrude from the forest are flooded with sunlight (which kills most microorganisms that cause decay) and so are apt to have sound wood.

Saw the sun-lit section of the log into 12-inch lengths and split and sliver it with your hand-axe by the method outlined in Chapter 10, Tripping With Tots And Teens. Then use a sturdy pocket knife or thin-bladed sheath knife to cut long thin slivers of wood from the heartwood splittings. This is your tinder. The key to making good, long shavings, as opposed to short, broken ones, is to move your knife blade back and forth in a sawing motion while applying only moderate pressure. Even a very dull knife will produce usable shavings if a sawing rather than whittling motion is used.

If you want to impress your friends, fish a floating log from the water. The outer inch or so will be wet but the center will be bone dry (which is why the log "floats"). Split the log and take your shavings.

Abandoned birds' and hornets' nests and thin strips of bark peeled from grape vines also make good tinder. So do cedar bark and cedar branches. In an emergency, you can even burn money! Wood robbed from a beaver house is excellent since it is very tough and dry, but for environmental reasons you should avoid using it, except in dire emergencies -- and even then take only a few sticks.

Leaves and grass have poor heat output and tend to suffocate a fire. Using leaves for tinder marks you as a tenderfoot -- that is, if your fire won't start.

Forget about using newspaper for tinder. Paper is hydrophyllic (loves water); it absorbs moisture from the air and becomes damp and useless on rainy days.

CONSTRUCTION
Set the fire according to Steps 1, 2, 3.

STEP ONE
Obtain two sticks about one inch in diameter and position them about six inches apart. Place a few pencil-thin pieces of kindling over them at right angles. Space the pieces of kindling about an inch apart.

Figure 16-1   Fire Building Procedures: Step 1.

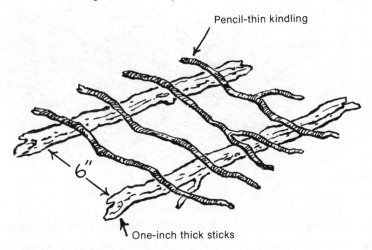

Pencil-thin kindling

6"

One-inch thick sticks

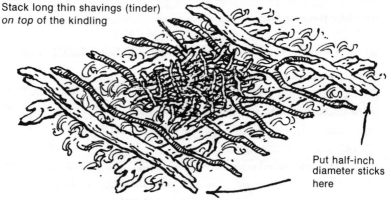

Stack long thin shavings (tinder)
on top of the kindling

Put half-inch
diameter sticks
here

Figure 16-2   Fire Building Procedures: Step 2.

STEP TWO

Stack long thin shavings (tinder) or small dry twigs *on top* of the kindling to a height of about one inch. Take care to "scientifically" place each shaving. A common mistake is to just throw the tinder on the kindling supports. Fires often fail due to insufficient oxygen, so position each shaving carefully to provide plenty of air space.

Next, put two sticks about one-half-inch in diameter over the ends of the inch-thick sticks at right angles to the fire base. These sticks will support the heavier kindling which you will pile atop the shavings.

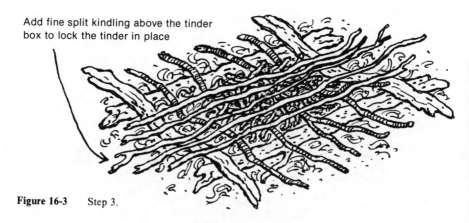

Add fine split kindling above the tinder
box to lock the tinder in place

Figure 16-3   Step 3.

STEP THREE

Systematically criss-cross two or three tiers of *fine split kindling* above the tinder box. Don't place too much wood on the fire

-- excess wood will draw heat from the young flame, and to start wet wood you need all the heat you can get.

Your fire is now ready for lighting. Note that the tinder box sits on a platform a few inches off the ground. There are three reasons for the platform. First, cold, damp ground will rob the fire of much of its heat during the early stages of combustion. Second, the platform permits a continuous draft, similar to that of a hibachi grill. When you make a fire in wet weather you are already fighting one variable -- wet wood. The raised platform eliminates a second variable -- lack of sufficient oxygen. Third, hibachi-type fires provide ample room to place a match directly *under* the flammable tinder, which ground fires don't. When you light a hibachi fire, the heat goes upward -- through the tinder -- and is quickly transmitted to the kindling above by the straight-through draft of the raised platform. The tinder box of a typical ground fire, on the other hand, is often awkward to reach, and as a result only the very edge of the tinder is usually lit. The young fire, then, must burn sideways to ignite the rest of the tinder. As everybody knows, heat goes upward, not sideways! If the platform has a major fault, it is its susceptibility to wind. By building a low, well-shielded platform, however, this problem can be eliminated.

LIGHTING THE FIRE

Not long ago I watched two teenagers attempt to start a perfectly built platform fire. The youngsters used fifteen matches, quit in disgust, and called me. Without touching a single piece of wood, I lit the fire with one match. As the kids looked on in awe, I explained that my magic personality was responsible for the flame. "My smile," I said, "radiated heat!" In reality, of course, I knew where to place the match; the youngsters didn't. Improper placement of the match is a major reason why well-built fires won't start. You must know *where* to put the match before you put it there. Confused? Look at it this way. A match produces its best heat immediately upon lighting. The more of this initial heat you can trap, the better are your chances of starting the fire. So practice with an unlit match. Be sure the match head can be placed directly beneath the driest, most flammable tinder; rearrange your fire to accomplish this if necessary. Too often the fire-builder lights the match before deciding where to place it. By the time the decision is made, the match has either lost much of its heat or the wind has blown it out.

Once you have found a suitable place beneath the tinder where the match can be held, you are ready to proceed to the lighting of the fire. Strike the match as close to the fire as possible, and quickly touch the first flicker of flame to the tinder. Hold the match stick as long as possible, then drop it. Don't pull the match back out of the fire; you will lose too much heat if you do.

Outdoors books would have you believe that a rugged north-woods guide can get a fire going within a minute or two under any conditions. This is hogwash. Even the most experienced woodspeople occasionally "cheat" by using candles, fire starters, paper, and yes -- gasoline. Firebuilding is a simple skill that is easily learned, but there is no magic involved. Although the rather elaborate procedure described in this chapter may seem like a lot of needless work and fuss, it always produces good results -- with a *single* match -- at those miserable times when you need a fire most.

HINTS

I have found it best not to waterproof matches; instead, I prefer to carry them in a waterproof plastic bottle with a screw-on lid. I place a wad of cotton beneath the lid of the bottle to prevent scoring of the match heads. Although there are commercially waterproofed matches available, I am skeptical of their performance, especially when they are stored for several months or years. Waterproof matches, I have found, don't light as efficiently as nonwaterproofed ones; the waterproof coating tends to smother the flame. If, however, you want to waterproof your matches anyway, the best method I have found is to coat each match individually with nail polish or lacquer. I don't like to dip matches in paraffin as is sometimes recommended; paraffin-treated matches are almost always difficult to light.

A suitable watertight match case can be made from a pair of shotgun shells. Stack matches into an empty 16-gauge shell and slide a fired 12-gauge case over the smaller shell for a cover. The dead primers of the shell casings provide a convenient striker for the matches. Several of these simple match cases can be scattered in different packs to provide an emergency match supply.

Always carry a candle. Candles are necessary to provide the sustained heat required to ignite wet wood. Include a small birthday candle in your waterproof match case.

An effective method of drying wet matches is to draw them briskly through your hair. Don't use your clothes, though; they are much too abrasive.

In the piney woods of the north and east, look for the balsam-fir tree. Its sap is nearly as volatile as kerosine. In summer, the tree produces half-dollar-sized resin blisters on its trunk. Lance a few blisters with a sharp stick and collect the pitch on a piece of wood or bark. Set the "resin cup" directly under your fire base and light it. Voilá! Fire every time -- with one match.

Bring along a butane lighter and save matches for emergencies. Also, carry some "Fire-Ribbon" or other chemical fire-starter. For spring river trips where a dunking requires a quick warming fire, assemble these kit materials:

A flattened half-gallon milk carton, a handful of thick shavings, and some splittings of scrap wood. Put everything into a nested pair of plastic bags. When the emergency strikes, dump everything on the ground; frizz up the milk carton and splash it with "Fire-Ribbon". Light the Ribbon and toss the wood on top. The carton will burn for about three minutes, the wood an additional five. That's enough time for you to search the woods for more fuel while your wet friend is being re-warmed by your instant blaze.

In a heavy rain: If there's no shelter and you don't have a rain tarp, prop one end of your canoe on a pair of paddles jammed through a seat brace. Then build a *small* fire under the canoe. When the blaze is going well, remove the overhead canoe and heap more wood on top.

Let's review the rules for making a successful fire:

1. Place sticks far enough apart on the fire base so there'll be adequate ventilation for the developing flames. I recommend that each stick (kindling and fuel) be separated by a *full radius*. Thus, two half-inch diameter sticks should be placed at least one-quarter inch apart. The most common reason fires fail is *lack of oxygen!*

2. Tinder should be *wafer-thin* -- no larger in diameter than

the thickness of a match. Trying to ignite wood larger than that on a damp day is a waste of time.

3. Don't heap the fire base high with wood during the developing stages of the flame. Unnecessary fuel just draws heat from the young fire and cools it. Pre-set pyramid style fires (alá Boy Scouts) look nice in handbooks but burn inefficiently. Once you complete Step Three, wood should be added one stick at a time and placed strategically so that you can "see light" between each one. Smoke is nature's way of telling you you're suffocating the blaze!

Before you dismiss fire-building as an unnecessary skill, you should realize that it is not uncommon for people who are lost to use their entire match supply and fail to start a fire. Your comfort and safety on a wilderness canoe trip depends upon the penny match and your ability to use it.

EXTINGUISHING THE FIRE

As a forester with the U.S. Forest Service some years ago I fought a twenty-acre fire in some scrubby alpine fir. The timber, I recall, was evaluated at about two thousand dollars, but the cost of extinguishing the blaze came to nearly one hundred thousand dollars. The fire was traced to a careless sheepherder, who was presented with the bill.

Most people don't realize that they are financially responsible for any forest fire they cause. This fact should not be taken lightly, for as the case in point illustrates, the expense involved in bringing even a small blaze under control can be exorbitant.

It should go without saying that your fire should be *dead out* when you break camp. In canoe country water is never a problem, and generous amounts of it should be used. Much of the canoe country of Minnesota, Canada, and Maine is rocky and has only a few inches of soil cover. To survive the high winds and rugged climate of the far north, trees form a shallow, far-spreading network of roots which extend many feet in all directions. Root systems of neighboring trees intertwine and provide stability for the struggling vegetation. Combined with a thin surface layer of highly flammable duff, this subterranean web of life provides an ideal pathway for the underground spread of fire. A fire may smolder in the soil for hours, or even days, and travel many hundreds of feet along these roots to flame up where oxygen and fuel is again abundant.

For this reason it is best to check the remains of a fire by touching your fingers to the ashes and charred wood. If the remains are hot enough to burn your fingers, they are hot enough to burn a forest.

Much of the current camping literature scorns campfires as an antiquated affectation. After all, modern trail stoves are eminently reliable and they don't blacken pots or produce foul-smelling smoke. Nonetheless, those of us who value the cry of the loon, the penetrating chill of a fog-borne morning, and the smell of fresh coffee simmering gently over wood coals, will continue to rely on fires -- occasionally at least -- for as long as there are cool clear rivers, star-lit nights, and sparkling sunsets.

17.
Trip Planning and Transportation

TRIP PLANNING

I always reserve the first weekend in May for my annual whitewater trip down the infamous Hell's Gate section of Minnesota's Kettle River. At this time of the year, Hell's Gate usually rates a high Class II or low Class III on the river rating scale -- an exciting run in an open canoe, and reasonably safe if you're properly prepared.

I prepare extensively for any canoe trip which includes rapids of Class III or greater difficulty. In early May this means a wet suit, a helmet, an extra paddle, fifty feet of throwing line, a waterproof first-aid kit, a knife, and a giant truck innertube for additional flotation.

On one particular Kettle River trip I was, to my chagrin, overprepared. This became apparent in the parking area near the point of departure. I was gingerly placing one foot into a leg of my wet suit when a smiling canoeist strode up. "Whatcha gonna use the wet suit for?" he asked. "The water temperature's only seventy degrees. The river's way down -- she won't even go a Class I today. I just *walked* through the first pitch! That innertube

is a great idea, though. Why don't you leave the canoe on the car
and ride the tube down through the riffles?''

I responded with a mumbled comment about an ounce of
prevention and hastily threw the gear back into the car. I spent the
remainder of the day swimming and tubing the rapids.

Although you can overprepare for a canoe outing, the fact
remains that good planning is the main ingredient in a safe canoe trip.

If you always paddle with an experienced group or club, you
won't have to worry about trip planning for the job will be done
for you. If you show up for a canoe trip inadequately prepared, the
trip leader will most likely either help you get properly prepared
or will ask you to shuttle cars instead of paddle. Thousands of
canoeists take canoe trips each year for which they are completely
unprepared. Often trip planning does not even consist of the most
elementary basic -- consulting a map of the river before embarking.
Most of these happy-go-lucky paddlers survive their ventures, and
many enjoy themselves immensely. Often they repeat the same
mistakes over and over again with no apparent bad effects. But a
few unlucky canoeists damage their equipment, their boats, and
their bodies. A very small number never lives to take another canoe
trip.

You can get away with a good deal of haphazard planning if
your trips will be taken on nonviolent waterways close to civilization
under carefully calculated climatic conditions. However, to embark
on a difficult wilderness venture without the most detailed preparation is to invite disaster. If the trip will be taken in an isolated area
where emergency help is generally unavailable, planning should
begin as early as possible -- preferably nine months or more in
advance of the date of embarkation. This will allow ample time to
secure maps, trip guides, food, and special equipment.

To insure a successful expedition, the following procedure and
timetable is recommended:

PLANNING SCHEDULE FOR A HYPOTHETICAL CANOE EXPEDITION INTO AN ISOLATED AREA

TRIP DATES: July 5 - July 20

Timetable

SEPTEMBER OF THE PREVIOUS YEAR. Hold an organizational meeting of those who will be going on the trip.

1. Discuss, in a general fashion only, the trip you plan to take. Since maps will probably be unavailable at this early date, do some rough planning using road or county maps.

2. Decide the purpose of the trip; for example, canoeing to reach a destination, leisurely paddling and fishing, or strictly fishing. Many trips have been spoiled because a few members wanted to go fishing while others wanted to paddle. All trippers must be in complete agreement as to the purpose of the trip.

3. Select a trip leader. There must be one person who will take the major share of responsibility for the organization and preparation of the journey. Obviously the leader should be the most experienced member of the group.

The trip leader should assign responsibility to group members as follows (for small groups, double up jobs):

Select a navigator, who will write for maps and trip guides (see Appendix A for sources), obtain permits, and so forth. The navigator should have an interest in route finding and a nose for research, and should round up all sources of information which pertain to the proposed trip.

Select a public relations chairperson. This individual should contact the chamber of commerce nearest the jump-off point in an attempt to locate a pen pal who is familiar with the waterway you intend to travel. When a pen pal is found, explain your trip and request information regarding its feasibility. Be sure to ask for weather information and river difficulty ratings. Also, ask your contact person how long he or she thinks it will take you to complete your voyage. When you receive this information, allow at least fifteen percent additional time for the unexpected. As explained in Chapter 14 (Wilderness Navigation), maps go out of date quickly and rivers can fluctuate greatly from week to week. Your river may be still in flood stage in early June, while by mid-August it may be too low for good canoeing. Unfortunately, neither your map nor your trip guide will indicate this. For these reasons it is unwise to undertake a major canoe expedition without corresponding with a person who is familiar with the local water conditions.

One individual should develop a rough menu for the group's consideration at a later meeting.

Select a quartermaster (usually the trip leader). The quartermaster should develop a complete equipment list including group items, (like tents and canoes) and an individual checklist.

The most experienced paddler of the group should undertake the responsibility of being training chairperson. At least two short check-trips should be taken by the group before embarking on the big adventure. Ideally, one trip should be a day session to concentrate on the mastery of whitewater technique and to find out which group members are best matched as paddling partners. A second trip should be an overnight affair. Test your equipment, your menu, and your rapport with other group members on this trip.

NOVEMBER OF THE PREVIOUS YEAR. Hold your second organizational meeting. It sometimes takes a month or more to obtain topographic maps in the scale you want. You may by this date still not have all your maps and trip guides, but enough should be on hand to begin planning in earnest. Attempt to accomplish the following at this meeting:

1. Go over the equipment checklist item by item. Be overprepared! Decide who will furnish the major items of equipment, like tents, canoes, stove, cooking gear, and so on.

2. Make sure each individual has adequate personal gear. For example, you should not permit the use of cheap plastic rain suits, poor-quality sleeping bags, badly constructed paddles, or inadequate footwear. You can only move as fast and as comfortably as the slowest member of the party, and one person with shoddy equipment can spoil it for everyone.

I vividly remember the ten straight days of driving rain we had on a canoe trip to Moosonee, Ontario, in 1974. One member of our group did not have waterproof footgear. By the fifth day of the trip, his feet were so wet and cold that he could barely continue. Luckily someone had an extra pair of rubber boots. Our frigid-footed friend gratefully accepted the boots (which fortunately fit) and completed the trip in comfort.

3. It is important that each individual be thoroughly committed to going on the trip. You just can't afford to plan for several months, buy special equipment, and then have someone back out at the last moment. To make sure this doesn't happen, compute the approximate cost of the trip, divide it equally, and set up a schedule of payments:

$25 due by January 1 (nonrefundable deposit to
    insure commitment)
One-quarter of the total cost due by February 15
Another quarter of the cost due by March 15
Third quarter of the cost due by April 15
The remainder of the cost due by May 1

It is essential that you have some working capital on hand in the early stages of the trip. If the trip is very long, you will have a sizable cash outlay for food, and some of this food may need to be advance-ordered from a camping shop or by mail. A common mistake is to wait too long to order food. Many camp shops and mail order houses have difficulty furnishing some food items after June 15.

4. Select a treasurer to handle incoming monies. The treasurer should prepare an account book which lists debits and expenditures made by members. The group can settle up in June.

5. Agree on a policy for the repair or replacement of damaged canoes and equipment. Most groups choose to split the cost evenly, regardless of who is at fault.

6. Arrange for the return to your starting point. If you are traveling by train, make sure you have up-to-date schedules. If you plan to fly back, find out what the charter pilot's restrictions are on transporting canoes and equipment. Some charter planes simply won't take canoes. If you will drive, who will shuttle your car(s)? These questions should be answered as early as possible in the planning stages of your trip.

JANUARY: Third organizational meeting.

1. Collect commitment money. Perhaps imbibe some fine wine to celebrate!

2. Finalize the equipment list and order what you need.

3. Check on maps and trip guides. If you don't have everything yet, send out follow-up letters.

4. Finalize the menu to everyone's satisfaction. Decide what can be bought at the local supermarket and check items to be mail- or equipment-shop ordered.

FEBRUARY: Fourth organizational meeting. Have a menu party. Order mail-order food items and prepare a list of foodstuffs to be presented to your grocer.

MARCH: Fifth organizational meeting. Have a map party. Cut, paste, tape, and waterproof all your maps and trip guides (each group member should have his or her own map set). Go over the maps and trip guides in detail and compare these with information received from your area contact person. Note any discrepancies among the materials. If information is lacking, now is the time to write (or phone) for it. You have only three months left until launch time!

APRIL: Sixth organizational meeting. Spring has arrived; the excitement mounts!

1. Go over any correspondence you have received since the last meeting. Tie up loose ends and socialize. Convince your spouse you are really going!

2. Firm up training session dates.

FIRST WEEK IN MAY: Seventh organizational meeting. The countdown begins! Have a food-packing party! Repackage food, make beef jerky, and so on.

SECOND WEEK IN MAY: Last meeting before the trip!

1. Have an equipment-packing party. Pack all group and personal gear, except those items you will wear or carry. Be sure to use a checklist so you don't forget anything.

2. Relax and celebrate! I assume you have all survived the practice canoe trips, you like the food, you get along well with each other, you are competent paddlers, and you have the right equipment. Nine months of detailed planning and preparation have gone into your canoe expedition. You are now ready to give birth to a great adventure!

Transportation

Perhaps the most difficult part of organizing a canoe trip is securing the transportation back to your starting point. Most canoeists simply run an auto shuttle. Shuttles, however, necessitate the use of two cars, and often you have only one. This is a real problem, especially for groups or families who are traveling together in a single vehicle.

The most obvious way to solve the transportation dilemma is to pay a local person or commercial outfitter to drive your car to the end of your trip. If you can arrange to have your car shuttled at the leisure of the driver (while you are on the water) rather than at a specific time, the cost will be much less.

An increasingly popular means of getting back to the starting point is by bicycle. For short trips where you won't be carrying much gear, merely set the bicycle in the canoe (wheels up) and take off (under paddle power, of course) downstream. Granted, your rig will attract stares of wonder and you will be besieged with wisecrack remarks, but you will have solved your transportation problem effectively. When your trip is completed your partner can watch the canoe and outfit while you peddle back to the car. Since most river shuttles are seldom more than twenty miles long (one way), you should be able to cover this distance easily in an hour and a half or so.

For long trips where you don't have room for a bike in the canoe, run your own shuttle by dropping off the two-wheeler at your take-out point. You can chain the bike to a tree, or if it is a valuable model, pay a local person to keep it for you until you finish the trip.

Another good way to shuttle yourself back to your car is to hitchhike. The important thing about hitchhiking, however, is to make sure you look like a canoeist rather than a bum, and after you've been out camping for several days it is frequently difficult to make the distinction. An often foolproof way to get a ride is to wear your life jacket and carry a paddle. Make sure oncoming motorists see the paddle and jacket and you usually won't have any trouble getting picked up. It is essential that you wait near a bridge or road close to the river, as your chances of getting a lift will decrease as your distance from the river increases. I have yet to wait more than twenty minutes for a ride in all the times I have hitchhiked. On several occasions sympathetic drivers took me right to my destination.

WHERE TO GO

Due to the impact of humans, wilderness waterways are changing so rapidly that it is impossible, or at least impractical, to give detailed descriptions of the best paddle routes. At this very moment there are canoeists who are planning trips into supposedly isolated areas, using outdated canoe books as their major source of information. Right now plans are underway to dam some of the finest canoeing waters in northern Canada; and in the United States the U.S. Army Corps of Engineers is continually channeling, straightening, and otherwise "improving" our rivers. As a result many exciting canoe trips of the past, as outlined in the literature, are nonexistent today. You will have to search diligently to find challenging waterways where you can be completely alone.

Surprisingly, some of your best wilderness canoeing will be on small, meandering streams and rivers close to home. Local rivers are often too shallow for good motorboating, too slow for whitewater thrills, and too inaccessible by road for good fishing. Such "unexciting" waterways may be more wild than the majority of those described in fancy guide books.

I would caution any canoeist against undertaking a wilderness trip of significance on the strength of a guide book alone. Even trip guides distributed by government agencies are apt to be outdated and inaccurate, and many of the best topographic maps available are many years old.

The best wilderness canoe trips will not be found in how-to-canoe books or published guides. Wilderness canoeists are often solitary people, and when they find a beautiful, isolated route, the last thing they want to do is advertise it. A wilderness trip described in print is an invitation to a wilderness despoiled. A good example is the infamous Chattooga River in North Carolina. Prior to the making of the film *Deliverance*, no one had ever heard of the Chattooga. Today this river draws hundreds of whitewater paddlers each season, many of whom come totally unprepared -- both in equipment and paddle skill.

Because of my great love for the wilderness, I prefer to remain secretive regarding my private haunts. Consequently there are no favorite floats described in this book. I leave the discovery of the last remaining wilderness waterways to you.

18.
Equipment Maintenance and Repair

Winter -- cold and bleak, and as far removed from the canoeing season as you can get. A quarter-year will pass before the earth begins to warm and the rivers run again. Until then, it's best to put your thoughts and efforts into the delights of the season -- skiing, snowshoeing, and indoor sports. Preparations for canoe travel can wait.

Don't you believe it! Winter is the one time when there is time to refurbish your well-used, well-worn canoeing outfit. Without diligent attention, all your delightful "toys" will rot away, rust away, and come apart at the seams.

Fortunately, equipment maintenance is a labor of love. The annual task of sanding and varnishing gunwales, of cleaning packs and re-oiling leather, of washing the sleeping bag and winterizing the camp stove, brings as much joy as a roaring fire and a good book on a frosty night. "Cleaning up your act" is proven therapy for the winter blahs. Here's what you need to do.

TLC^2 (TENDER LOVING CANOE CARE)
Wash your canoe immediately after each trip. Scrub the floor with a stiff broom to remove ground-in dirt and remove stubborn

spots on the hull with strong liquid cleansers. A coat of good paste wax keeps fiberglass, Kevlar, and Royalex hulls looking new and prevents aluminum ones from oxidizing. The special fiberglass boat waxes that contain mild abrasives are worth using because they keep the boat finish mirror-smooth and easy to clean. Surface scratches on fiberglass canoes usually disappear after a good rubbing with boat wax.

Yoke pads: If your canoe has capsized or has been washed during the season, there's apt to be water trapped inside the foam-filled yoke pads. The confined water can't readily evaporate, so it'll seep into the wood blocks and cause them to rot. Now is the time to drill a few 3/8-inch diameter holes through the wood yoke pad blocks (as suggested in Chapter 3) so the water can escape.

Painters: Mountaineers regularly wash their ropes. They know that ground-in dirt is highly abrasive. I usually coil and soak my lines in a bucket of soapy water, then rinse and dry them at room temperature. This is a once-a-year procedure. My polyethylene tracking lines have been maintained by this procedure for the last fifteen years, and they're still in fine shape.

Paddles: Wood-tipped paddles don't hold up no matter how careful you are with them. The remedy is to tip them with stainless steel (kits are available from Perception, Inc. Box 64, Liberty, South Carolina 29657) or fiberglass. Steel is much tougher than glass, of course, but it's also noisier...and noticeable. I prefer glass.

A piece of 7-ounce fiberglass and some epoxy (I prefer West System) resin is all you need. Remove the finish from the paddle blade about two inches back of the tip and paint the resin onto the wood. Then, wrap "bias-cut" (diagonal to the weave) glass around the tip. (Note: The glass cloth *will not* wrap a tight curve if you don't apply it on the bias!) Work enough resin into the glass to barely fill the weave of the fabric.

When the resin is dry, sand it smooth and varnish it with a product that contains ultraviolet inhibitors. Re-glassing paddles is an annual chore.

Woolens, down, synthetic products:

Woolens: Advertising to the contrary, wool is still the premiere material for canoe travel. A good wool shirt can be worn day in and day out for years and retain its insulative value and new look. None of the synthetics can compare.

Woolens should be washed, not dry cleaned. Special wool soaps aren't really necessary; any mild detergent will do. Ivory Snow is excellent as are the best "kind to your hands" dishwashing liquids. The key is to handwash in lukewarm water, and avoid rough handling. I pre-soak garments for three minutes, then hand rinse and spin-dry them in a washing machine. Spun-dry shirts are hung on wooden hangers out of direct sunlight to dry; sweaters are laid flat on absorbent towels. Good wool is resilient; it can be stretched or shrunk to shape.

For example, the sleeves on most shirts are too long for me, so I shrink them by washing them (just the sleeves) in very hot water (one minute soak). The shirt is then spun-dry and placed in a "hot" clothes dryer. Careful monitoring (every three minutes) of the drying process produces the exact sleeve length I want. When the sleeves have shrunk, they'll hold their size for the lifetime of the garment. This procedure is not unique: For years, lobster fishermen have "boiled" their wool mittens to make them warmer and more resistant to wind. This is the same principle used in the manufacture of world-famous "Dachstein" mittens and sweaters.

Down-filled products: Down-filled products should be washed, not drycleaned. Drycleaning -- especially with common perchloroethylene -- removes the natural oils and reduces loft. Washing a down sleeping bag or jacket is time-consuming but easy. Here's how.

Handwash the product in a tub of lukewarm soapy water. Ivory Snow, Woolite, or other gentle soap works fine. Special down soaps, while useful, are not essential.

Gently work suds into the article, but don't knead or squeeze the down. Tightly woven nylon shells absorb water reluctantly, so be patient. If your bag or jacket is very dirty, you may want to let it soak for a few hours.

Rub heavily soiled spots with a sponge doused with extra soap. Don't use harsh detergents or cleaning solvents.

Rinse the product *thoroughly* (at least twice) in luke-warm water. You absolutely positively must get all the soap out. During the final rinse, force as much water out as you can, but don't wring the fabric shell. Wringing can tear the fabric baffles, which contain the down.

Pick up the well-rinsed bag with both arms and place it in a large clothes basket. Then take it to your local laundromat for drying. If the laundromat has an ''extractor'' (high-speed centrifuge) use it to remove the final rinse water. If not, spin-dry the bag in a washing machine. One pass through the extractor or two cycles through the washer will remove nearly all the water.

Dry the sleeping bag in a large commercial dryer. Small home driers concentrate the heat over too small an area. Set the dryer on the lowest possible heat setting and throw in a couple of tennis balls or sneakers with the laces removed to break up the down clumps. Check the dryer frequently to be sure it really puts out LOW heat. If you can't control the heat, wedge a magazine in the dryer door (safety button locked down) so the machine will bleed heat. Stop the dryer every five or ten minutes and check the condition of the bag. Complete drying takes about two hours.

My expensive down sleeping bag has been washed eight times over the past twelve years by this method and it still retains all of its original loft, and the fabric shell is like new!

HOW TO WASH SYNTHETICS

Synthetics, like polyesters and polypropylenes, should *never* be drycleaned because the solvents can melt the fibers. Hand or gentle cycle machine washing in luke-warm water is the best practice.

Because polyester sleeping bag fills are tacked into place (there's new technology in the wind; the next decade should see loose-filament synthetics which can be blown into tubes like down), special care must be used so you don't rip the stitching, which secures the batting. For this reason, washing by hand is better than machine.

Polypropylene garments should be washed after every trip. Dirty polypropylene smells bad, doesn't insulate well, and pills readily. Polypropylene undergarments should probably be washed every few days on a canoe trip. Woolens can remain dirty for weeks without affecting their performance or longevity.

Don't overwash sleeping bags. Once a year is plenty for the synthetics (which tend to retain odors); every two years is sufficient for down.

You'll prolong the life of your down and synthetic products by air drying them in strong sunlight for several minutes during each day of your trip. I always sun-dry my sleeping bag for several hours before I put it away for winter storage.

Storage: In between outings, store down and polyester bags and garments in oversized, breathable stuff sacks (a pillow sack works fine) or on hangers. Don't keep them confined in watertight bags for long periods. Continued compression of the fill can permanently reduce loft.

Patching garments and sleeping bags: This work is simply a matter of sewing on a patch of matching material, which is often more difficult than it sounds, because "matching material" isn't always easy to find. Many down and polyester products come with nylon stuff sacks made of identical fabric, and I'm not above cutting these up to get the patching material I need. Most stuff sacks that come with sleeping bags and jackets are too small, anyway. Making a new oversized stuff sack is easy!

Veteran campers agree that Bandaids make the best field patches for torn nylon. Absolutely nothing sticks to nylon better than the sticky wings of a Bandaid, which remain glued to the fabric through repeated washings.

Tent maintenance: A shake-out and thorough sun-drying between trips keeps your tent looking like new. Abrasion is the main enemy of tent fabrics, and for this reason, careful washing -- especially the outside floor and fly -- after each trip is essential. Tent makers suggest you use only mild soaps, not harsh detergents, but I disagree. The minimal damage to waterproof coatings which results from using detergents is more than offset by the amount of ground-in dirt they remove. My old Cannondale Susquehanna is now twelve years old. It has been washed with strong detergents at least 50 times and remains absolutely waterproof.

Every other season I re-coat seams with Thompson's Water Seal. I dislike seam "glues" that get sticky in summer, brittle in winter.

Don't forget to replace your parachute cord tent lines every few years. Nylon degrades in ultraviolet light, so looks are not always a measure of strength.

Care of your packs: Packs should be washed inside and out with warm soapy water (I use dishwashing detergent) and allowed with warm soapy water (I use dishwashing detergent) and allowed to dry thoroughly before you store them. I clean leather with saddle soap and then rub in a leather preservative. Surface mold on leather straps and fittings is easily removed with a 25 percent solution of bleach in water.

You can restore areas of sun-bleached canvas by painting on canvas waterproofing compounds or Thompson's Water Seal. Worn nylon fabrics may be re-coated (it's expensive to cover large areas) with Kenyon RE-COAT, which you can buy at most camp shops.

Figure 18-1   Packs are best stored on wooden dowels hung from the ceiling. Mildew is a major enemy of pack fabrics and stitching so your storage method should provide plenty of ventilation.

Packs should be stored on nails or wooden dowels hung from the ceiling. Mildew is a major enemy of pack fabrics and stitching so your storage method should provide for plenty of ventilation.

Everyone knows that canvas packs or tents will rot if they're stored wet, but nylon ones can mold too! Certain microorganisms attack the polyurethane coatings used to waterproof nylon. Once the coated surface of a pack or tent begins to "peel", the only remedy is replacement! So be sure all your "software" is bone-dry before you put it away for the winter.

You can extend the life of a packsack by installing a double bottom -- a job easily done by your shoemaker. And you can make pack edges and stitching abrasion-proof by coating these areas with epoxy resin.

Most Duluth packs have closing flaps that are too short. These can be lengthened by sewing matching material to the pack flap. To avoid remounting severed leather fittings, cut off the flap at its midpoint and sew the extra fabric into place -- a job easily accomplished on a light-duty sewing machine.

Rx for your camping stove: Most stove problems can be attributed to dirty fuel and varnish build-up from gasoline left in the stove for long periods. Varnish clogs valves and causes erratic operation. The remedy is complete disassembly and thorough cleaning of the stove parts -- hardly a good time, and not at all easy without the right tools.

So empty all gas from your stove after each trip, and burn the tank dry at the end of the camping season. If your stove has a built-in filter (most Optimus models do) remove and clean it with gasoline.

Stoves equipped with pumps have leather washers that must be kept oiled. Any oil works, but boot greases and automotive synthetics seem to last longest. Coleman and Optimus are now supplying synthetic pump washers that are inferior to the traditional leather ones. Check the plumbing section of your hardware store -- some leather stool washers fit some stoves perfectly!

A lot of good camp stoves are junked because they won't hold pressure, a problem commonly attributed to a blown safety valve. For Optimus and Phoebus stoves, the remedy is simple and inexpensive; just replace the fuel tank filler cap (which contains the valve) with a new one. Coleman units are more complicated and require factory servicing.

Sharpness is an ongoing process: Keeping your knife and axe sharp and rust-free is an ongoing process. Camp axes should be sharpened with a fine mill file using the procedure illustrated in Figure 18-2 then trued on an oil stone. Knives should be sharpened on Wachita or Arkansas oil stones, used in conjunction with special cutting oils (kerosine and WD 40 is less expensive and works fine).

Figure 18-2 Here's the best way to sharpen an axe in the field. When using this method, care must be taken to prevent the file from going too far forward (a bad cut could result). For the utmost in safety, equip your file with a handle and guard (impractical accessories on extended canoe trips).

cutting oils (kerosine and WD 40 is less expensive and works fine). If you want an exceptionally fast-working edge, get one of the new diamond impregnated stones which require water for a lubricant.

When storing your sheath knife, remember that acids in leather can discolor and dull the blade. So grease your edged tools (RIG UNIVERSAL, available at gun shops is the *absolute best* rust preventative) before you sheath them. Some conscientious campers cover their blades with Saran Wrap before sheathing them for long-term storage.

That's about it for basic maintenance of your canoe camping gear. Hardly back-breaking drudgery, is it? Fact is, the cleaning and repair of each item brings forth pleasant memories of past trips; every canoe dent and paddle scratch recalls an encounter with a specific rapid or portage trail. Scars, nicks, gouges and tears in equipment, signify honest hard use, a reason why some canoeists are reluctant to make repairs.

On the other hand, some paddlers are maintenance freaks and don't know when it's time to quit. Even the best cared-for gear won't last forever. Products can be over-patched, over-epoxied, over-sewn. When an item in my camping closet has "had it", I carefully remove and save all still usable items (like buckes, leather straps, and sections of unworn canvas) and keep them for repairing my other equipment.

Appendix A
Map Sources
and Canoeing
Technique Books

The U.S. Geological Survey is the most complete and least expensive source of topographic maps. Indexes to topographic maps for each of the fifty United States are available free from the Geological Survey. Maps can be ordered directly from the appropriate USGS office listed below, or can be purchased from one of the many private map dealers whose names and addresses appear in the indexes. Each state index also contains a complete listing of city libraries which carry USGS maps.

STATE TOPOGRAPHIC MAPS

To order maps of areas west of the Mississippi River, write to:

> *Branch of Distribution*
> *U.S. Geological Survey*
> *Federal Center*
> *Denver, Colorado 80225*

To order maps of areas east of the Mississippi River, write to:

> *Branch of Distribution*
> *U.S. Geological Survey*
> *1200 South Eads Street*
> *Arlington, Virginia 22202*

To order Canadian topographic maps, write to:

Map Distribution Office
Department of Energy, Mines, and Resources
615 Booth Street
Ottawa, Ontario
Canada K 1A OE9

STATE GEOLOGICAL SURVEYS

Every state has a geological survey office, and this is a good place to get up-to-date topographic maps. Although you can obtain identical maps from the U.S. Geological Survey at slightly less cost, your state will usually process orders faster (it is not uncommon to wait two or three weeks for U.S. Geological Survey maps, while state geological survey offices generally ship maps within a few days after the request is received).

Geological Survey of Alabama
P.O. Box Drawer O
University of Alabama
University, Alabama 35486

Department of Natural Resources
3001 Porcupine Drive
Anchorage, Alaska 99504

Arizona Bureau of Mines
University of Arizona
Tucson, Arizona 85721

Arkansas Geological Commission
State Capitol Building
Little Rock, Arkansas 72201

Division of Mines and Geology
Department of Conservation
P.O. Box 2980
Sacramento, California 95814

Colorado Geological Survey
254 Columbine Building
1845 Sherman Street
Denver, Colorado 80203

Connecticut Geological and Natural History Survey
Box 128, Wesleyan Station
Middletown, Connecticut 06457

Delaware Geological Survey
University of Delaware
16 Robinson Hall
Newark, New Jersey 19711

Department of Natural Resources
Bureau of Geology
P.O. Box 631
Tallahassee, Florida 32302

Department of Mines, Mining, and Geology
19 Hunter Street S.W.
Atlanta, Georgia 30334

Division of Water and Land Development
Department of Land and Natural Resources
P.O. Box 373
Honolulu, Hawaii 96809

Idaho Bureau of Mines and Geology
Moscow, Idaho 83843

Illinois Geological Survey
121 Natural Resources Building
Urbana, Illinois 61801

Department of Natural Resources
Geological Survey
611 North Walnut Grove
Bloomington, Indiana 47401

Iowa Geological Survey
16 West Jefferson Street
Iowa City, Iowa 52240

State Geological Survey of Kansas
University of Kansas
Lawrence, Kansas 66044

Kentucky Geological Survey
University of Kentucky
307 Mineral Industries Building
120 Graham Ave.
Lexington, Kentucky 40506

Louisiana Geological Survey
Box G, University Station
Baton Rouge, Louisiana 70803

Maine Geological Survey
State Office Building
Room 211
Augusta, Maine 04330

Maryland Geological Survey
214 Latrobe Hall
Johns Hopkins University
Baltimore, Maryland 21218

Massachusetts Department of Public Works
Research and Material Division
99 Worcester Street
Wellesley, Massachusetts 02181

Michigan Department of Natural Resources
Geological Survey Division
Stevens T. Mason Building
Lansing, Michigan 48926

Minnesota Geological Survey
2624 University Ave. W.
St. Paul, Minnesota 55114

Mississippi Geological Survey
Drawer 4915
Jackson, Mississippi 39216

Division of Geological Survey and Water Resources
P.O. Box 250
Rolla, Missouri 65401

Montana Bureau of Mines and Geology
Montana College of Mineral Science and Technology
Butte, Montana 59701

Nebraska Conservation and Survey Division
University of Nebraska
113 Nebraska Hall
Lincoln, Nebraska 68508

Nevada Bureau of Mines
University of Nevada
Reno, Nevada 89507

Geologic Branch, Department of Geology
James Hall, University of New Hampshire
Durham, New Hampshire 03824

New Jersey Bureau of Geology and Topography
John Fitch Plaza
P.O. Box 1889
Trenton, New Jersey 08625

New Mexico State Bureau of Mines and Mineral Resources
Campus Station
Socorro, New Mexico 87801

New York Geological Survey
New York State Education Building, Room 973
Albany, New York 12224

North Carolina Division of Mineral Resources
P.O. Box 27687
Raleigh, North Carolina 27611

North Dakota Geological Survey
University Station
Grand Forks, North Dakota 58202

Ohio Division of Geological Survey
1207 Grandview Avenue
Columbus, Ohio 43212

Oklahoma Geological Survey
University of Oklahoma
Norman, Oklahoma 73069

Oregon State Department of Geology and Mineral Industries
1069 State Office Building
1400 S.W. Fifth Avenue
Portland, Oregon 97201

Pennsylvania Bureau of Topographic and Geological Survey
Harrisburg, Pennsylvania 17120

Rhode Island has no Geological Survey

South Carolina Division of Geology
P.O. Box 927
Columbia, South Carolina 29202

South Dakota State Geological Survey
Science Center
University of South Dakota
Vermillion, South Dakota 57059

Tennessee Department of Conservation, Division of Geology
G-5 State Office Building
Nashville, Tennessee 37219

Texas Bureau of Economic Geology
University of Texas at Austin
Austin, Texas 78712

Utah Geological and Mineralogical Survey
103 Utah Geology Survey Building
University of Utah
Salt Lake City, Utah 84112

Vermont Geological Survey
University of Vermont
Burlington, Vermont 05401

Virginia Division of Mineral Resources
P.O. Box 3667
Charlottesville, Virginia 22903

Washington Division of Mines and Geology
P.O. Box 168
Olympia, Washington 98501

West Virginia Geological and Economic Survey
P.O. Box 879
Morgantown, West Virginia 26505

Wisconsin Geological and Natural History Survey
University of Wisconsin
1815 University Avenue
Madison, Wisconsin 53706

Geological Survey of Wyoming
P.O. Box 3008
University Station, University of Wyoming
Laramie, Wyoming 82070

OTHER GOVERNMENTAL AGENCIES

Maps of local waterways may be obtained from the U.S. Army Corps of Engineers. A few of their field offices are listed below:

U.S. Army Corps of Engineers
219 Dearborn Street
Chicago, Illinois 60604

U.S. Army Corps of Engineers
P.O. Box 59
Louisville, Kentucky 40201

U.S. Army Corps of Engineers
1217 U.S. Post Office and Custom House
180 East Kellog Boulevard
Saint Paul, Minnesota 55101

U.S. Army Corps of Engineers
111 East 16th Street
New York, New York 10003

U.S. Army Corps of Engineers
P.O. Box 17277
Foy Station
Los Angeles, California 90017

The U.S. Coast and Geodetic Survey has a large assortment of topographic maps, aerial photographs, and surveys. Write for a free index.

For Aerial Photographs:
>   *Coast and Geodetic Survey*
>   *Rockville, Maryland 20852*
>   *Attn: Photogrammetry Div. C-141*

For Topographic Maps:
>   *Coast and Geodetic Survey*
>   *Rockville, Maryland 20852*
>   *Attn: Map Information Service, C-513*

Abbreviated guides and maps to canoeable rivers and streams are often available from your state's department of natural resources and conservation.

CANOEING TECHNIQUE BOOKS

>   A WHITEWATER HANDBOOK FOR CANOE AND KAYAK,
>   *by John T. Urban*
>   *Appalachian Mountain Club*
>   *5 Joy Street*
>   *Boston, Mass. 02108*

>   BASIC RIVER CANOEING, *by Robert McNair*
>   *American Camping Association, Inc.*
>   *Bradford Woods*
>   *Martinsville, Indiana 46151*

>   PATH OF THE PADDLE, *by Bill Mason*
>   *Van Nostrand Reinhold Ltd., Toronto, Canada 1980*

Absolutely the best guide to the art of paddling whitewater. Over 650 photographs and illustrations.

>   CANOEING, by The American National Red Cross
>   Doubleday & Company. Inc.
>   Garden City, New York 1977

Nothing in the way of modern paddling technique, but a wealth of solid canoe lore and proven whitewater procedures. All sorts of classical information on traditional paddling methods, sailing, poling, and much more.

Appendix B
Guidelines
for the
Group Leader

These are suggested items for overnight trips. See Chapter 10, Tripping With Tots and Teens, for the specifics of using these and other items.

Forms

____ Swim form (certification of swimming ability)
____ Medical history form.
____ Medical release form.

Equipment

____ Knife
____ Whistle
____ First-aid kit (waterproof)
____ Silver duct tape for repair
____ 50 feet (or more!) of three-eighths inch nylon rope; aluminum carabiner.
____ Matches in waterproof container, candle, chemical fire-starters.
____ Gasoline trail stove.

_____ Nylon trail tarp.

_____ 100 feet of parachute cord and six tent stakes for rigging the
tarp.

_____ Folding saw.

_____ Hand axe (in sturdy sheath).

_____ Shovel (Aluminum tube with one end flattened).

_____ Emergency fire-making kit (plastic bag filled with kindling
and flattened milk carton).

_____ Leaf and lawn size garbage bags or extra rain jacket.

_____ Flashlight (waterproof).

_____ Sewing and repair kit.

RULES OF THE RIVER

1. The leader leads. No one passes the leader. Ever!

2. The most experienced canoeist (next to the leader) paddles
"drag." The drag canoe never passes anyone. Ever!

3. There should be one experienced leader and one capable
"drag" paddler for every four canoes.

4. Every canoe should carry a whistle, especially the lead and
drag boats. Whistles should be blown ONLY in the event of
emergency.

5. Each canoe keeps visual contact with the canoe BEHIND
it, not ahead of it. Rationale: It's easy to drop back to take up the
slack; it's not so easy to push ahead and catch a fast team.

6. Emergency equipment (first-aid kit, fire-starters, etc.)
should be carried in both lead and drag canoes. If only one set of
emergency gear is carried, put it in the drag boat.

7. In the event of a capsize, the first responsibility of nearby
canoes is to pick up the swimmers. Only after the canoeists are
rescued should their canoe and equipment be salvaged.

Appendix C
Neglect
and the
Proper Way

Here's a not-so-simple quiz that will test your understanding of backcountry ethics. Answers and rationale follow. Hint: Some questions have more than one right answer, and some answers are "open to interpretation."

I hope you'll duplicate this quiz (permission is granted by the publisher) and share it with friends, with church and Scout groups, with fishermen, hunters, birders, hikers, canoeists, and with everyone who cares deeply about the future of our wild places.

NEGLECT AND THE PROPER WAY

QUESTIONS

_____ 1. The best way to dispose of fish entrails is to: a)Throw them into the river or lake, b)Bury them at least 100 feet from water, c)Leave them on a prominent rock (well away from the camp area) for seagulls, d)They are biodegradable so it makes no difference how you dispose of them.

_____ 2. To properly dispose of human waste: a)Bury it at least 12 inches deep, 100 feet from water, b)Human waste degrades quickly; it should not be buried! c)Bury it 4-12 inches deep, at least 100 feet from water.

_____ 3. It's okay to dispose of biodegradable wastes (food scraps and such) in Forest Service outhouses, box latrines, and chemical toilets: a)True, b)False, c)Open to interpretation.

_____ 4. What's the correct way to dispose of steel and aluminum cans? a)Burn them out, pound them flat with the back of an axe or rock, and pack them out in a strong plastic bag, b)Burn them out then bury them! c)Bury them at least 100 feet from water, d)Any of the above methods are acceptable.

_____ 5. How should you dispose of glass bottles in the backcountry? a)Break them into fine pieces and bury them, b)Pulverize them to a powder and bury them at least 100 feet from water, c)Burn them out in a hot fire then bury them, d)If you bring bottles into the backcountry, pack them out!

_____ 6. To keep water from entering your tent in a heavy rain, dig a shallow trench around it so the run-off will drain harmlessly away. a)True, b)False, c)Open to interpretation.

_____ 7. If you have a *small amount* of uneaten food, toss it into the bushes. Animals will dispose of the food quickly and completely. a)True, b)False, c)Open to interpretation.

_____ 8. It's okay to construct log benches and tables at your campsite as long as you use cord, not nails. a)True, b)False, c)Open to interpretation.

_____ 9. Best way to dispose of aluminum foil is to: a)Bury it, b)Burn it, c)Pack it out, d)Any of these methods are satisfactory.

_____ 10. It's okay to play loud radios during *daylight* hours. a)True, b)False, c)Open to interpretation.

_____ 11. Pounding nails into trees so you'll have places to hang things, improves the campsite for the next party. a)True, b)False, c)Open to interpretation.

_____ 12. Leave your axe or hatchet at home: It is not essential to your comfort or survival. a)True, b)False, c)Open to interpretation.

_____ 13. Bright-colored equipment -- canoes, tents, packs and clothing -- detracts from the "wilderness experience." Choose "earth tones" instead. a)True, b)False, c)Open to interpretation.

_____ 14. You may bathe and wash clothes and dishes in a waterway as long as you use "biodegradable" soap. a)True, b)False, c)Open to interpretation.

_____ 15. Always bring a strong plastic bag for garbage...and PACK OUT the contents! a)True, b)False, c)Open to interpretation.

_____ 16. Use a campstove for all your cooking. It is unethical to build fires in wilderness areas. a) True, b)False, c)Open to interpretation.

_____ 17. You are responsible! a)To check the remains of your fire by hand before you leave the area; if ashes are hot enough to burn your hand they're hot enough to burn a forest! b)To bring the right gear and clothing for the worst conditions you may encounter, c)To help others who are in trouble, d)To educate others in the "proper way" to treat wilderness areas, e)All of the above.

_____ 18. Ecology-minded outdoorspeople will row or paddle rather than use motors. The noise of motors frightens wildlife and the oil/gasoline scum and carbon-monoxide exhaust is harmful to fish and aquatic organisms. a)True, b)False, c)Open to interpretation.

_____ 19. To insure a restful sleep, the wise camper will always place evergreen boughs or a bed of green leaves beneath his or her sleeping bag. a)True, b)False, c)Open to interpretation.

_____ 20. You are responsible to call unsafe and illegal practices which you observe to the attention of the person(s) involved ... and to report violations of land and water use regulations to the appropriate authorities (if practical). a)True, b)False, c)Open to interpretation.

END OF TEST

ANSWERS

1. B is correct, though C is acceptable if: 1)You are in an area where seagulls are common, and 2) the waterway *is not* heavily fished.

2. C. The top *foot* of soil contains the greatest number of decay organisms (bacteria and fungi), so breakdown will occur most rapidly in this area. The idea is to bury wastes deep enough

so animals won't dig them up, yet shallow enough so they'll decompose quickly.

3. Absolutely false! Garbage should be buried or packed out, never thrown in latrines. Bears commonly upset latrines to get at food buried among the human waste. The mess which results is indescribable!

4. A is correct. Steel cans degrade in around 75 years. Aluminum cans require *hundreds* of years! Cans should *always* be packed out!

5. D is correct. It may require one million years for a glass bottle to "return to nature." For this reason, bottles should always be packed out! Better yet, they should *never* be brought into the backcountry!

6. False! Trenching creates soil erosion. It is unethical and in most places, illegal to ditch tents. Use a plastic groundcloth *inside* your tent and you'll stay dry in the heaviest rains.

7. Absolutely false! This upsets the ecology of animals and causes them to become dependent on man. Chipmunks, squirrels and raccoons get used to being fed and will chew through packs and boxes to get at food. And bears will become bold and downright dangerous!

8. False. Many people take to the backcountry to get away from the trappings of civilization. Your "improvements" may be interpreted by them as full scale "development!"

9. C. It requires a very hot fire to burn aluminum foil completely. Partially oxidized foil is the scourge of the backcountry. Bottles and cans have been outlawed in many federal wilderness areas because people won't pack them out. Aluminum foil may be next!

10. No way! It's never all right to inflict your noise on others.

11. False. It's unethical, illegal, and it hurts the trees!

12. This is debatable. Purists would say "true," but I disagree. When the woods are drenched from a week long rain, you need a small axe, saw and a knife to make fire. First, saw off a 12 inch length of dead log and split it with the axe to get at the dry wood inside. Then slice fine shavings (tinder) from the heartwood and you'll have a roaring fire in no time.

Axes don't damage forests; irresponsible people do! Score

your answer correct if you are in philosophical agreement with either viewpoint.

13. C. (purists would disagree). Bright-colored equipment is essential to the safety of an expedition in remote country. If you float local streams and *never* make remote trips -- and are bothered by bright colors -- you may wisely choose earth tones. Otherwise, vivid hues simply make good sense. I don't mind seeing an orange tent or a red canoe: But I do mind litter, noise and graffitti!

Score your answer correct if you agree philosophically with these viewpoints.

14. No way! When bacteria attack biodegradable products they reproduce and use up oxygen which harms fish and aquatic organisms. Just because a product is "biodegradable" doesn't mean it is good for the environment!

15. True! A responsible outdoorsperson *always* packs out his/her trash!

16. C. Many outdoorspeople (myself included) *prefer* to do all their cooking on a stove. However, it is ethical and legal to build fires in most publicly owned wilderness areas, and that includes sand and gravel bars in navigable rivers. Nonetheless, you are *strongly* urged to use a stove instead of a fire whenever possible, especially in well-traveled and "ecologically sensitive" areas. No conscientious outdoorsperson would think of making a campfire on delicate vegetation!

Score your answer correct if your heart was in the right place!

17. E. Don't take these responsibilities lightly. You *are* responsible for any forest fire you cause, and penalties are severe. So make sure your flames are dead out! If you don't know what to bring on a canoe trip, read a book about it *before* you go. And *do* help others in trouble and educate everyone you meet about "neglect and the proper way."

18. False. The *sound* and smell of motors is certainly offensive to many people -- the reason why they are banned from some lakes. However, motors do little, if any damage to lake and river ecosystems.

19. Absolutely false! It is illegal and unethical to cut green trees. Use an air mattress or foam pad; it's more comfortable!

20. True: Whenever possible, use the "honey rather than guns" approach. Most damage to ecosystems is the result of ignorance not wanton vandalism. People will usually do the "right thing" once they've been properly and patiently educated. Be a spokesperson for the environment. And practice what you teach!

SCORING THE TEST

Each question is worth one point. A score of 20 is possible.

19-20 . . . . . ENVIRONMENTAL EXPERT!
17-18 . . . . FIRST-CLASS SCOUT
15-16 . KNOWLEDGEABLE TENDERFOOT
13-14 . . . . . . FUN-LOVING FLOATER
      Sorry, your good times are being had at the expense of the environment!
12 or less . . . BACKCOUNTRY BUMPKIN!
      You need help! Take someone along who earned a higher score.

Index

Books available through Survival Medical Outfitters, P.O. Box 10102, Merrillville, Indiana 46410. Check, money order, VISA, and Mastercard accepted; please include expiration date of card. Write or call (219) 769-0585.

Commercial orders must be addressed to Stackpole Books, P.O. Box 1831, Cameron and Kelker Streets, Harrisburg, Pennsylvania 17105. For fast service use the toll free number. Call 1-800-READ NOW. For library telemarketing orders, call 1-800-LIBRARI. In Pennsylvania, call (717) 234-5041. Please call between 8:30 a.m. and 4:00 p.m. EST.

WILDERNESS MEDICINE
William W. Forgey, M.D.

An informative medical procedures manual written specifically for outdoorsmen interested in preventing, diagnosing and treating common illnesses and injuries. Emergency medical and surgical techniques are described in simple terms. Devoted to the selection of medications, both prescription and non-prescription and their use under wilderness conditions. **Paperback**, 5½ x 8½, 120 pages, photos, diagrams, illus. 0-934802-14-9 **$9.95** Canadian $12.95

"... a clear, concise guide to treating the gamut of outdoor mishaps, from insect bites and fishhook removal to more serious problems such as broken bones and heatstroke."
Sports Afield 11/84

HYPOTHERMIA - Death by Exposure
by William W. Forgey, M.D.

Hypothermia is the lowering of the body's core temperature to the point that illness and death can result. It can be prevented. It can be treated. But only if you know how. Hypothermia is the greatest potential danger for anyone traveling in the outdoors -- whether fishing, hunting, camping, climbing, or even driving down an Interstate Highway. Outdoors medical expert, Dr. William Forgey, explores the causes, methods of prevention, advances in clothing, field treatments, hospital care, and the basics of physiology and physics of hypothermia in terms everyone can understand. Paperback, , 6x9, 172 pages, illus., index, glossary, bibliography.
ISBN 0-934802-10-6 **$9.95** Canadian $12.95

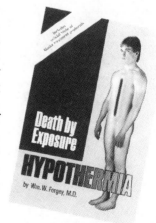

CANOEING WILD RIVERS
Cliff Jacobson

An easy reading manual, of source material, canoeing tips, advanced techniques, and gear recommendations by a weathered expert. **Paperback**, 340 pages, color photos, illus.

0-934802-17-3 **$14.95** Canadian 17.95

> *"If you've ever dreamed of canoeing Alaska's arctic rivers, or for that matter, any waterway in North America, then **Canoeing Wild Rivers** is the first book you should obtain."*
> Alaska Outoors 11/84

> *"This book, **Canoeing Wild Rivers,** by Cliff Jacobson is the one I recommend above all others ... It is not a re-hash of previous writers, but the accumulated learnings of much personal experience."*
> Verlen Kruger ['84]
> Ultimate Canoe Challenge member

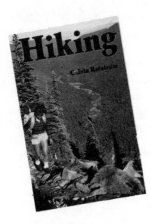

HIKING
Calvin Rutstrum

A comprehensive, procedural coverage from the short urban walk to the extensive wilderness trek, with analysis of equipment, outdoor living methods, and modern hiking ethics. **Paperback**, 6x9, 125 pages, photos, illus.

0-934802-20-3 **$8.95** Canadian $11.95

BACK COUNTRY
Calvin Rutstrum

A volume of adventures, trips and events from the Northern Wilderness during the first part of this century. **Paperback**, 6x9, 255 pages, Les Kouba illus.

0-934802-11-4 **$14.95** Canadian $17.95